Understanding Teacher Expertise in Primary Science
A Sociocultural Approach

Anna Traianou

Goldsmiths College, University of London, UK

SENSE PUBLISHERS
ROTTERDAM / TAIPEI

A C.I.P. record for this book is available from the Library of Congress.

Paperback   ISBN: 90-77874-88-7
Hardback   ISBN: 90-77874-89-5

Published by: Sense Publishers,
P.O. Box 21858, 3001 AW
Rotterdam, The Netherlands

Printed on acid-free paper

Cover picture by Mila Panizo

NEW DIRECTIONS IN MATHEMATICS AND SCIENCE EDUCATION

Volume 1
Learning Science:
A Singular Plural Perspective
W.-M. Roth, *University of Victoria, Canada*
Paperback ISBN 90-77874-25-9 Hardback ISBN 90-77874-26-7

Volume 2
Theorems in School:
From History, Epistemology and Cognition to Classroom Practice
P. Boero, *Universita di Genova, Italy* (Ed.)
Paperback ISBN 90-77874-21-6 Hardback ISBN 90-77874-22-4

Volume 3
The Culture of Science:
Its History in Person
K. Tobin, *The Graduate Center, City University of New York*, USA & W.-M. Roth, *University of Victoria, Canada* (Eds.)
Paperback ISBN 90-77874-33-X Hardback ISBN 90-77874-35-6

Volume 4
Understanding Teacher Expertise in Primary Science:
A Sociocultural Approach
A. Traianou, *Goldsmiths College, University of London, UK*
Paperback ISBN 90-77874-88-7 Hardback ISBN 90-77874-89-5

CONTENTS

Acknowledgements   ix

Preface   xi

PART A

1   **The Emergence of the Subject Knowledge Requirement within UK Research on Primary Science Education.**   3
Primary Science in the 1960s   3
Primary Science in the 1970s   8
Primary Science in the 1980s   12
Primary Science in the 1990s   17
Primary Science Beyond 2000   21
Conclusion   22

2   **The Subject Knowledge Requirement**   25
"Small range" Constructivism   25
"Big Ideas" Constructivism   32
Sociocultural Approaches to Knowledge and Understanding   35
Conclusion   41

3   **The Pedagogical Content Knowledge Requirement**   43
Subject Specific Teaching Knowledge   43
Pedagogical Content Knowledge for the "Big Ideas" of Science   48
Sociocultural Approaches to Science Learning and Teaching   55
Conclusion   60

PART B

4   **Methodological Implications of a Sociocultural Perspective for Studying Teacher Expertise**   65
The Use of Qualitative Case Study in this Study   67
Context of this Study   68
Conclusion   71

5   **An Expert Primary Science Practitioner's Perspective**   73
Coral's Perspective on her own Science Subject Knowledge   73
Coral's Views About the Nature of Children's Science Learning   79
Coral's Views about her Teaching of Science   86
Discussion   89

6   **An Example of Expert Primary Science Practice**   93

First Phase: Introduction   95

Second Phase: Generating Children's Interest in Investigating Friction   97

Third Phase: Investigating Friction   102

Fourth Phase: Discussing findings about the friction on different surfaces   109

Fifth Phase: Investigating lubricants   117

Sixth Phase: Discussing Children's Findings about the use of Lubricants   121

Discussion   123

7   **Conclusion: Primary Science Expertise-in-Action**   129

The Growth of Emphasis on Subject Knowledge   129

Assessing Constructivist Approaches to Primary Science Teacher Expertise   132

Understanding Coral's Expertise   134

Implications for the Professional Development of Teachers   141

References   145

Subject index   155

Author index   161

ACKNOWLEDGEMENTS

My thanks go to the classroom teacher who gave generously of her time, sharing her thoughts and reflections about knowledge, learning and teaching with me.

I would like to express my appreciation to Patricia Murphy for her guidance in writing this as a thesis when I was a doctoral student at the Open University. I am indebted to Martyn Hammersley for his continual encouragement and support as well as for his willingness to comment and discuss numerous drafts of chapters.

I am grateful to Dennis Atkinson, Rosalyn George, Claudine Kirsch and Soo Miller for providing the kind of colleagueship which I find invaluable.

Also thanks to my extraordinary friends Mila, Toni, Natalie and Lia who constantly encouraged me to keep going!

Finally my love and thanks go to my family, Pantelis Traianos and particularly my father Grigoris Traianos for their unconditional support and interest in my work.

This book examines the very influential idea that science subject knowledge plays an essential role in the classroom practice of primary school teachers. In recent years, this idea has come to be seen, both by many researchers and by policymakers, as a major component of teacher expertise. Indeed, it is often argued that the effective teaching of primary science depends on teachers' adequate understanding of scientific knowledge and of the ways in which this knowledge can be taught effectively to children.

Within research in primary science education, this emphasis on subject knowledge arose, to a large extent, from the growing influence of constructivist perspectives on learning and teaching. These perspectives are by no means homogenous, but they do share some important features in common. Above all, they emphasise the importance of establishing learners' prior conceptions about the phenomena being studied and the need for teachers to challenge these conceptions directly during teaching. It is argued that, in order to be able to do this effectively, primary teachers must have sound science subject knowledge and an appropriate understanding of constructivist theories of learning and teaching. Since the 1990s, the definition of teacher expertise has been extended to include pedagogical content knowledge, which is seen as the kind of knowledge that "translates" what teachers know about science, children's learning and teaching into effective pedagogy.

In order to explore these issues, in this book I will focus on two constructivist lines of thinking about expertise in primary science that have been influential within UK research. My aim is to examine the arguments and evidence on which they are based, and the assumptions they involve about knowledge, pedagogy, and learning; and to compare these with the rather different perspective provided by sociocultural theory.

This book is inspired by the belief that research on primary science education has not taken adequate account of sociocultural perspectives on knowing and learning, which treat these as necessarily situated and contingent. Above all, these perspectives stress that expertise is defined *in action* by relevant communities of practice: its character is tied to the perspectives and activities of those who are recognised as experts. This is not necessarily in conflict or incompatible with constructivism. However, it does provide a rather different view of expertise in primary science. Thus, the core of this book employs a sociocultural perspective to explore in-depth the perspectives and classroom practice of a teacher who is regarded locally, and to some extent more widely, as an expert primary science practitioner. The aim is to articulate what this can tell us about the nature of expertise in this field and its role in classroom practice.

In the current climate of government-led interventions around what primary teachers ought to know and how they ought to teach science, in the UK and also elsewhere, it is essential that we focus on how practitioners can enact their expertise in order to develop children's scientific understanding.

ORGANISATION OF THE BOOK

The book is divided into two parts. The first is concerned with the assumptions about knowledge, learning and teaching that underpin the two constructivist lines of thinking about primary teacher science expertise that are currently influential in UK research. In the first chapter, changes in ideas about primary science are traced, and in particular the rise of emphasis on teachers' subject knowledge, and on the importance of pedagogical content knowledge. In the following two chapters, constructivist views about primary science expertise are examined, in some detail, and compared with sociocultural views of knowledge and learning.

In Part B, I begin by discussing the implications of a sociocultural perspective for the methodological approach used to study teacher expertise in my own work (chapter 4), and then present a case study of a primary science teacher who was recognised as an expert practitioner. In chapter 5, I investigate the ways in which this teacher understands her own expertise. This involves an exploration of her views about scientific knowledge and its role in teaching, and her beliefs about the learning and teaching of science. Following this, in chapter 6, I provide a detailed analysis of an episode from her teaching, in order to describe the ways in which an expert practitioner enacts her expertise. This case study allows some assessment of the relationship between currently dominant views about primary science expertise and the form that such expertise can take in the classroom. In the conclusion, I summarise the argument as a whole, and examine the implications of my study for the education and professional development of primary teachers.

PART A

THE EMERGENCE OF THE SUBJECT KNOWLEDGE REQUIREMENT WITHIN UK RESEARCH ON PRIMARY SCIENCE EDUCATION

In this first chapter, I discuss the main reforms of primary science that took place during the past forty years in the UK, and how they lent support to increasing emphasis on the importance of subject knowledge for effective primary science teaching. I will argue that debates about the subject knowledge requirement have been influenced by changing views about the learner and the learning process, assumptions about the relationship between the nature of scientific activity and its products, and ideas about the value of teaching science in primary schools. I will also point out that, quite often, political factors have intervened to affect decisions about what and how to teach primary science.

The first section of this chapter deals with the curriculum reforms that took place in the 1960s. The second section describes some of the changes that occurred in ideas about the teaching of primary science during the 1970s. The third section focuses on the appearance of constructivism in science education and the introduction of the Science National Curriculum. And the last section describes the appearance of the distinction between subject knowledge and pedagogical content knowledge during the 1990s and current ideas about effective primary science teaching.

PRIMARY SCIENCE IN THE 1960s

It is often suggested that the beginning of the reform of UK primary science can be traced to the curriculum developments that took place during the 1960s. These developments re-activated discussions about the content and role of science in the curriculum, and how it should be taught.

At that time, science was not regarded as a core element of the primary school curriculum, which was still struggling to escape from the legacy of the *elementary* tradition, with its emphasis on the basic skills of literacy and numeracy and on the inculcation of pupil discipline (Richards, 1983). Where science was taught, it was treated simply as one more stimulus to children's intellectual, emotional and physical development. For the most part, it involved the study of natural history, since encouraging children to explore aspects of the natural world built on their innate curiosity. Therefore, it could enable them to acquire an enduring love of nature and develop good observational skills, both of which were deemed necessary for the subsequent stages of scientific learning. This reflected an inductivist conception of science which prevailed at the time (Hodson & Prophet, 1986).

An important contrast with the elementary tradition was the child-centred *developmental* (or progressive) tradition, which had begun to be mentioned in official reports on primary education from the 1930s onwards. The precise characteristics of this tradition are much debated (Blenkin & Kelly, 1981). In general though, influenced by the writings of Jean-Jacques Rousseau, Frierich Froebel, Johann Pestalozzi, Maria Montessori and John Dewey, its supporters are usually identified as embracing "a broad set of educational values that are more centred on the child and the contribution of education to his or her continuing process of development, than on the child as someone being prepared to become some future "finished" educational "product" in fulfillment of society's demands" (Hargreaves, 1986, p. 169). Thus, typically, developmental educators de-emphasise subject divisions and focus on the process of knowing, rather than on its product. This is taken to mean that the central aim of teaching is to help children develop their ability to learn rather than to help them master a body of knowledge. Developmental educators see themselves less as specialists in a particular academic subject and more as *gardeners* (Claxton, 1990), responsible for providing the necessary conditions to enable growth to take place. They believe that children are intrinsically well motivated by direct, inquiry-oriented experiences and learn primarily through unstructured, play-like activities. They also favour a more co-operative relationship between teacher and children in the learning process, one which encourages children to play an active part in their own learning and development (see Blyth 1965).

The developmental tradition was closely associated with curriculum developments in primary science education in Britain in the 1960s. Thus, when, in 1961, the Ministry of Education expressed concern about the narrow content and poor quality of science teaching in primary schools, the emphasis was placed on finding ways in which improvement could be achieved whilst retaining the main principles of the developmental tradition.

The Appearance of the Process Approach to Primary Science

Some changes in the teaching of science had already been attempted in a few schools in the 1950s. Conran (1983), for example, argues that some primary teachers who were interested in science began to consider science teaching in terms of a series of practical investigations performed by the children themselves. Within this approach, observation remained the main skill that teachers were trying to promote, although teaching science also focused on developing children's interests, attitudes and awareness of the natural world; on "exploring and appreciating (to some extent) patterns and relationships; on acquiring knowledge and developing the ability to communicate it" (p. 19). In some schools, the content of science was also broadened to include physical sciences in their curriculum. And, in order to overcome the problem of ill equipped classrooms, many teachers started to use everyday, commonplace materials in children's investigations. Thus, children were encouraged to discover and explore the world around them and to ask questions, especially of the kind which could be answered by direct observation. However, among these teachers, there was little understanding of progression in children's science learning, or of the contribution of science teaching to the child's overall intellectual development.

In 1963, in order to support such initiatives in schools, the Science Masters' Association (SMA) and the Association of Women Science Teachers (AWST), which now together form the Association for Science Education (ASE), established a committee to consider the nature of primary science. In its report, the committee argued that "we are concerned more with the developing of an enquiring attitude of mind, than with the learning of facts" (ASE, 1963, p.2). The ASE, before it established its primary science committee, had been concerned for some years about secondary school curricula and it developed the view that inquiry and experimentation should be a central feature of secondary science (Wastnedge, 1968). Around the same time, a similar view was expressed in the reform efforts of the National Science Foundation (NSF) in the United States. Taking into account the views of leading scientists, the NSF initiatives attempted to organise science curricula around the structure of scientific disciplines as modes of inquiry rather than bodies of knowledge, and laboratory work was seen as providing experiences designed to help students learn for themselves by operating as "scientists in the classroom" (Raizen, 1991, p. 18). This approach to learning *about* science by *doing* science became known as *discovery* learning. In Britain, "discovery learning" first appeared in the Nuffield Secondary Science projects (see for example, Nuffield Chemistry 1967), but soon influenced the primary projects, in which it became known as the "process approach" (see Wastendge, 1967).

The emphasis on discovery learning was further reinforced by the writings of Jean Piaget, especially his idea of the child as a lone discoverer, motivated to create and solve problems in an attempt to understand and organise the world around him/her (Hodson, 1996; Wood, 1988). Furthermore, Piaget's descriptions of how such unstructured, self-directed observations and experimentation develop, through a series of stages, into sophisticated formal reasoning processes provided a guide to the issue of progression, and suggested a role for the primary teacher as the *facilitator* of the learning process.[1]

Piaget's ideas took some time to become widely known in Britain. His work was initially received with hesitation. During the 1950s, however, a number of books were published which interpreted Piaget's theory for teachers, and some training colleges began to disseminate it, especially in the field of mathematics. Of particular importance in relation to the teaching of science was the work of Susan Isaacs, who reinterpreted Piaget's ideas in the light of observations of children engaged in concrete problem-solving situations arising directly from their own interests (Harlen & Qualter, 2004). She noted that if children were treated as intelligent human beings, there would be very little in the way of learning and understanding that they could not master. Initially, though, this had little observable impact in schools.

Explicit support for Piaget's theory was offered by the publication of the Plowden Report in 1967, which appealed to his theory in support of the argument that knowledge is best acquired through activity and experience.

In relation to science, this emphasis on *action* and *doing* blended well with the notion of science as a process of inquiry and exercised significant influence both in secondary and primary science curricula.

The Picture of Good Primary Science Teaching in the 1960s

It was against this background of general educational reform that the *Nuffield Junior Science* project (1964–1966) and the Science *5-13* project (1967–1975) were set up to help those teachers who wanted to use science as a means for educating children.

Based on Piaget's theory about children's natural drive to discover the world around them and on the view of science as a process of inquiry, the Nuffield Junior Science project (NJS) expressed the belief that children's practical problem solving is "essentially a scientific way of working" (Goodwin & Wastnedge, 1995, p. 78). Therefore, the task of a school "is not one of teaching science to children, but rather of utilising the children's own scientific way of working as a potent educational tool" (p. 78). In turn, the term *scientific way of working* (or *how to think scientifically*) was interpreted to mean the ability to isolate a problem, and, in working towards its solution, to be able to observe, investigate, communicate and most crucially to *hypothesise* and *predict*. Apart from the last two of these learning processes, which could be considered to be more characteristically scientific, the others were seen as general learning processes. For some authors, this approach to science learning blurred the distinction between science and other subjects and suggested an integrated approach to learning (e.g. Harlen, 1978).

According to the director of the NJS project (Wastnedge, 1967, 1968), science teaching should focus on helping children develop their abilities to ask their own scientific questions, isolate a scientific problem and find its solution through careful investigation. Furthermore, *what is learned* was seen to be inextricably linked with *how it is learned*. The project stressed that, given the increasing body of scientific knowledge, it was impossible to prescribe what one should know. Therefore, the only plausible criteria for selecting and organising scientific knowledge for the purposes of teaching can derive from children's own questions, interests and needs:

> We concluded, and believe very strongly, that a child should raise his/her own scientific problems, partly because isolating a problem is an important part of scientific thinking, partly because the ever increasing body of knowledge make it increasingly ridiculous to prescribe what any child should know, but mostly because we do not believe that anyone can ask a completely significant question for someone else.

> This should not be interpreted as meaning that knowledge is not important. Obviously it is, but the content of what is learned should take its true place in relation to how it is learnt. (Wastnedge, 1968, p. 346)

Thus, the NJS project introduced a way of teaching science as a process of inquiry, and provided an answer to the problem of the narrow content of science by allowing children's interests to decide what scientific knowledge they needed to know. The project seemed to value the application of science – that is, useful knowledge which can be established through practical investigation and applied to solve problems-more than abstract concepts and principles alone. To disseminate its findings, the project team set up in-service courses for teachers and produced books with background scientific information and topic-related activities, from which teachers could make their own programmes according to their children's interests and abilities.

The project's successor, *Science 5–13*, built on this work, but differed by providing teachers with explicit statements of the objectives for children's learning. Thus, although the child's motivation and the need for learning were still regarded as rooted in experience, the project included about 150 behavioural objectives which were grouped into three stages related to the Piagetian staged theory of intellectual development (Ennever & Harlen, 1972). These learning objectives aimed to guide the provision of opportunities for learning and to form a basis for monitoring individuals' progress. Parker-Jelly (1983) argues that the project exerted significant influence on a range of policy statements and curriculum projects which were to emerge in the 1970s, such as *Match and Mismatch* (Harlen, Darwin, & Murphy, 1977), the *Sciencewise Series* (Parker & Ward, 1978) and the *Learning Through Science* project (Richards et al., 1980).

Thus, the picture of good primary science teaching that was predominant during the 1960s and 1970s was one which regarded science as a unique vehicle for children's overall intellectual development, and scientific teaching as a process of inquiry through which learners acquire useful knowledge. Children should be encouraged to ask questions and find out answers for themselves until they are satisfied. To teach science successfully, primary teachers needed to have an understanding of how to recognise an appropriate scientific question, how to design experiments, evaluate evidence and draw valid conclusions; though they should also have adequate scientific knowledge on which to draw when guiding children's investigations.

However, during this period other views also emerged about the teaching of primary science, which emphasised the teaching of abstract concepts of science. For example, in 1963, a project dealing with this was set up by the Ministry of Education. Based at the Oxford University Institute of Education, the project became known as the *Oxford Primary Science Project* (OPSP). Its main principle was that it is impossible to ignore that children will bring their own scientific experiences into school and, therefore, it is vital to include in the teaching of primary science the contribution of scientific knowledge in their interpretation of the environment (Redman, Brereton, & Boyers, 1968, 1969). Thus, the project took a diametrically opposite starting point from the Nuffield Junior Science project, which had been established in the same year, by prioritising four scientific concept groups, thought by a group of scientists to be the most important ones for young children's scientific learning[2]. The project considered how these concept groups could be broken down into smaller units, by taking into account what was known about children's intellectual development, and how these units could be understood by children through practical activities. It was thought that the child at the primary stage "may be able to make abstractions about the scientific experiences which he has, and to form scientific concepts in a simple, unsophisticated form" (p. 17). The project produced a book for teachers describing activities related to the four science concept groups. However, the project's materials did not attract much attention at the time. For some authors, this is explained by the dominance of the child-centred approach to the teaching of the whole primary curriculum (Osborne & Simon, 1996a).

PRIMARY SCIENCE IN THE 1970s

Despite the curriculum developments of the 1960s and 70s, and the variety of curriculum materials produced for teachers to stimulate and support scientific activities with young children, the quality of science teaching did not seem to change dramatically (see Black, 1980; Boyle, 1990). It was suggested, that to a large extent secondary science teaching continued in its old mode of memorising facts, with little practical work, whereas primary schools continued to focus on nature study and training in observation. Kerr and Engel (1983), pointed out that although many primary teachers seemed to be aware of the existence of important curricular developments in primary science, and ranked highly objectives which could be achieved through planned scientific activity, there seemed to be little scientific activity carried out in primary classrooms. It was also suggested that some primary teachers who followed a "process approach" to the teaching of science engaged children in practical activities which focused exclusively on developing children's understanding of processes, neglecting what was necessary to develop concepts more explicitly.

One of the reasons offered to explain the failure of these projects to be taken up by primary teachers related to the latter's lack of confidence in teaching science, which in turn was associated with their poor science background and their failure to recognise the potential contribution of science to the curriculum. Whittaker (1980), for example, pointed out that primary teachers had neither sufficient understanding of the scientific process nor adequate knowledge of science to organise open-ended activities and to encourage the development of specific skills by carefully guiding their pupils' own interests. She argued that teachers needed practical help to be able to use the ideas and the materials that exist. Furthermore, an HMI report (DES, 1978) argued that the major obstacle in the implementation of the curriculum materials was the lack of appropriate scientific knowledge among teachers. The report proposed steps to improve the situation which included the careful deployment of teachers who did have such expertise.

Thus, in order to improve the quality of primary science teaching, financial support was given during the 1980s for in-service courses, and Local Education Authorities (LEAs) were invited to apply for Education Support Grants for primary science. Part of the plans of those LEAs which received grants was to employ advisory teachers to work in classrooms with other teachers (Harlen, 1995). Primary schools were also encouraged to develop policy statements for science and to create a post within their staffing of coordinator for science. These activities were intended to provide help to teachers in understanding and using the existing curriculum materials.

Criticisms of the Process Approach

However, during the 1970s criticisms had begun to emerge of the curriculum materials themselves. Some of these criticisms related to the absence of a common content for the science activities that young children were to be engaged in. Wynne Harlen (1978), for example, argued that although the idea of allowing children to select the content of the practical activities according to their interests is attractive, in practice teachers find it very difficult to follow the interests of a whole class of children. Even more importantly she pointed out, some children may not be interested in anything sufficiently to want to investigate, and therefore teachers may have to offer them specific problems. The absence of a common content could also mean that there would be repetition of experiences, especially when children moved schools, or that large gaps would appear in children's scientific understanding.

It was argued by some that the main problem that the lack of common content indicated was that what science was taught was left to the choice of primary teachers, many of whom did not have the appropriate scientific understanding. As Kerr and Engel (1983), put it: "at present the content of primary science is left almost entirely to chance, a state of affairs which puts a considerable strain on conscientious teachers who lack sufficient background and experience of science" (p. 48). In turn, this argument is closely related to ideas about children's learning in science. In her influential article *Does Content Matter in Primary Science*, Harlen (1978) argued that the choice of content should not be left to "chance, but should make sure that all children have the opportunity to gain basic ideas that lay a foundation for a gradually more sophisticated understanding of their world" (p. 618).

This shift in emphasis within discussions of primary science, from processes to content, is not unrelated to other changes that occurred during the 1970s and early 1980s. For example, in primary science education, attention was given, virtually for the first time, to the assessment of children's performance.[3] This led to consideration of children's learning in science being not only in terms of their understanding of processes but also in terms of their understanding of concepts. More specifically, the *Assessment of Performance Unit* (APU), which was established in 1974 by the Department of Education and Science (DES), to "promote the development of methods of assessing and monitoring the achievement of children in school and to seek to identify the incidence of underachievement" (p. 9) developed a framework for assessment in primary science based on assumptions concerning the nature of the subject, its aims and objectives, and what children might be expected to be able to do as a result of their education. After consulting a number of interested bodies, such as the Association for Science Education, science was defined as "an experimental subject concerned fundamentally with the solving of problems in scientific and everyday situations" (Gott & Murphy, 1987, p. 6). This view of science accepted the importance of processes, procedures and concepts of science in solving problems. From this perspective a framework for assessment was produced which included six categories. Five of these categories were process-based, whereas the sixth one involved the application of science concepts. In turn, thirty seven concepts were identified which were written in the form of general statements. The results of the APU surveys in the early 1980s indicated that the level of pupil performance was particularly low in relation to the more specific scientific skills (e.g. hypothesising and predicting) and in the application to scientific ideas. This focused future efforts to improve science teaching on these areas.

Furthermore, the 1970s found education experiencing a change in climate away from the progressivism of the Plowden era. This change may have influenced the re-emergence of discussions about the teaching of abstract concepts of science in the primary school. The latter could be seen as the consequence of a series of responses to the Plowden report, which began to make their appearance soon after its publication, challenging the assumptions of a child-centred education. In 1969, for instance, *Perspectives on Plowden* appeared, in which R. S. Peters argued that the general view of education taken in the Report was not appropriate to the practical needs of that time.

Around the same time several Black Papers were published (collections of critical articles predominantly from the political right) which, among other things, criticised child-centred education for failing to teach children discipline and respect for authority. In one of them, Bantock (1969) argued that Rousseau's dichotomy between book learning and discovery learning is, at the very least, problematic, since it is possible to discover a great deal from books. These criticisms were further reinforced in 1976 when, in a speech at Ruskin College, the then prime minister, James Callaghan, talked about the "unease felt by parents and teachers about the new informal methods of teaching" and gave voice to the idea of "a core curriculum of basic knowledge" (Darling, 1994, p. 100). He also insisted that the views of politicians, parents and others should be taken into account and that educational debate could not be left exclusively to professional teachers. More support for the criticisms was provided by the publicity given to the failings of an individual primary school (William Tyndale School), which used what was labelled as a progressive approach to teaching. Around the same time a research report was published and widely reported, which claimed that children in "formal" classrooms made progress in English, reading and maths which was significantly superior to those taught "informally." The report included the findings of an empirical study on how far primary school children progressed over the period of a year in different classes where the teaching style was classified as "formal" "informal", or "mixed" (Bennett, 1976). Demands were expressed, especially by the press, to find out what had gone wrong in primary schools.

Harlen (1995) argues that such criticisms created a more sympathetic climate for the monitoring of standards, and made reception of work of the Assessment of Performance Unit (APU) easier. Also, the criticisms that undermined the intellectual credibility of child-centred education led some authors to question whether the "process approach" was the most appropriate way to teach primary science (e.g. Driver, 1975). Such authors put forward arguments for adjusting the policy about content in primary science and for moving away from the "process approach" towards a view of teaching which pays attention to how children acquire both an understanding of processes and an understanding of content. Their arguments were associated with debates about the role of science in the curriculum, and with the emergence of a new interpretation of Piagetian theory about children's learning in science, what became known as *constructivism*.

The Changing Picture of Good Primary Science Teaching

Throughout the late 1970s and early 1980s increasing concern was expressed about science and its role in the curriculum. Within the Association for Science Education, there was pressure to review the whole science curriculum (both primary and secondary) in order to establish an appropriate balance between the specialist and generalist aspects of science education. It had been argued that secondary science teachers continued to see the main purpose of science education as the supply of future scientists, with the result that two very different kinds of school science existed: academic science and non-academic science (Young, 1976). The curriculum developments of the 1960s and 1970s, especially the Secondary Nuffield projects, were said to have contributed to this division, by being essentially elitist and producing course materials intended for the minority of students who could cope with heavy conceptual demands (Boyle, 1990). These two kinds of school science were considered to be mutually exclusive; O-level and A-level courses had become increasingly abstract, whereas courses dealing with the everyday applications of scientific concepts were reserved for those not entered for examination. The likely consequence of this dual policy towards science education, it was suggested, was the emergence of two kinds of citizens: the scientifically literate and the scientifically illiterate. Thus, it was argued that there was a need for reform to produce a broad and balanced curriculum, which would offer to all pupils equal access to scientific literacy.

This argument for reform seems to reflect the principles that dominated the reform of science education in the United States at that time. During the 1980s concern had shifted to the needs of academically disadvantaged students, and more broadly all those who were not destined for scientific and technical careers. Politicians and reform activists linked the quality of science education less to the excellence of the research establishment (central to the reform in the 1960s) than to the technical competence of the American workforce in the name of global competition. As Turner and Sullenger (1999) put it, in this atmosphere "science for all and scientific literacy became the watchwords of education reform, both in the United States and abroad" (p. 7).

Thus, by the end of 1970s, influenced by the argument of "science for all", science in primary schools was officially recognised both to be important for the overall education of children, but also to be poorly practiced (see DES, 1978,

1985). In this way, an approach to the teaching of primary science began to emerge which was trying to balance a process approach to learning with the acquisition of more abstract scientific ideas. Discussing the content of primary science, Harlen (1978) argued that what seemed to be required "are content guidelines that are firm enough to ensure that children encounter the range of ideas and facts which are relevant to understanding their environment, yet are loose enough to enable teachers to use a variety of routes to arrive at them" (p. 620). These content guidelines included statements such as: "all things are pulled down towards the earth; the amount of this pull is the weight of an object", "some substances dissolve in water very well, others only a little and some not at all" (p. 622). Children were supposed to acquire such ideas through a variety of practical activities. This approach to the teaching of primary science was also embraced by the HM Inspectorate (see DES, 1978). [4]

As I mentioned earlier, the search for an effective approach to the teaching of primary science which stresses the role of abstract scientific concepts was encouraged by the appearance of constructivism. This is discussed in the next section.

PRIMARY SCIENCE EDUCATION IN THE 1980s

In Britain, constructivism initially appeared in the context of secondary science education. By the end of the 1980s, it had established itself as the dominant approach to learning and teaching science among those writing about both primary and secondary education. Its assumptions about how children learn science, the nature of scientific activity, and what science teaching should involve, influenced decisions about the content of the Science National Curriculum (DES, 1989), and led to a reconsideration of the character of science teaching and consequently what teachers need to know in order to teach science effectively.

During the 1970s, research in secondary science education began to focus on the description and interpretation of students' conceptions of various scientific phenomena. Until that time, most of the research into children's ideas of science aimed to assess children's conceptions against the accepted scientific ones. Students' misconceptions were considered as an indication of some "defect" in teaching and learning. The re-discovery of the earlier work of Jean Piaget (1971), the arrival of post-positivist philosophies of science and the appearance of psychological perspectives such as those expressed in the work of David Ausubel (1968), Jerome Bruner (1966), Robert Gagné (1970), and George Kelly (1955), gave an impetus to the pursuit of a new research tradition in education, and in science education in particular (Gilbert & Watts, 1983). The term *constructivism* was used to label this emerging research tradition. It incorporated a wide range of theoretical perspectives, which appeared to share the assumption that the children being studied "must at a minimum be considered knowing beings", and that "the knowledge they possess has important consequences for how behaviour and actions are interpreted" (Magoon, 1977, p. 652).

Thus, by the early 1980s there was a growing body of research into children's ideas of a variety of science topics. Most of this research involved secondary school pupils (e.g. Bell, 1981; Erickson, 1978), although there were also examples of research into the ideas held by younger children (e.g. Osborne & Freyberg, 1985). Such studies suggested that children bring to school their own interpretations of aspects of the physical world, which are often inimical to learning the ones held by the scientific community. Terms like *alternative frameworks* (Driver & Easley, 1978), *conceptual frameworks* (Driver & Erickson, 1983), and *minitheories* (Claxton, 1993) were used to label children's intuitive ideas, and to indicate that these are different from those of school science. Consequently, some science educators began to suggest that there is a need to look more carefully, and in detail, at pupils' own understandings and ways of thinking about scientific ideas, and to use this information in planning teaching strategies.

Of course, the notion that learning depends on the learner relating new experience to what he/she already knows was not new. It had been a central feature of many cognitive theories, and was an idea familiar to teachers. As Kerr and Engel (1983) put it, "good practice has always included listening carefully to individual children's ideas and then beginning from the vantage point of the learner's own experience" (p. 46). Constructivism, however, claimed to provide not only further evidence in support of the argument that new learning depends on previous learning, but also a better articulated theory of how children learn science and a better understanding of science as a human activity. Furthermore, constructivists argued that they were offering a "new pedagogy" for the effective teaching of science; one which aimed to "empower people to act more effectively in their daily lives" by enabling them to develop useful conceptual tools (Millar & Driver, 1987, p. 57).

More specifically, constructivist perspectives rejected the empiricist assumption that knowledge is passively built up from sensations generated by an observer-independent world. Instead, they presented knowledge in terms of "conceptual structures that epistemic agents, given the range of present experience within their tradition of thought and language, consider viable" (von Glasersfeld, 1989, p. 124). Accordingly, constructivist perspectives blurred the distinction between public forms of knowledge (knowledge as it is presented by scientists) and personal understanding (knowledge of the world as it is constructed by the individual), by suggesting that in both cases the construction of meaning is influenced by the personal beliefs and the values of the culture in which people live. Furthermore, by arguing that observations are theory-laden, constructivism also blurred the distinction between the processes and content of science. As Driver (1975) put it:

> As theories have been discarded and others adopted, observations themselves have taken on a different significance. Observations are not absolute; what is observed is viewed through the spectacles which all those initiated into that branch of science wear. (p. 801)

Based on this view of knowledge, learning science came to be seen as an adaptive process of self-organisation through which individuals reconstruct their conceptual frameworks towards more viable or useful ones in order to carry out a task in a more effective way. As mentioned earlier, this view of learning science was based on a different interpretation of Piaget's theory, one which stressed learners' ability to be *active* and *reflective* in the learning process. In particular, within *Piagetian constructivism* the learner was considered to be an intelligent adaptive problem-solver, who brings his/her conceptions to the learning process and constantly tests them against experience. Encountering a perturbation relative to some expected result, the learner may be actively induced to reconstruct his/her conceptions in order to re-establish a relative equilibrium between previous knowledge and the new experience (Driver, 1984).

From a Piagetian constructivist point of view, the teaching of science should aim to facilitate conceptual change by addressing the learner's existing conceptions. In turn, practical activities, therefore, ought to be selected on the basis that they provide the necessary evidence which would force learners to confront the mismatch between their existing ideas and those accepted by the scientific community.

Thus, by arguing that "children's ideas should be taken seriously", Piagetian constructivism offered a new approach to the teaching of science, one which differed from didactic methods of teaching that failed to recognise the importance of children's conceptions in the learning process. It also differed from the "process approach", which assumed that children learn *about* science (learn the content of science) by *doing* science (getting involved in their own investigations) by arguing that children's everyday ideas need to be elicited and challenged directly, so as to help them modify their initial understanding towards a desired scientific one. Driver (1975), for example, pointed out that if during the teaching of science children are left alone to choose their own questions to investigate, there is a danger that their enquiries will be set within the context of the science theory they already know, so that no conceptual change would be achieved. Furthermore, the "process approach" was also criticised for reflecting an inadequate understanding of the nature of scientific activity. It was argued, that there was no empirical evidence to support the existence of a clearly describable method of science. The commonly listed processes of science (observing, predicting, hypothesising, etc.) are aspects of children's general cognitive functioning, and therefore science can lay no special claim to them (Millar, 1989).

On both sides of the Atlantic, during the 1980s and 1990s, many projects were set up to explore the nature and implications of learners' prior knowledge of science. Some of these projects suggested particular teaching sequences to help children reconstruct their initial understanding. Such sequences usually involved an elicitation phase, during which the teacher would try to probe learners' thoughts on the topic in hand and help them to clarify their ideas through engagement in individual work or group discussion (see Nussbaum & Novick, 1982). A second phase followed, in which the teacher should ensure that there is a direct contrast between the learners' view and the desired scientific view. This could be achieved by presenting the "desired" view, or by somehow making it emerge from the class. During a third phase, the teacher should provide opportunities for the learners to see how the desired view is used in explaining a specific phenomenon and applying it to other examples. The teacher was seen as the facilitator of the process, responsible for creating the sort of environment necessary to help the learners to reconstruct their initial understanding (e.g. Driver & Oldham, 1986).

The Picture of Good Primary Science Teaching in the 1980s

Most of the studies mentioned in the previous section involved secondary school children and were aimed, primarily, at teaching secondary science more effectively. Soon, however, Piagetian constructivism appeared in primary science education as a theory which could provide a better explanation for how children learn. During the 1980s the aim of teaching science in the primary school was still to help children learn how to learn. Harlen and Osborne (1985), for example, argued that a rationale for primary science should start from a vision of the way in which we want children to learn and of the kind of learning we wish to promote, rather than in terms of teaching specific items of scientific knowledge. It has also been argued that constructivism in primary science facilitated the acceptance of defining the science content areas to which children should be introduced and suggested an interrelated view of the processes and content of science (Harlen, 1999).

In order to help teachers develop their understanding of a Piagetian constructivist approach to learning and teaching science, a project was set up in 1987, funded by the Nuffield Foundation. The project, which became known as *Science Processes and Concept Exploration* (SPACE), aimed to explore children's conceptual understanding in science and the possibility of children modifying these ideas as the result of relevant experiences (SPACE, 1987—1990). The project carried out research in primary classrooms and its starting point was the ideas children bring to the learning process. Appropriate science activities were designed to enable children to test out their initial ideas and those of others against evidence, so that reconstruction of their initial understandings could be achieved. The project did not set clear objectives of what children should be expected to learn. Instead, it was suggested that the direction of development should be set out in broad terms to give guidance as to what it is sensible to expect of children at various points and that it should be possible to define the "big ideas" relating to both science content and procedures. In turn, these should be presented as aspects of development to which practical activities contribute. In the first phase of the project, from 1987 to 1989, eight concept areas were studied (Electricity; Evaporation and Condensation; Everyday Changes in Non-Living Materials; Forces and their Effect on Movement; Growth; Light; Living Things; Sensitivity to their Environment; Sound). The second phase of the project (1989—1990) included the study of a further ten concept areas (Earth; Earth in Space; Energy; Genetics and Evolution; Human influences on Earth; Processes of life; Seasonal Changes; Types and Uses of Materials; Variety of Life; and Weather). The research findings led to the development of classroom materials, known as *Nuffield Primary Science* (1993).

Thus, by the end of the 1980s, a new view of good primary science teaching was established, which emphasised the interrelated nature of content and processes and stressed the importance of children's prior conceptions in shaping their learning process. Learning was seen as a process of conceptual change, which takes place as children get engaged in practical activities, and are offered opportunities to reflect on and test their ideas against experiences designed to induce cognitive conflict. Good teaching requires the teacher to elicit children's alternative ideas, plan progression for them and devise experiments which will challenge their conceptions and will help them to acquire the scientific view. And teachers' knowledge of the theoretical constructs of science was seen as an essential prerequisite for effective constructivist teaching (see Harlen, 1999).

Piagetian constructivist perspectives provided a unified approach to the teaching of science for both primary and secondary education, and they influenced decisions about the Science National Curriculum, which was introduced for the first time in 1989. Its emergence and main principles, together with its implications for the teaching of primary science, are discussed next.

The Introduction of the Science National Curriculum

The 1980s ended with the introduction of the National Curriculum, consisting of ten "core" and "foundation" subjects plus religious education, and accompanied by a programme of attainment tests. Science was established as a "core" subject in the curriculum and had to be taught to every child in state schools in England and Wales (DES, 1989).

In general, the idea of a national curriculum was cautiously welcomed. Some saw it as an important means through which children are introduced to "*valued skills, interests, attitudes, concepts and knowledge*" (Richards, 1983, p. 3). However, within British society and its teaching profession, there was considerable disagreement over what is to be "valued", and the content of the new national curriculum inevitably reflected that conflict. As Blyth (1978) had remarked many years earlier: "Everybody agrees that curriculum matters. This is probably the extent of agreement about curriculum" (p. 25). Such debates, together with accumulated criticisms of progressive approaches to education, made it easier for the involvement of politicians to appear necessary in sorting out educational matters. According to Darling (1994), the National Curriculum emerged within a climate which considered the freedom enjoyed by schools and local education authorities to determine the nature of the education provided for primary school children as a crucial weakness in a failing system. Moreover, the new, intensive programme of assessments tests, with school performances made public, introduced a system of "accountability" which put enormous pressure on schools and teachers. Nevertheless, the Science National Curriculum was conceived as an attempt to give all pupils throughout their compulsory education an exciting, broad and balanced experience of science (Jennings, 1992). It stressed the importance of continuity, progression and equal opportunities in primary and secondary science education; although it made clear the need for differentiation, to allow "the highest existing standards to be maintained for the most able" (DES, 1985, p. 13). The Science National Curriculum included clear objectives (attainment targets) for the knowledge and understanding, as well as the skills and aptitudes, which pupils of different abilities and maturity should be expected to have acquired at or near certain ages (DES,

1988). Its first version (DES, 1989) consisted of seventeen attainment targets and multiple statements at ten levels for each one. Fifteen of these targets (AT2–AT16) dealt with knowledge and understanding, one attainment target (AT1) was concerned with the development of investigative skills, whereas the last one (AT17) dealt with the nature of science (this was not intended to be assessed at Key Stages 1 and 2)[5]. In addition to this, and in relation to the Government's claim that regular testing would lead to the raising of standards, it was decided that pupils would be subject to formal testing at ages seven, eleven, fourteen, and sixteen. Furthermore, it was stressed that equal emphasis should be placed on content and process, both in teaching and testing.

However, the Science National Curriculum was soon found to be inconsistent with the assumptions which underlie a constructivist approach to learning. Harlen (1995), for example, argues that there was an "incompatibility between a curriculum structure which specifies objectives and the steps towards them and a view of learning which takes the learner's ideas as the starting point" (p. 93). Furthermore, although science educators had seen the concern for conceptual understanding as intimately linked with the processes of investigation, the inclusion in the curriculum of processes and content in separate attainment targets was thought to discourage attention to their interrelationship (Black, 1993).

Primary teachers found the form of the Science National Curriculum unfamiliar, and even at odds with the science they were used to teaching. Their anxieties centred on interpreting curriculum statements and assessment, but the numerous ambiguities and inconsistencies within the different attainment targets of the Science National Curriculum, together with the lack of assessment requirement guidelines, did not make its understanding or implementation easy. On some occasions, teachers at both primary and secondary levels began to teach to attainment targets, believing mistakenly that these represented what was to be taught, rather than to work from programmes of study, which were designed to facilitate an investigative approach to learning (see Smith, 1994).

PRIMARY SCIENCE IN THE 1990s

The prescription of content was one of the most significant features of the changed primary curriculum, and one result of this was that a lot of attention came to be placed on teachers' ability to teach this content effectively. For example, in 1995, in the review of inspection findings conducted for the UK Office for Standards in Education (OfSTED, 1993/94), the inspectors argued that some primary teachers' low level of subject knowledge, especially in relation to physical sciences, was detrimental to their teaching performance:

Since the beginning of the 1980s, some attempts to define an adequate level of subject knowledge had been made in policy documents concerning the training of primary school teachers (DES, 1983, 1985). In particular, these recommendations stated that at least two years A-level study of a subject related to the primary school curriculum should be an essential part of initial teacher training courses, and that one of the criteria for selection for postgraduate teaching training courses should be a curriculum relevant degree (Calderhead & Miller, 1985). But, among science educators and researchers, such recommendations were seen as introducing a wide and intense programme of studies which could only encourage rote teaching and learning (Johnson, 1997). Instead, they suggested that teachers' adequacy of subject knowledge should be defined in terms of their conceptual understanding: their ability to apply their understanding of the concepts including in the curriculum in giving explanations of relevant phenomena (Russell et al. 1992).

Nevertheless, during the 1990s the issue of the kind and amount of subject knowledge needed by primary teachers to teach science effectively became central in research on primary science education. Some studies suggested that many primary teachers lacked conceptual understanding of some of the main concepts of science, and that where teachers did have some understanding, their knowledge was not in accord with that of scientists (e.g. Kruger & Summers, 1989). Following on from this, many teaching materials were produced and professional development courses were launched in order to help teachers acquire the desired scientific understanding.

It is worth noting here that similar findings about primary teachers' lack of science subject knowledge–particularly in the physical sciences, and confidence in their teaching of science were also reported in other English-speaking countries (Abel & Roth, 1992; Australian Foundation for Science, 1991).

Such studies increased the force of debates about the knowledge primary teachers need to possess in order to teach science effectively and the extent to which teachers' subject knowledge influences effectiveness.

For some researchers, primary teachers are only capable of acquiring understanding of a small range of scientific concepts (Summers & Mant, 1995). Others argued that primary teachers are capable of acquiring understanding of a range of broad scientific principles (Harlen & Holroyd, 1995). These researchers also stress that in discussing teachers' subject knowledge emphasis should be placed on teachers' understanding of the nature of a particular scientific orientation.

With regard to the issue of the extent to which teachers' science subject knowledge influences the effectiveness of teaching, different views were expressed. For example, while Harlen, Holroyd and Byrne (1995) argued that teachers' poor subject knowledge seemed to affect their confidence and forced them to adopt various coping strategies, such as "teaching as little of the subject as the teacher can get away with it", they also claimed that teachers' knowledge about how to teach science may go "a long way to compensating for lack of scientific knowledge" (p. 99). Others placed more emphasis on teachers' knowledge of scientific concepts as an essential condition for effective teaching (Osborne & Simon, 1996a, 1996b; Summers, 1994).

Research on Teacher Effectiveness

Further support for the subject knowledge requirement was provided by research on teacher effectiveness, which originated in the United States, in the mid-eighties. This kind of research shifted its focus from the identification of patterns of teacher behaviour, which had been claimed to improve academic performance among pupils, to the study of the knowledge and beliefs which underlie effective teaching behaviour (e.g. Berliner, 1989; Buchmann, 1984). In Britain, until that time there was little research about the role of subject knowledge in teaching, although, there had been some studies on the professional socialisation of teachers (e.g. Lacey, 1977; Zeichner & Tabachnick, 1985).

Some of the research on teacher effectiveness was interested in teachers' knowledge of the content being taught. Shulman's work is one of the main examples of this type of research. He developed a model for conceptualising practice, which included a *knowledge base* for teaching and a *pedagogical rationale for action*; the "steps" that a teacher follows every time he/she teaches a subject (Wilson, Shulman & Richer, 1987, p. 106). Of importance, here, are his notions of *content knowledge* (or *subject knowledge*) and *pedagogical content knowledge*, which are at the core of the knowledge base for teaching; that is "the body of understanding, skills and dispositions that a teacher needs to perform effectively in a given teaching situation" (p. 106). Content knowledge refers to "the amount and organisation of knowledge per se in the mind of the teacher", whereas pedagogical content knowledge is "the particular form of content knowledge that embodies the aspects of content most germane to its teachability" (Shulman, 1986, p. 9). Thus, within Shulman's model, teachers' understanding of subject knowledge is considered to be one of the most influential factors shaping teaching. As he puts it: "most teaching is initiated by some form of "text", a textbook, a syllabus, or an actual piece of material the teacher or student wishes to have understood" (p. 14), and therefore, the teacher needs to comprehend the text before he/she decides how to teach it.

Shulman's work soon became influential in research on science education, especially in the United States and Australia. Indeed, many projects focused on the identification of the main dimensions of teachers' science pedagogical content knowledge with the aim of producing a model of teacher cognition which could be used for the purposes of teacher training (e.g. Gess-Newsom & Lederman, 1999).

The notion of science pedagogical content knowledge also shaped views about primary science expertise within UK research. More specifically, during the 1990s the group of researchers who carried out the bulk of research into teachers' understanding of scientific concepts expressed concerns about primary teachers' knowledge of constructivist pedagogy. It was argued, for example, that primary teachers still follow the *process* approach in their teaching of science thereby restricting children from developing understanding of scientific concepts. In order to address these concerns, this group of researchers launched continuing professional development courses, which aimed to help practicing teachers to acquire *curricular expertise* or *subject specific teaching knowledge* in relation to specific scientific topics. It was claimed that these term embraced both content knowledge and pedagogical content knowledge, thereby identifying the subject knowledge and specific pedagogical skills a teacher should possess in order to be able to help children acquire scientific understanding of a topic (Summers, Kruger & Mant, 1997a, 1997b). These researchers also supported a version of constructivist teaching, which stressed that in order to induce conceptual change, it is important that chil-

19

dren are introduced to abstract scientific concepts *before* their engagement in practical activities.

This view of the teaching of primary science is not unrelated to criticisms of the constructivist perspective that began to emerge during the late 1980s. Some of these criticisms related to the epistemological principles of constructivism, especially its antirealist stance and the implications of this stance for the teaching of science. Ogborn (1995), for example, argued that the abandonment of "realism as policy" has "led to a loss of nerve in science teaching, leading some to doubt the point and value of teaching science" (p. 3). Similarly, Matthews (1994) rejected constructivism for being subjectivist, empiricist, personalistic, and idealistic, and for tacitly assuming that "a child in isolation can discover and vindicate scientific truths" (p. 147). And Osborne (1996), drawing on Rom Harré's realist philosophy, suggested that a realist conception of the subject matter of science need not lead to didacticism and can supplement constructivist pedagogy by making a place for telling, showing or demonstrating" (p. 74). Such criticisms usually claim that all that is beneficial in constructivist pedagogy, mainly the elicitation of children's conceptions, can be preserved and used in other teaching approaches which could be more effective in helping children reconstruct their initial understanding.

Around the same time, Vygotskian views on learning appeared in the literature of science education research (see Koch, 2006). These views emphasised the role of language and communication in the development of children's scientific understanding, and influenced changes in ideas about the nature of effective learning and teaching. In this way, within UK research on primary science education, a *socio-constructivist* version of learning and teaching emerged, which argued that children reconstruct their everyday ideas as they test these ideas and the ideas suggested to them by more knowledgeable others within children's *zone of proximal development* (Driver et al. 1994; Harlen & Qualter, 2004). [6]

Following on from this, in 1997, Harlen discussed pedagogical content knowledge as a broad framework that "enables" (p. 7) teachers to use their subject knowledge to support a socio-constructivist approach to the learning and teaching of science designed to help children acquire understanding of broad scientific principles.

These debates took place during a time when the British Government was expressing the view that teacher training should be conducted, as much as possible, in schools on an apprenticeship basis; a proposal that is based on the idea that teaching is a practical accomplishment that involves acquiring a battery of techniques to be deployed in the delivery of a pre-specified curriculum (see Alexander, Rose, & Woodhead, 1992).

Further support for this approach to teacher education was given by the introduction of the Initial Teacher Training Curriculum (DfEE, 1998), which detailed the scientific understanding and pedagogical skills required of beginner teachers[7].

Similar documents were prepared in many countries during the 1990s (e.g. the U.S. National Science Education Standards, 1996). Such standards-driven documents raised additional issues about the level of knowledge and pedagogical strategies that beginner teachers ought to possess and how this should be assessed (Nichols & Koballa, 2006).

PRIMARY SCIENCE BEYOND 2000

The beginning of the twenty-first century has been characterised by a worldwide trend towards standards-based education (see Appleton, 2006). In UK, this has been accompanied by further development in testing regimes, especially in relation to the assessment of student teachers' understanding of subject knowledge. Many science teacher educators, for example, now use multiple-choice tests to assess student teachers' science knowledge (such as that produced by the University of Cambridge Local Examinations Syndicate). At the same time, it has been suggested that, although primary teachers' science knowledge is better than previously, they still lack understanding of the purpose of practical work in science learning, and confidence in engaging children in scientific investigations (Millar & Osborne, 1998).

Among UK primary science researchers, debates continue around the kind and amount of teachers' science subject knowledge, as well as about the kind of pedagogical content knowledge, that is necessary. Indeed, currently, it is possible to identify two constructivist lines of thinking about teacher expertise. For one group of researchers, those whom I will call "small range" constructivists, the education of primary teachers should include their learning of a small range of scientific concepts and pedagogical skills. This knowledge should help primary teachers to introduce children to abstract scientific ideas prior to their engagement in practical activities. On the other hand, a second group of researchers, those whom I will call "big ideas" constructivists argue that primary science expertise requires their understanding of a broad range of scientific principles, as well as knowledge of the components of a particular scientific orientation. In turn, for these constructivists this knowledge is essential in helping teachers to use a socio-constructivist approach to the learning and teaching of science, through which children construct understanding of abstract scientific principles.

More recently, questions about the character of teachers' science subject knowledge have been linked with broader discussions about the nature of scientific literacy. Some commentators have stressed the interdisciplinary nature of primary teaching, and have examined the place of science within an interdisciplinary school curriculum (see Roth, Tobin, & Ritchie, 2001). Others have argued that science learning should move beyond teaching children about the main concepts of science to include cognitive abilities that will enable them to use scientific knowledge in evaluating the effects of human activity to the natural world (e.g. Hodson, 1998; National Research Council, 1996).

Moreover, sociocultural interpretations of Vygotsky's theory have appeared in science education research. These are framed by the assumption that knowledge and learning are necessarily situated within the activities of a science classroom community. As a result, they raise new questions about the nature of teachers' subject knowledge and their pedagogical. Nevertheless, their influence on primary science education research remains limited.

CONCLUSION

I have focused my discussion in this chapter on the main reforms of primary science that took place in UK during the past forty years, and how these lent support to an increasing emphasis on the importance of subject knowledge for primary science expertise. I began by describing the curriculum developments that took place during the 1960s, which were influenced by the child-centred tradition and aspects of Piaget's stage theory. The picture of "good" primary science teaching that became predominant during the 1960s and 1970s was one which portrayed science teaching as a process of inquiry through which learners acquire useful knowledge. To teach science effectively, primary teachers needed to have an understanding of the process of inquiry and sufficient scientific knowledge to be able to guide children's inquiries.

However, during the 1980s, "good" primary science teaching came to be redefined, as a result of dissatisfaction with the "process approach", criticisms of child-centred education, discussions about the need for a broad and balanced science curriculum, and the appearance of Piagetian constructivist theories of learning. The emergent picture of "good" primary science teaching was one which maintained the principle that science teaching should aim to contribute to the overall intellectual development of the child, but it assumed that the content and process of science were interrelated, and that children bring prior conceptions to learning that need to be challenged directly during teaching. Furthermore, increased importance was given to the acquisition of abstract concepts as an outcome of learning.

Within this picture of science teaching, particular emphasis came to be placed on teachers' understanding of the theoretical constructs of science, since this was seen as an essential prerequisite for effective constructivist teaching. This stress on subject knowledge was further reinforced by the introduction of the Science National Curriculum, the appearance of prescribed content knowledge which primary teachers had to teach, and the introduction of tests designed to assess children's learning of this knowledge. As a result, during the nineties, the subject knowledge requirement became a major component of considerations of teacher effectiveness.

Around the same time, the distinction between subject knowledge and pedagogical content knowledge came to be made in the literature dealing with primary science education research. Furthermore, researchers saw the need to adjust their picture of "good" primary science teaching. From the point of view of "small range" constructivists, teaching should include introducing children to a limited range of abstract scientific concepts prior to their engagement in practical activities. For "big ideas" constructivists, teaching should engage children in activities where they are offered opportunities to test their own hypotheses and those of more knowledgeable others against scientific evidence.

So, at the beginning of the twenty-first century, debates about teacher expertise continue to focus around the kind of subject knowledge and pedagogical content knowledge that are necessary to ensure the effective teaching of primary science. However, these discussions take place in a climate where, on the one hand, there is increased criticism of Piagetian constructivism and a growth in influence of socio-constructivist and sociocultural perspectives, while on the other hand, from the direction of policy, there is an increasingly standards-driven view of teacher education.

NOTES

[1] Hodson (1996) argues that in the United States the major impetus to discovery learning came from the writings of Jerome Bruner (1966) and Joseph Schwab (1962). In his influential essay "The teaching of science as enquiry" Schwab emphasises scientific inquiry as both content and method, and argues that laboratory experience should precede classroom teaching, and that the laboratory manual should 'cease to be a volume which tells the student what to do and what to expect" and be 'replaced by permissive and open materials which point to areas in which problems can be found' (Schwab, 1962, p. 55).

[2] These concept groups were Energy, Structure, Change and Life.

[3] Some work on assessment had been carried out on the *Progress in Learning Science* project (1973-1977, see Parker-Jelly, 1983).

[4] It should be mentioned here that in the history of primary science, this is not the first time that discussions about the balance between teaching science for its utility and teaching science for its abstract concepts has taken place. Layton (1973), for example, argues that in the reform of elementary education that took place in the mid-nineteenth century a similar debate- between the teaching of 'science of common things' and the teaching of 'pure science' – led to the exclusion of science from the elementary curriculum and the reduction of its content to the study of natural history, with an emphasis on observation.

[5] Since 1989, there have been four revisions of the Science National Curriculum (1991; 1995; 1998; 2000), which reduced the number of Attainment targets to four.

[6] This is defined as 'the distance between the actual development level determined by independent problem-solving and the level of potential development as determined through problem solving under adult guidance or in collaboration with more capable peers' (Vygotsky, 1978, p. 86).

[7] A revised version of the UK Initial Teacher Training Curriculum, was produced in 2001 (Teacher Training Agency, 2001). A new revised version of this curriculum will be implemented in initial teacher education courses in 2007

THE SUBJECT KNOWLEDGE REQUIREMENT

In discussing teachers' science subject knowledge what is often implied is that, in order to be effective, a primary teacher must have a level of subject knowledge above some specified threshold. This has been suggested by Harlen (2000), for example, who argues that teachers need to have a "foundation for building a framework for teaching science" (p. 7). However, among researchers in primary science education in UK there are different views about what this foundation should consist of, which are shaped by different interpretations of constructivism. Thus, for "small range" constructivists, the foundation of teachers' knowledge should consist of teachers' adequate *conceptual understanding* of a small range of science concepts included in the English Primary Science National Curriculum.[1] By contrast, for "big ideas" constructivists this foundation should take the form of adequate conceptual understanding of broad scientific principles along with understanding of the nature of a proper scientific orientation.

In this chapter, I discuss in detail the assumptions about the nature of knowledge and how it develops that underpin these two constructivist views and the methods used to determine teachers' adequacy of subject knowledge. In the course of this, I will draw on a sociocultural perspective of knowledge and learning. This perspective stresses the complex interdependence of knowledge and action, and argues that knowledge and understanding are necessarily situated in the specific activities of communities of practice.

"SMALL RANGE" CONSTRUCTIVISM

"Small range" constructivists argue there is a substantial lack of *conceptual understanding* among primary science teachers about many areas of the primary Science National Curriculum, and that a considerable number of them experience great difficulty in acquiring the necessary scientific understanding.

On this basis, they argue that it may be unrealistic to expect that primary teachers, especially the ones with no science qualifications, to acquire adequate knowledge of all the concept areas included in the primary Science National Curriculum. Osborne and Simon (1996b), for example, claim that the science knowledge that primary teachers need to possess in order to teach science effectively to children can only be determined by a careful consideration of what science concepts most primary teachers are able to acquire adequate knowledge of. Without such knowledge primary teachers are considered to be unable to identify correctly children's prior understanding or to plan their teaching so as to help children acquire the scientific view.

And so such authors concentrate their efforts on defining a more limited range of significant science concepts that primary teachers are capable of understanding. Summers and Mant (1998), for example, discuss the aspects of the concept of *energy* that should be included in the Science National Curriculum, arguing that these aspects should replace those aspects of *balanced* and *unbalanced forces* that teachers find difficult to understand.

"Small range" constructivists give little emphasis to the development of teachers' problem-solving *procedural understanding*: their knowledge of the procedures needed to figure out what a scientific problem is about, and to collect and interpret evidence in order to address it. However, they are concerned with teachers' acquisition of practical skills, such as how to wire a circuit. Indeed, they often imply that the development of problem-procedural knowledge should follow the acquisition of simple concepts and process skills. Moreover, they suggest that scientific concepts can be broken down into smaller parts and taught to teachers separately. These researchers, for instance, have identified, in order of difficulty, seven "simple concepts" (p.13) associated with aspects of electricity, which were easily understood by most primary teachers who participated in an in-service course on the topic. This points to a *sequential* view of knowledge acquisition on the part of these constructivists: the idea that simple concepts, facts and process skills (lower functions of cognition) are basic in individuals' knowledge, and they exist as prerequisites to learning more complex or higher-order functions of cognition, such as complex concepts and problem-solving procedural knowledge (see Greeno, Pearson, & Schoenfeld, 1999).

It is important to note here that the sequential view of knowledge acquisition is part of a broader psychological approach, which is often referred to as *cognitivism*. Cognitivism was developed during the 1950s and 1960s in order to explain why students fail to or succeed in acquiring academic knowledge (see Murphy, 1999). It assumes that the mind and the environment are separate and have somehow to match one another. It uses computational methods and metaphors to model human learning and understanding, and is based on the assumption that there are certain universal features of human cognition (e.g. cognitive structures, short-term memory) that explain human thinking in general. Moreover, it assumes that human thinking involves logical deduction using context-free rules. In particular, within this approach knowledge is seen as a property of the individual mind, acquired during the course of solving problems thrown up by the environment. During this process, encoded symbols from the environment are stored in the individual's memory in hierarchical structures that stand in one-to-one correspondence with the problem in the world. Each time an individual has to solve a new problem, he/she compares the information received from the environment with existing structures in the brain in a search of correspondence or difference. Thus, for cognitivism, a problem in the external world is represented inside the individual's head and is solved using specific rules. From this point of view, learning and understanding depend on changing knowledge representations, and acquiring or strengthening expert rules that would solve a given problem more efficiently (Bredo, 1997). From a sequential perspective, learners are expected to learn, first of all, the properties of the concepts of a discipline, and then the procedures by which such concepts are used to solve paradigmatic problems within the discipline. Such problems are clearly stated and have one correct answer, and concepts are treated as products or *units of cognition* which can be acquired in all-or-none integral steps (White, 1979). Understanding each of these steps implies that the individual possesses adequate description of its properties; and that, based on this description, he/she is able to correctly classify instances as examples or non examples of the specific concept (Klausmeier, Ghatala, & Frayer, 1974). And, since it is the learner who is responsible for doing the problem solving in this model, cognitivism places particular emphasis on what an individual brings to a given problem. It suggests that the same data, such as a set of examples or non examples of a concept, will have different impact on the conclusions drawn by various individuals or by the same individual at different points during his/her learning. Thus, in order to lead an individual to a certain conclusion, one needs to be aware of his or her prior academic knowledge and search strategy. The term *misconceptions* is often used to refer to individuals' defective understanding of some of the properties of a specific concept.

Cognitivism is a feature of some *constructivist* perspectives, especially those influenced by Piaget's approach, within which knowledge is "constructed in a slow process that begins with a simple sensory-motor schema during early childhood and progresses to complex schema without physical referents from the late teens onwards" (Roth, 1999, p. 6). Such perspectives place emphasis on learners' everyday ideas, that is the ideas that individuals construct in their everyday interactions with the world. They argue, for example, that everyday knowledge can be an obstacle to the successful acquisition of academic knowledge (Gilbert & Osborne, 1980). From this point of view, in order to ensure the effective acquisition of academic knowledge attention is given not only to individuals' prior academic understanding but also to their everyday understandings. Indeed, this is the approach to knowledge that underlies "small range" constructivism.

Acquiring Understanding of a Small Range of Science Concepts

For "small range" constructivists, teachers should be capable of constructing conceptual structures during their everyday interactions with aspects of the physical world. However, teachers' understanding of scientific concepts is treated as sharply distinct from their everyday conceptualisations – the ideas that teachers construct in their everyday interactions with the physical world (Summers & Mant, 1995). Sometimes, this view of scientific concepts is associated with a *modest realist* perspective in which science is seen as involving a body of scientific propositions produced by the systematic testing of ideas against the real world. Each of these scientific propositions is treated as having a precise and fixed meaning that describes the *universal properties* present in all the phenomena being described. By contrast, everyday conceptualisations of a science concept (e.g. *force*) are seen as imprecise; they involve a variety of meanings or beliefs, which are specific to the situations they describe. The term *misconceptions* is often used to describe such intuitive beliefs-ideas which are at odds with the currently accepted view of the science community.

At the core of this distinction between scientific and everyday knowledge is the belief that scientific knowledge is the product of a distinct form of reasoning about the physical world. Osborne (1996), for example, argues that the methods, procedures and criteria that scientists use to test hypotheses against the real world, to judge specific evidence for and against theory etc, are distinct from the ones used by other disciplines or by individuals in their attempts to understand their surroundings. On such a view, it is inappropriate to assume that teachers can acquire adequate understanding of scientific concepts through their everyday interactions with the physical world, though it is possible that some implicit understanding of a science concept may be obtained through such interactions. Summers et al. (1998), for instance, argue that some of the primary teachers who participated in an in-service course designed specifically to help teachers develop their scientific understanding of aspects of *energy conservation,* appeared to hold everyday ideas about the topic which were close to the scientific understanding of it. Thus, many teachers seemed able to explain energy conservation in terms of "saving" or using "less energy" (p. 311), though they appeared to be unaware that their everyday understanding was close to the scientific version of this concept.

In general, researchers who share this approach to judging the adequacy of teachers' knowledge emphasise that scientific understanding can only be ensured if teachers are introduced to the correct definition of specific scientific concepts, so that they acquire an adequate description of the properties and relationships of each scientific concept and a clear understanding of the ways in which such properties and relationships are used to explain all instances of it. In turn, they argue that teachers' introduction to scientific definitions should take place during in-service education courses and should precede teachers' involvement with practical activities. In this way, teachers are expected to reconstruct their misconceptions and be able to use the predefined scientific explanation in explaining correctly relevant aspects of the physical world.

Of course, the process of acquiring an adequate understanding of a science concept is not smooth. It is possible that teachers may not acquire an understanding of all the relevant properties of a scientific concept, or that they may continue to use their misconceptions as well as their scientific understanding in explaining the same aspect of the physical world. Summers (1994), for example, commenting on the scientific understanding acquired by primary teachers who participated in in-service courses, says that "the scientific understanding achieved is likely to be partial and "messy" with, for example, misconceptions existing alongside scientific views and teachers unsure of their new knowledge" (p. 185).[2]

Thus, from this point of view teachers' *adequate conceptual knowledge of science* refers to teachers' possession of an adequate description of the universal properties and relationships of scientific concepts, and to their ability to use this knowledge in explaining correctly aspects of the physical world. Of course, primary teachers are not expected to acquire adequate descriptions of *all* scientific concepts, or even of all of those included in the primary Science National Curriculum. This is judged simply not to be feasible. However, since for these researchers scientific concepts can be broken down into smaller parts, they argue that it is possible to identify the parts that primary teachers can easily understand and need.

Defining Teachers' Adequate Understanding of a Small range of Science concepts

The methods employed to define teachers' adequacy of science knowledge are usually semi-structured interviews and multiple-choice questionnaires. The interviews are carried out with a small sample of teachers to explore teachers' views of the specific concept. The interviews often precede the use of questionnaires, which usually aim to establish the prevalence of misconceptions in a larger sample of teachers (see Kruger, Palacio, & Summers, 1990, 1992).

The type of interview often used in these studies is a variation on the Interview-About Instances (IAI) technique, which was developed in the late 1970s by Roger Osborne and John Gilbert to investigate students' understanding of everyday words that are used in subtly different ways in science. The IAI method consists of dyadic discussions with participants, using a deck of cards as a focus. These cards contain line drawings depicting situations such as "a book lying on a table", or real objects such as a "jumping toy car" (Summers & Kruger, 1990, 1992) and 3D models (e.g. Mant & Summers, 1995), which are used to prompt discussion about a particular aspect of a situation, such as the role of energy. The method rests on the choice of appropriate instances, so as to expose critical aspects of teachers' knowledge. This is because, at the core of the design of the IAI technique, lies the assumption that understanding of science concepts is determined according to the individual's ability to correctly classify instances as examples or non examples of a concept (Osborne & Gilbert, 1979, 1980). It is important to note that since the method rests on selection of an appropriate set of instances the researchers' decisions about what the dimensions of an adequate description of a concept are, shape the findings.

The presentation of selected instances follows a particular order, which sometimes is the one that is described in the Science National Curriculum. During the interview, for each instance, the interviewer describes the situation and then asks the interviewee a focus question. Some of these questions require the teacher to decide whether a particular concept is contained in the specific instance. For other instances, the interviewer may explain to the teacher the meaning of the concept that is included in a specific instance (e.g. *net force*) before he/she presents the teacher with a number of different statements, from which the teacher is asked to decide which one describes the instance best (Summers & Kruger, 1993). On other occasions, the focus question aims to encourage the teacher to talk for a few minutes about a specific concept (Kruger & Summers, 1989). For each response, further questions are asked by the interviewer, aiming to clarify teachers' meaning or probe further to elicit teachers' understanding of the specific concept.

Quite often some of the instances used during the interviews are included in the questionnaire, together with a number of statements, from which the teachers are asked to choose whether they think the statement is true or false (and two more choices are included: "don't understand" and "not sure"). Sometimes, these statements are ideas that have been expressed by other teachers during interviews. Since the aim of such interviews and questionnaires is to identify teachers' existing knowledge, particular emphasis is placed on not helping teachers with their responses (Summers et al., 1998).

The adequacy of teachers' science knowledge is determined by the analysis of their responses to interviews and questionnaires. Thus, teachers who possess inadequate scientific knowledge are those who are unable to classify correctly the specific instances included in the interviews and questionnaires as examples or non examples of a specific science concept, or can only classify correctly a few of these. By contrast, teachers who classify correctly most of these instances are taken to have "complete" scientific understanding or, in other words, adequate subject knowledge. It is assumed that teachers' ability to classify correctly a limited number of instances associated with a particular concept and to give reasons for their decisions in terms of a predefined explanation informs their ability to use the same concept correctly in the future. It is believed that, each time a teacher is faced with a situation which relates to an aspect of the physical world, he/she should be able to recall the correct scientific concept and classify this situation as an instance or a non instance of the specific scientific concept.

In evaluating this first type of constructivism, a key issue for consideration is whether adequacy of knowledge measured by interviews and questionnaires actually captures teachers' practical science expertise.

Questionable Assumptions About "Small Range" Constructivism

As already noted, for "small range" constructivism teachers' ability to explain experience correctly is a matter of matching the properties and relationships specified in a set of sentences with the properties and relationships present in the instances being described. There is a tacit belief here in *representationalism*, the idea that symbols mirror reality (Bredo, 1999). Yet a belief in *representationalism* could only be sustained if each scientific concept gathered together identical instances or at least very similar ones. Under such conditions, the application of such concepts would be unproblematic, and their involvement in science generalisations could make the application of other terms unproblematic. For example, the statement that a *force is* a *pull or* a *push* could be used to provide a precise and adequate explanation of all the instances associated with *force*, if it could be asserted that the instances associated with the terms *pull* or *push* are identical (the extension of the concept). In such a case, of course, the extension only needs to include one instance which could be the very idea of "force", "pull" and "push". This suggests an essentialist account of concept application. However, in practice, instances are not identical. For all the complexity of language, experience is much more complex and richer in information. Physical objects and events are never self-evidently identical with one another or possessed of a common essence (Barnes, 1974, 1982). Given this, teachers' ability to make sense of experience is a much more complex matter than a cognitivist view of mind allows; it is fraught with ambiguity and uncertainty. Responding to a situation involves exercising judgments about which concept is applicable in the particular situation, judgements that are often influenced by teachers' perceptions and interpretations of the specifics of the situation and which cannot be easily codified or made entirely explicit (Bruner, 1966).

Following on from this, uncertainty or even failure in the task situation does not necessarily indicate lack of expertise on the part of teachers because understanding takes place over time and in context, rather than necessarily occurring at a fixed and predictable point. Indeed, some researchers argue that, given the dynamic nature of cognition, interviews "can only provide clues to ongoing cognitive processes" (Welzel & Roth, 1998, p. 40). Teachers may fail to respond adequately to interview and questionnaire demands, but reconstruct their understanding in a more scientific direction as they reflect on the problem later.

Finally, unlike the problems dealt with in interviews and questionnaires, those faced by teachers in classrooms may not be well-defined and therefore will need to be actively framed as problems before they are solved. Children's questions and ideas about scientific concepts and phenomena may be expressed within contexts that are far more ambiguous and complex than the instances teachers are asked to respond to in constructivist research of this kind. Given this, in order for teachers to deal with such cases they may need to figure out the nature of the situation first, before they decide which concept is most appropriate to use (Bruner, 1986). Figuring out the situation may include framing and reframing the problem depicted in an instance, and trying out a number of different concepts to explain it, testing hypotheses, discussing the instance with children in the classroom or reading about specific concepts in resource textbooks. In doing this, teachers may need the problem-solving procedural knowledge of science to which "small range" constructivism gives little emphasis. Moreover, decisions about how to respond to situations that arise during teaching are often made on the spot, which heightens the need for contextual judgment and teachers' reliance on their pedagogical expertise. However, the courses based on this approach do not introduce teachers to ways of thinking about ill-defined problems or pedagogical strategies for dealing with such problem-situations.

It can be suggested, therefore, that even if a range of science concepts can be defined that primary teachers are able to apply correctly in explaining a limited number of situations associated with them, this still leaves open the possibility that teachers may not be able to apply the same concepts successfully in all future situations. In other words, in some situations teachers may still express misconceptions about concepts which they previously appeared to understand adequately.

In summary, there are some serious questions to be raised about this way of approaching teachers' adequacy of subject knowledge. Some of these concern the assumptions about the nature of knowledge, and about teachers' development of scientific understanding. Others relate to the methods used to assess adequacy of teachers' understanding. Above all, there are significant questions about the relationship between the understanding that teachers display in interviews and questionnaires and their practical expertise: their ability to use scientific knowledge in classroom situations.

"BIG IDEAS" CONSTRUCTIVISM

A second group of researchers in UK primary science education, those which I called "big ideas" constructivists, argues that the foundation of subject knowledge that primary teachers need to possess in order to teach science effectively consists of conceptual understanding of a small number of broad scientific principles that are included in the primary Science National Curriculum, along with procedural understanding characteristic of a proper scientific orientation.[3] Discussing the importance of teachers' conceptual understanding of the "big ideas" of science, Harlen (1997) says:

> Why "big ideas"? Because these are, in the end, what we want children to understand–not particular muscles in the arm, not the particular position of that image in the plain mirror, but the general ideas that help to explain muscle action wherever it happens and all the phenomena where images are formed. (p.7)

In turn, the necessary procedural understanding involves understanding that science begins with observation, and raising questions about what has been observed, and proceeds through predictions and hypothesising, planning and carrying out an investigation, collecting and interpreting data. Such understanding is associated with a view of science as a cooperative activity in which scientists use past and present ideas to produce knowledge that is conjectural, and is built up through the systematic testing of ideas against evidence (Harlen & Qualter, 2004).

"Big ideas" constructivists believe that the understanding of science develops as individuals interact with their own experience and with the ideas of others, and involves conceptual change. On such a view, procedural understanding is the means for acquiring conceptual understanding. In other words, knowledge of how to do science develops interactively with knowledge of concepts of science. Thus, this approach to teachers' subject knowledge places emphasis on problem solving aspects of procedural knowledge, those which "small range" constructivists consider higher order and perhaps beyond the reach of primary teachers.

Another difference is that, while "small range" constructivists draw a sharp distinction between teachers' everyday conceptualisations of physical phenomena and scientific concepts, "big ideas" constructivists argue that there are similarities between these; and that teachers' misunderstandings can be seen as resulting from their making inappropriate links between experience and knowledge or from use of misleading everyday language. More specifically, drawing on a Piagetian constructivist perspective of the learner, "big ideas" constructivists argue that throughout their lives teachers construct conceptual structures as they test their ideas against experience (Harlen, Holroyd, & Byrne, 1995). These structures may involve ideas that are at odds with the accepted scientific ones. As a result, teachers' everyday ideas may be linked to specific events as opposed to the "big ideas" of science that are used to explain a wide range of events. It is possible, though to foster and develop further teachers' ability to test their ideas against evidence, to the point that it takes the form of scientific inquiry, thereby helping them to make appropriate links between knowledge and experience. In other words, teachers need to be offered opportunities to develop procedural capability, so as to be able to test their existing knowledge against scientific evidence and use the evidence to make appropriate links between this knowledge and experience. Such reconstruction may also take place as teachers discuss their ideas with more knowledgeable adults, who may suggest different ideas for them to test. Indeed, influenced by Vygotsky's work, this group of researchers emphasise the role of social interaction in the development of scientific understanding.

Following on from this, "big ideas" constructivists describe teachers' knowledge of science as a network of links between scientific concepts and experience, which can be extended as teachers make new links between scientific concepts and ways of acting and interpreting evidence. Thus, developing teachers' procedural understanding is seen as the key to educating primary science practitioners. This is not just because this understanding is fundamental for helping teachers acquire conceptual knowledge of the "big ideas" of science, but also because it is closely related to the ways in which teachers should help children develop their own scientific understanding in the classroom.

Nevertheless, teachers' adequate conceptual understanding of the "big ideas" of science is regarded as central to effective teaching, since without it teachers' are not in a good position to guide children's scientific learning.

Defining Teachers' Adequate Understanding of the "Big Ideas" of Science

Like the first type of constructivism, "big ideas" constructivists also use interviews to determine teachers' adequacy of scientific understanding. The method used for determining teachers' adequate knowledge of the Big Ideas of science is similar to the Interview-About-Instances method described earlier in this chapter. During such interviews, teachers are presented with *events* associated with specific scientific ideas. The means for presenting the chosen events to teachers are either coloured photographs, or simple equipment; and the related "big ideas" of science provide the framework for analysing teachers' responses. For example, in order to explore teachers' understanding of energy and electricity, they were presented with a battery-operated circuit which included a switch and a bulb (Harlen, 1996). This event was the focus of the interview which aimed to explore teachers' understanding that current flow needs a circuit of suitable materials, switches make and break the circuit, and that the battery supplies electrical energy which is changed in the bulb to heat or light energy. Teachers were asked to discuss the particular event and to arrive at a *collaborative explanation* for the event, that is, an explanation that is satisfactory for both the teacher and the interviewer. During these interviews, the interviewer was checking constantly that what was suggested made sense to the teacher in terms of the evidence presented and other evidence that could be recalled.

Helping teachers in their explanations differentiates this approach from the previous one, in which teachers are not offered any kind of support in the interviews or questionnaires. For "big ideas" constructivists this kind of support is judged to be appropriate because what is taken as teachers' knowledge is not the knowledge that teachers appear already to possess but the understanding that they can achieve under the guidance of another more capable adult, and within the teachers' zone of proximal development.

Thus, during discussions of a particular event, in some cases the teacher will provide the information and in other cases the interviewer will propose ideas to test out. In this way, the teacher not only develops his/her conceptual understanding but also his/her procedural understanding of science. Of course, not all of the "big ideas" included in the primary Science National Curriculum are easily understood by primary teachers. For example, ideas such as, current flow needs a circuit of suitable materials, and that switches make and break a circuit, are easily understood by most primary teachers. By contrast, the idea that the battery supplies electrical energy which is changed in the bulb to heat/light energy, is less easily understood. Nevertheless, it has also been suggested that given the opportunity, teachers can develop adequate understanding of many scientific concepts (Harlen, 1999).

Despite these important differences, this approach to teachers' expertise, like the first one, treats knowledge from a cognitivist perspective. It seems to be assumed, for example, that once teachers have achieved a collaborative explanation for a particular event, they have acquired adequate knowledge for applying the concept in the future, both in the classroom and in other contexts. Indeed, doubts that might surround the interpretation of problem-solving situations seem only to be treated as acceptable during teachers' *acquisition* of subject knowledge. These are not regarded as a significant part of teachers' responses to situations that arise during teaching, at least not when they relate to a concept of which teachers have already been shown to possess adequate understanding. Instead, it is expected that such problem-solving situations are well defined, and that they can be resolved either by the retrieval of the correct big idea of science or by the application of a clearly defined scientific procedure.

What I am arguing, then, is that, despite their important differences, the two constructivist approaches to teachers' subject knowledge I have discussed share some limitations in common, especially in terms of their interpretation of the relation between teachers' knowledge and their classroom expertise. They assume a universalistic view of scientific knowledge: the idea that the concepts of science are abstract, precise entities which can be internalised into the mind of the individual teacher. Moreover, both approaches treat teachers' understanding as taking the form of *acquired*, commodity-like knowledge that is essentially decontextualised and available to be *applied* across situations. From this point of view, once primary teachers have acquired the correct understanding of scientific concepts and/or of scientific procedures, they should be able to apply them in the future, both in classrooms and in other situations.

As mentioned in the beginning of this chapter, my questioning of these assumptions is based on some recent developments in the study of cognition. These emphasise that the construction of knowledge cannot be seen independently from the situation in which it occurs. A sociocultural approach to cognition offers a rather different picture of knowledge, understanding and learning, one which may have important implications for how teachers' adequacy of science knowledge is defined and for how it relates to classroom practice.

SOCIOCULTURAL APPROACHES TO KNOWLEDGE AND UNDERSTANDING

Unlike cognitivist approaches to mind, which treat the concepts and ideas expressed in language as representing the situations they describe - and therefore, as having an existence independent from the situation in which they were produced - sociocultural theories view the concepts and ideas expressed in language as the products of a particular line of societal activity which take their meaning from the context of that activity.

Like "big ideas" constructivists, they draw on Vygotsky's work, but this time in treating language as providing the means or tools for social coordination and adaptation (Lave, 1993; Wertsch, 1985). Vygotsky's work primarily contrasted practical ways of thinking associated with traditional society and the more theoretical and abstract ways of thinking introduced by modern educational institutions. Thus, it was directed toward modernisation and the learning of abstract scientific concepts.

Although it is difficult to generalise across this tradition as a whole, at this point, it is perhaps important to clarify the main theoretical insights which are endorsed by most psychologists of the Vygotsky school. In particular, Vygotsky's theory is concerned with the social development of mind: the ways in which a person's higher mental functions develop through social interaction (Axel, 1992). These higher mental functions – the mental capabilities such as thinking, believing, remembering, wishing, desiring, hoping, imagining, and so on – are embedded in or mediated by language. Language is an essentially social phenomenon, in the sense that it presupposes the existence of a *set of shared social meanings* (e.g. the theoretical propositions of physics) against which any communicative act has its reality. Such sets of shared social meanings are the products of a *culture*. Cultures are constituted by the socially significant forms of activity of a community: "historically evolved human attributes, abilities and modes of behaviour" (Leont'ev, 1983 cited in Davidov, 1988, p. 23).

Within Vygotsky's theory, it is only through the appropriation of such socially significant forms of activity that the individual becomes capable of the higher mental functions. *Activity*, therefore, becomes the unit of analysis; it is the mediating agent between the individual and culture/society. In other words, higher mental functions must be understood as internalised forms of social activity. On such a view, *appropriation* is a process in which these social activities are translated from the social plane onto the individual plane, where they emerge in restructured form as the individual's higher mental functions (Backhurst, 1988). This transformation of cultural to individual knowledge takes place in the *zone of proximal development* (ZPD). In this endeavour, linguistic expressions become the *means* by which individuals construct understanding of a situation and participate in the activities of a particular community. When there is problem in acting, the meaning of these expressions has to be negotiated and socially constructed. Thus, within Vygotsky's theory individual actions and mental representations are understandable as integral elements of the activity systems in which they function, take shape, and which they in turn constitute (Engeström, 1988). In other words, thought and speech are instruments for the planning and carrying out of tasks, just as eyes and hands are.

Influenced by Vygotsky's theory, sociocultural approaches to cognition hold that "what we take as knowledge and how we think and express ideas are the products of the interaction of groups of people over time" (Putman & Borko, 2000, p. 5). Throughout their lives, individuals participate in various communities of practice, ranging from scholarly disciplines such as Science and History to groups of people sharing a common interest, including those operating in particular classrooms. Each of these communities, generates tools, a set of shared social meanings, which its members use to interpret and negotiate their interpretations with one another, thereby enabling them to continue to act successfully in the activities of that community. In the course of this process, people develop, often tacitly, rich networks of links between specific tools and situations, which are employed to make sense of future situations. And because situations are not fixed or identical, each time an individual uses a tool to construct understanding of a new situation that resembles an old one, he/she develops a better understanding of both the tool and the situation itself. As Brown, Collins and Duguid (1989) put it:

> People who use tools actively rather than just acquire them build an increasingly rich implicit understanding of the world in which they use the tools and of the tools themselves. The understanding, both of the world and of the tool, continually changes as a result of their interaction. (p. 33)

An important implication of sociocultural approaches to knowledge is that an individual's understanding of the concepts, theories and ideas of a particular community is a *dynamic* process resulting from acting in situations and negotiating with other members of the community. Furthermore, such understanding is constructed first on a social plane before it becomes internalised by the individual, and is best described as an "evolving spiral" (Patricia Murphy, personal communication), in which lower mental functions (e.g. concepts and facts, and simple process skills) and higher mental functions (problem-solving procedural knowledge, complex concepts, perception, remembering, etc.) develop interdependently as individuals participate in socially and culturally organised activities.

This is a very different approach from treating understanding as involving the application of a static set of concepts and procedures, as within cognitivist approaches to mind. For example, in their attempts to act successfully in an activity of a specific scientific community, individuals may initially perceive the task as unfamiliar and feel unable to understand it. On such occasions, the situation in which the blockage occurs forms the practical background for the thinking. Individuals may decide to examine the actual site of the problem, to look around, negotiate it with other members of the community, choose which tools could be used to make sense of it, to help determine the nature of the problem. Testing the proposed solution involves practical action to see whether anticipated consequences occur, that may lead to further thinking, testing and acting until a solution is reached which is acceptable to the members of the particular community. Thus, for sociocultural theorists the *activity* becomes the unit of analysis rather than the individual's mental structures.

Following on from this, sociocultural theorists emphasise the *ambiguity* and *contingency* of understanding. They argue that because knowledge as organised for a particular task can never be sufficiently detailed, sufficiently precise to anticipate exactly the conditions of action, the individual needs to be prepared to deal with contingency. As Keller and Keller (1993) put it:

> An individual's knowledge is simultaneously to be regarded as representational and emergent, prepatterned and aimed at coming to terms with actions and products that go beyond the already known. (p. 127)

Sociocultural perspectives direct our attention not to the individual who tries to build understanding independent of others, but instead to individuals as they are becoming functioning members of their communities before they become selves. It is important to note here that, unlike cognitivist theories which assume that novices' ability to understand the expert depends on the possession of identical cognitive structures or representations of the task, within sociocultural perspectives novices' ability to understand the expert depends on their ability to engage in and carry out successfully the activities of the relevant community (Roth, 1999). On this view, the "master" or *expert* is relatively more skilled than the novice in terms of having a broader understanding of the important features of a cultural activity. However, the expert's depth and breadth of understanding is still developing in the process of carrying out the activity and in deciding which tools to use in order to guide others successfully in it (Rogoff, 1990). Following on from this, the essence of an individual's understanding is its *functionality*: the ability to employ knowledge as a resource in order to achieve situated, contextualised goals emanating from problem-solving situations in the communities of practice to which they belong (see Greeno, Pearson, & Schoenfeld, 1999).

Sociocultural Approaches to Knowledge and Understanding of Science

Sociocultural approaches to the knowledge and understanding of science draw on a view of *science as practice* to argue that scientific culture is made up of all sorts of bits and pieces – material, social, and conceptual - that do not stand in any unitary relation to one another. The problems that scientists solve in the laboratory are frequently ill-structured; they may not provide all the information needed or they provide so much that the scientist has to make crucial decisions about which information to use as a basis for a solution. In such situations, scientists appear to use a variety of problem-solving approaches depending on the material, conceptual, and social resources available. On such a view, instruments, facts and interpretations of phenomena are collaboratively constructed, meanings and courses of action are negotiated, determined by consensus, or dictated by someone in power by bringing together the material, conceptual and social elements available in specific settings (e.g. Collins & Pinch, 1993; Latour & Woolgar, 1979). Following on from this, sociocultural theorists view science as a form of *discourse*: "a social activity of making meanings with language and other symbolic systems in some particular situation or setting" (Lemke, 1995, p. 8). And they stress that the essence of doing science is the ability to examine the coherence of evidence and knowledge claims.

In turn, they describe the process by which novices become functioning members of a particular scientific community in terms of *enculturating* learners into the practices of a particular scientific community, so that novices learn, through *cognitive apprenticeship*, "the language, behaviours and other culturally determined patterns of communication of the scientific community" (Roth, 1993, p. 147). The metaphor of *enculturation* is associated with *situated practice* theory. This theory, while it is related to Vygotsky's perspective, is quite distinctive because it considers cognition not solely as a property of individuals, but as being "stretched over" the individual, other persons as well as physical and symbolic tools (Sfard, 1998). Work on situated practice focuses on everyday ways of thinking and knowing: the ways in which individuals solve problems that arise in the performance of everyday activities of the *community of practice* to which they belong. In particular, it argues that problems found in everyday activities, such as those which arise when Liberian tailors learn to sew (Lave, 1988) or when grocery shoppers compare prices, are complex and often ill-structured; they may not provide all the information needed or they might provide too much. In such situations, individuals appear to use a variety of problem-solving approaches, depending on the specific situation (Scribner, 1985).

Furthermore, it has been suggested that problems which might be considered by outsiders as identical tasks were solved by means of different strategies. This indicates an inextricability of tasks from the setting. In other words, problems always change with the setting and become different problems altogether. Thus, within situated practice, learning and knowing lie in the relationship between the individual and the environment, where *environment* refers to both the physical, historical and cultural surroundings as well as to the problem solver's ideas and beliefs relevant at the moment. And, since learning and knowing involve changes in activity in an environment *co-constructed* with others, they are considered to be *distributed* phenomena rather than residing solely in the heads of individuals (Roth, Tobin, & Ritchie, 2001).

An implication of a situated view of learning is that novices become functional members of a particular scientific community of practice as they observe and practice *in situ* the behaviour of members of this community. Brown, Collins and Duguid (1989), for instance, argue that following extended membership in the activities of a culture, novices pick up relevant jargon, imitate behaviour, and gradually start to act in accordance with its norms. Thus, learning a subject, such as physics, involves more than introducing learners to abstract concepts and self-contained examples. It involves exposing novices to the ways in which the members of a scientific community look at the world and how they use their conceptual and procedural tools to solve well and ill-defined problems. Initially, such exposure is expected to help learners develop a *tacit* understanding of what makes a relevant scientific question or what is legitimate or illegitimate behaviour in a particular activity.

Novices become fully-fledged members of a specific scientific community as they participate in *joint authentic activities* with experts, during which, they learn, through a process of cognitive apprenticeship, how to conduct research from the beginning, through to the end of a research project (Roth, 1995, 1996). And, this involves learning about the tools of science, about how to identify a problem and how to proceed to its solution, by trying out different concepts, raising questions, testing a proposed idea, negotiating and discussing the proposed solution with other members of their community until a solution is sought which is acceptable by the other members of the community.

Moreover, learning the discourse of science involves learning how to argue over the efficacy of the warrants of science for knowledge claims. This is a difficult process because everyday language is often inconsistent with scientific discourse. Thus, an important part of learning science is to offer learners opportunities to express their everyday conceptions in order to learn how to "identify when and how their everyday discourse is compatible with the discourse of science and to figure out ways to resolve inconsistencies" (Tobin, & McRobbie, 1999, pp. 218—219). This process takes place within the context of a specific activity, and involves a process of negotiation and consensus building with the other members of the learners' community of practice.

It is worth noting here that, sociocultural approaches to the learning of science have some similarities with the view of how scientists' understand scientific concepts which was suggested by Thomas Kuhn (1970, 1977) and developed further by Barry Barnes (1982). According to this view, the concepts and laws of science are *tools* or *conventional representations* of the physical environment which are used to group, order and pattern the objects and processes encountered in nature according to their similarities and differences. Understanding of these conventions is acquired by carrying out paradigmatic procedures, which highlight the relations of similarities and differences currently accepted by the specific scientific community. From this point of view, *paradigms*, that is to say the problem-solutions that students and scientists encounter during their education or research career as *exemplars* of how the specific scientific community does its job, are the means by which new members of the scientific community acquire understanding of scientific generalizations. And, because instances of these generalisations are not all identical, this understanding is not static but dynamic: it develops each time a scientist uses a tool to solve a particular problem. Moreover, there are sometimes problems where nothing seems the natural concept to apply. And, this is because each time a scientist decides to use a tool in a new situation, he/she needs to assert resemblance between the new situation and a previous one. The idea of resemblance involves the individual's judgment that similarity outweighs difference. And this judgment arises from the "the routine operation of the agent's own perception and cognition – something which is contingent and revisable" (Barnes, 1982, p. 26). Like sociocultural theorists, for Kuhn and Barnes misconceptions are seen as part of learning how to do science rather than as a deficit in the acquisition of a correct description of the properties of a specific science concept.

Sociocultural Implications for Teachers' Adequacy of Subject Knowledge

From a sociocultural perspective, teachers' science subject knowledge consists of a rich, dynamic and evolving network of links between the ways in which a particular concept is used in a number of different situations and of the situations. This network would develop and change each time a teacher uses a particular concept to act successfully in a specific situation. Furthermore, teachers' understanding of scientific discourse would be seen as emergent, with the aim being to come to terms with actions and products that go beyond the already known. And it would be described as an evolving spiral, in which simple concepts, facts and process skills and complex concepts, procedural knowledge, perception, remembering and feelings of uncertainty develop interdependently as teachers participate in socially and culturally organised activities.

It is important to note here that like constructivist perspectives, sociocultural theorists also emphasise the crucial role that knowledge plays in practice (see Edwards, 2005; Tobin, 1998). However, given that they recognise the essential and inseparable roles of cultural tools, social activity, and individual efforts, sociocultural theorists argue that the assessment of an individual's knowledge should be based on how this person performs, and not on what this person says about his/her own performance or what he/she can and cannot do in artificial situations.

Some sociocultural theorists have used interviews and questionnaires to assess secondary students' knowledge of aspects of physical science. Welzel and Roth (1998), for example, interviewed 13 grade 6-7 students at the end of a four-month classroom unit on simple machines. Prior to and at the end of the unit, students were tested in a number of ways which included their responses to paper-and-pencil questions about three real-life situations that illustrated applications of levers, pulleys and inclined planes. However, unlike constructivist interviewing, these interviews were designed to take into account the dynamic and situated nature of cognition by regulating the complexity of the tasks that were offered to the students, allowing students sufficient time for the development of situated cognition, and by explicitly participating in the cognitive activities of the interviewees. Indeed, the aim of such interviews was to assess the "maximum level of complexity that interviewees can enact *at a specific moment in time*" (p.40, emphasis mine).

However, more usually, a sociocultural perspective directs our attention to the study of teachers' performances in the activities of their communities of practice in order to assess adequacy of subject knowledge. And, teachers can be seen as participating in a variety of communities of practice, such as those formed by staff in a particular school, those made up of teachers and mentors in initial teacher education and continuing professional development courses, and that constituted by the teacher interacting with children in a particular classroom. In turn, the nature of the problem situations that teachers deal with depends on their context, and different problems require different kinds of solution, which in turn require differential use of cultural tools. Indeed, sociocultural theorists emphasise that learning is a process of boundary crossing mediated by access to different communities of practice (Engeström, Engeström, & Karkhainen, 1995; Lave, 1993). Furthermore, they point out that developing expertise is a matter of social relationships and identities within different communities of practice, in which novices learn how to use tools of various kinds to solve the problems of the specific community (Lave & Wenger, 1991). And, they argue that, increasing access and participation, within and be-tween different communities of practice, would increase "individual and collective knowledgeability" (Guile & Young, 1998, p. 114).

On this view, adequacy of subject knowledge is a complicated issue which in-volves assessing their use, and limitations on their use, of cultural tools, in relation to particular tasks, in particular contexts, and in particular moments in time. Thus, one way to determine adequacy of teachers' subject knowledge is functionality: their ability to make decisions on which concepts are more appropriate to use and how these should be used in problem solving situations of different communities of practice, including situations that arise as they participate in their science class-room communities.

CONCLUSION

In examining the two main constructivist approaches to teachers' science subject knowledge I have identified some differences between them. These relate to their assumptions about the relationship between conceptual and procedural knowledge and to their views of the role that social interaction plays in the construction of teachers' scientific understanding. In turn, these differences have implications for determining what form teachers' science subject knowledge should take.

For "small range" constructivists, teachers' knowledge in science develops in a sequential manner: the concepts, facts and practical problem skills are basic in teachers' knowledge, and exist as prerequisites to learning more complex or higher-order functions of cognition, such as complex concepts and problem-solving procedural knowledge. Following on from this, "small range" constructiv-ists, argue that teachers' subject knowledge needs to consist of a limited range of simple science concepts and practical process skills, and these should be intro-duced to teachers during initial or continuing professional development courses.

By contrast, "big ideas" constructivists adopt a socio-constructivist perspective on knowledge. This argues that teachers can acquire adequate understanding of broad scientific principles through their testing of their prior conceptions and the ideas offered to them by more knowledgeable others against scientific evidence. In turn, teachers' subject knowledge is treated as involving an expandable range of broad scientific principles and a particular approach to doing science. In line with this, it is argued that the education of teachers should offer them opportunities to develop adequate understanding of problem-solving, not just because it helps them to extend their own scientific understanding but also because it is central to chil-dren's learning of science.

Despite their differences, both approaches treat teachers' understanding of scientific knowledge as acquired, commodity-like knowledge that is essentially decontextualised and available to be used across situations. This is evident in their approaches to the assessment of teachers' adequacy of their science subject knowledge, which they define according to their ability to retrieve or collaboratively achieve the correct scientific knowledge and apply it in their explanations of well-defined situations that are included in interviews and/or questionnaires. From this point of view, both approaches to teacher expertise assume that once teachers acquire adequate understanding, of either a set of simple concepts or of a range of broad scientific principles, they are able to apply these in the classroom with the use of appropriate means. And in this way, they underestimate the complexity of practice.

These criticisms derive from sociocultural perspectives, which treat the concepts, theories and ideas of a scientific community as tools: the products of a particular line of inquiry which can only take on meaning in that context. Drawing on Vygotsky's work, they stress that understanding of the scientific discourse is often messy and contingent and depends upon processes of interpretation and negotiation of the problem at hand. Thus, teachers' science subject knowledge should be conceived as a dynamic process resulting from acting in situations and negotiating with other members of their communities. Moreover, its adequacy should be determined by functionality: by assessing teachers' ability to employ tools skilfully in order to achieve specific goals.

NOTES

[1] Conceptual understanding refers to the individual's ability to explain aspects of the world by identifying correct links among 'items' of knowledge (see Hiebert & Lefevre, 1986).

[2] It should be noted here, that researchers who share this approach to teachers' adequacy of science knowledge use the term misconceptions to refer not only to teachers' intuitive beliefs but also to teachers' partial understanding of a science concept (see for example, Summers & Mant, 1998).

[3] Examples of such principles are "water exists as solid, liquid and gas", "switches make and break the circuit", "the battery supplies electrical energy which is changed in the bulb to heat/light energy" (see Harlen, 1996, p. 6).

THE PEDAGOGICAL CONTENT KNOWLEDGE REQUIREMENT

As I pointed out in Chapter 1, primary science teacher expertise is often seen as involving not just subject knowledge but also *Pedagogical Content Knowledge* (PCK). Indeed, both "small range" and "big ideas" constructivists recognise the role of pedagogical content knowledge, though they view it differently. For "small range" constructivists, teachers' pedagogical content knowledge comprises a body of separate components which specify in detail the knowledge and skills that primary teachers ought to possess in order to make "accessible" to children their own knowledge of a small range of science concepts. These researchers refer to this list of components as *teachers' subject specific teaching knowledge* or *teaching knowledge*. By contrast, for "big ideas" constructivists emphasis is placed not on specific components that enable the transfer of subject knowledge in the classroom, but rather on teachers' understanding of how to use their subject knowledge to support a *socio-constructivist* learning and teaching approach through which children construct their own understanding of the "big ideas" of science.

In the first part of this chapter, I examine in detail the assumptions about learning and teaching that appear to underlie each of these two constructivist approaches to primary teachers science PCK. In the second part, I discuss the implications of sociocultural perspectives for this aspect of primary science expertise.

SUBJECT SPECIFIC TEACHING KNOWLEDGE

For "small range" constructivists, the notion of teachers' subject specific teaching knowledge includes the following components:

- The conceptions and preconceptions that children of different ages and backgrounds bring with them to the learning of a topic.
- The strategies most likely to be fruitful in developing the understanding of learners.
- The most useful analogies, illustrations, examples, explanations and demonstrations.
- Appropriate scientific terms and language to use with children.
- What to emphasise (not just what is the case, but critically, what is not the case).

- How to simplify validly what are often very complex ideas.
- Simple technical knowledge of equipment to be used in children's investigations. (Summers et al., 1997b, p. 332)

As I argued in chapter 2, "small range" constructivists argue that teachers need to possess adequate knowledge of a small range of science concepts in order to be able to develop adequate subject specific teaching knowledge. However, they also argue that because teachers often lack adequate subject knowledge, they are often unable to develop adequate subject specific teaching knowledge. Following on from this, "small range" constructivists claim that in order to ensure the effective teaching of science it is important for researchers to identify the aspects of scientific knowledge that teachers need, and are able to acquire, in relation to a particular scientific area, and the subject specific teaching knowledge that is necessary for teaching these aspects effectively to children. Once such knowledge is identified by researchers, it should be included into resource materials and/or be introduced to teachers during professional development courses, so as to be "transferred directly to the classroom" (Summers et al., 1997a, p. 106).

This group of researchers also place emphasis on teaching teachers how to set a series of clear conceptual objectives. This is seen as an essential part of the effective application of subject specific teaching knowledge. Drawing on a sequential view of knowledge acquisition, "small range" constructivists argue that in setting conceptual objectives, teachers should be able to decompose their subject knowledge into smaller parts according to children's age and abilities. As they put it, teachers should include in their conceptual objectives the "simpler more limited form" (p. 23) of a specific piece of scientific knowledge. Moreover, teachers should be able to choose the right order for their conceptual objectives, since such objectives determine not only what knowledge children are to learn but also the sequence in which effective teaching of this knowledge can take place. It has been argued that presenting ideas in the wrong order detracts from the effectiveness of teaching (p. 116). Teachers also ought to include in their conceptual objectives the teaching of practical problem-solving skills. Such skills include, for example, children's understanding of how to wire a circuit, or how to connect electric components in series and in parallel. Once children acquire the necessary scientific knowledge, they can then apply it in solving more complex problems, such as the building of an electric device which indicates when it is raining.

For "small range" constructivists adequacy of teachers' subject specific teaching knowledge seems to be inferred from the degree of effectiveness of their teaching, which in turn, is determined according to "pupil learning outcomes" (Summers et al., 1997a, p.1) – the extent to which, following teaching, children's understanding of specific scientific ideas conforms to or deviates from the conceptual objectives laid down by the teacher at the beginning of the session. Moreover, it has been suggested that children's failure to acquire a specific scientific idea can be attributed to "inadequate teaching knowledge" on the part of the teacher (ibid. p. 115).

This group of researchers, also seems to suggest that in order for teachers to be able to use effectively in their teaching the components of subject specific teaching knowledge, they must acquire adequate understanding of a particular interpretation of constructivist teaching, which should be presented to them during professional development courses. It is argued that the most effective teachers from those who participated in a course associated with the teaching of electricity were the ones who used in their own practice the same teaching approach that was introduced to them during the course. These teachers also employed in their teaching the representations of scientific concepts and most of the analogies, demonstrations, practical activities, etc. that were introduced to during the course.

Like with teachers' science subject knowledge, "small range" constructivists' believe that children's everyday ideas about aspects of the physical world are "scientifically incorrect" or misconceptions (Summers et al., 1997a, p. 94). And, they argue, that scientific concepts should not be expected to be discovered by children through practical work. Following on, this group of researchers argues that, in order to change children's misconceptions towards a desired scientific concept, the classroom teacher must: a) explicitly tell children and show them the desired scientific view prior to children's engagement in practical activities and b) contrast children's misconceptions with scientific evidence during practical activities. Commenting on their approach to the effective teaching of primary science, "small range" constructivists argue that it relies on "getting the right mix" between "ready-made scientific explanations' and asking children "to make their own interpretations, speculations and predictions" (ibid. p. 116).

Thus, their teaching approach begins with the elicitation of children's misconceptions. This usually takes place at the end of a practical task set up by the classroom teacher. Its aim is to help the teacher identify the main misconceptions, ensure children's understanding of practical problem skills (e.g. how to wire a circuit) and prepare learners for the presentation of the scientific view, which follows. "Small range" constructivists argue it is important that teachers select and use appropriate *scientific language* in their presentations of scientific concepts, and are very careful in their choice of everyday words to facilitate their explanations. Teachers are also encouraged to combine their verbal description of these ideas with suitable visual aids. It has been pointed out, for instance, that teachers who used visual aids, such as flip charts, in their teaching of electricity were more effective than teachers who described verbally the same concept to the children. Moreover, as I argued earlier, Summers et al. place particular emphasis on the teacher's use of analogies and demonstrations for "reinforcing" and "developing" children's understanding of already scientific ideas (p. 31). Like with the choice of scientific terms and visual aids, analogies and demonstrations should be selected prior to teaching. Teachers are also encouraged to "revisit continuously" (p. 112) their conceptual objectives, so as to offer children opportunities to consolidate their understanding of an already introduced concept. During revision of a conceptual objective, the teacher's role is to elicit children's possibly continuing misconceptions and to advance them towards the desired scientific concept, either through classroom discussion where the scientific view is re-presented or by engaging them in practical work. For example, one of their effective teachers wanted to revisit her conceptual objective that an electric current consists of electrons moving in one direction. Therefore, she asked the children to express their ideas about what is happening in a simple circuit that included a battery and a bulb. Although, most children were able to explain that a complete circuit is needed for the bulb to light, one child expressed the view that electrons go along one of the wires only as far as the bulb. The teacher next emphasised to the rest of the class that if that child's idea was correct, "you don't need this wire then, do you?" and then asked the children to predict "what happens if you take it off" (p. 29). Through further classroom discussion the correct scientific explanation was offered by some children. It was intended that the contrast between the scientific explanation and children's continuing misconception would convince them to accept the scientific view.

The role of practical activities, then, is to provide the necessary evidence which would change children's misconceptions towards a specific conceptual objective. Practical activities are organised in a structured way to enable learners to arrive at the same endpoint. For example, during the above discussion some other children seemed to hold the conception that current is used up as it passes through the bulb. In order to help them change their ideas for the desired one, the teacher offered them a simple circuit and ammeters and asked them to measure the amount of electricity in the wires by placing the meters at different points in the circuit. The teacher told the children where to place the ammeters, so that they could confirm that the measurement was the same all over the circuit. Their seeing that the measurement was the same all across all the circuit was expected to convince learners to accept the scientific view. And, it is argued that this should be encouraged by the teacher during discussion following the practical activity, by emphasising not only the scientific view but also what is *not* the scientific view. Following on from this, "small range" constructivists argue that it is important that the classroom teacher selects appropriate practical activities and has adequate knowledge of *technical equipment*, so as to enable the children to see the appropriate scientific evidence.

It is possible, of course, that children may still retain their misconceptions after their engagement in practical activities. It is argued that, on such occasions, further scientific evidence should be provided to them by the classroom teacher in order to convince children about the scientific view.

Questionable Assumptions about Teachers' Subject Specific Teaching Knowledge

The assumption that children acquire knowledge of scientific concepts through the teacher explicitly telling them about and demonstrating the desired concepts seems to confuse a constructive with a passive view of the learner and the learning process. On the one hand, it seems to draw on the Piagetian principle that children are capable of constructing everyday ideas about aspects of the physical world and that the reconstruction of their ideas requires conceptual change. On the other hand, it ignores the constructivist principle that in order for conceptual change to occur, learners need to be offered opportunities to reflect on and problematise their everyday ideas, so as to determine the value of their conceptual structures by judging how well they "fit" with their experiences and how well they enable them to solve problems they experience (see Murphy et al., 2000). In Summers et al work, there is no evidence that children's ideas become available for reflection during the learning process. For example, although teachers' knowledge of children's misconceptions and the elicitation of such misconnections is the starting point of teaching, the aim of elicitation is to help the teacher assess children's existing knowledge against specific conceptual objectives, rather than to engage children in discussion and reflection.

Moreover, the belief that the presentation of the scientific view, and subsequent scientific evidence, will convince learners to accept the correct scientific concept implies the existence of an inherently structured world with distinct and clearly identifiable phenomena that can be easily restructured inside the individual's head (see the discussion in chapter 2). It has been argued, though, that seeing the world around us in terms of specific objects and properties is not a self-evident process; and that children structure their world differently from their teachers (see Roth, 2006; Roth et al., 1997). Moreover, it has been pointed out that all observation involves interpretation and that interpretation arises from the interplay of existing understanding and the world (e.g. Feyerabend, 1975; Hanson, 1965). In other words, what one can understand depends on what one already knows. This suggests that children who do not yet have the relevant background may be unable to see what a particular scientific explanation, analogy, or practical activity is showing.

Thus, this approach to primary science expertise treats children as *passive recipients* of scientific knowledge who only acquire an adequate representation of a scientific explanation by being told or shown it. In this respect, the form of teaching implied by this conception of pedagogical content knowledge parallels *transmission* teaching (see Torff, 1999). The teacher's role can be best described as the *deliverer* of the scientific knowledge and simple process skills that they have included in their conceptual objectives.

In turn, the scientific understanding that children may have been shown to have acquired during teaching is tied to problems that have been clearly stated and required one correct answer. By contrast, the relevant situations they come into contact with subsequently may be ill-defined; they may not provide all the information needed, or may provide so much information that the problem solver has to make crucial decisions about which information to use as the basis for a solution. For this reason, despite having been taught a concept "effectively", children may be unable to respond successfully to problem situations in the future, unless these are a close match to those in which children were originally taught the concept. At the same time, assessing the effectiveness of teaching by comparing the performance of the same learner over repeated tests also assume that the construction of knowledge and the process of learning takes place inside the individual's head and in isolation from processes of interpretation and perception of the problem presented in a question. However, if the learner has a different interpretation or perception of a given task, judgments about the child's performance could be misleading, because the learner may organise his/her thinking differently. From this point of view, learning outcomes which indicate that children failed to acquire a particular conceptual objective may not be the result of the teacher's inadequate knowledge of subject specific teaching knowledge, or even children's inability to acquire the specific piece of knowledge. Such outcomes may simply indicate that the children are thinking in a different and not necessarily inadequate way.

In much the same way, "small range" constructivists regard teachers as passive recipients of subject specific teaching knowledge. Indeed, their assumption that this knowledge can be transferred directly to the classroom implies that all classroom situations where a particular scientific concept is taught are for practical purposes identical. However, classroom situations are not identical, and teachers often need to adapt their teaching to children's needs. The means that teachers have used effectively in teaching a particular scientific concept to one class or group of children may not be appropriate for use with another class or group of children or with the same children on different occasions. Thus, even if teachers have effectively used their subject specific teaching knowledge of a scientific concept with a group of children this still leaves open the possibility that this knowledge may not be effective in teaching the same concept in the future. Moreover, in selecting the means for representing a particular scientific concept to children, teachers must exercise judgments about which analogy, practical activity or scientific term is most appropriate to use in order to promote the children's learning. Such judgments sometimes have to be made on the spot, as teachers respond to children's questions. In such situations, teachers may have to develop new practical activities, or use different terms and analogies. Yet there is very little room for developing this kind of teachers' understanding in Summers et al.'s notion of subject specific teaching knowledge. Indeed, primary teachers are advised to ignore any of the children's questions that they are unable to answer.

There are then some serious problems with the notion of subject specific teaching knowledge. Some of these concern their views about the nature of the leaner and the learning process. Others relate to their assumptions about teaching and teachers' education.

PEDAGOGICAL CONTENT KNOWLEDGE FOR THE "BIG IDEAS" OF SCIENCE

As noted earlier, a rather different approach to teachers' pedagogical content knowledge has been developed by "big ideas" constructivists concerned with the effective teaching of the "Big Ideas of Science." Within this approach, the emphasis is placed not on the specification of a list of components that ensure the effective representation to children of the teacher's own subject knowledge but on teachers' understanding of how to use their conceptual and procedural understanding of science to support a *socio-constructivist* learning and teaching approach. Following on from this, "big ideas" constructivists argue that pedagogical content knowledge enables teachers to know the scientific understanding they are aiming for, to identify children's everyday ideas, select appropriate resources and practical activities for the children. It also helps them to organise their teaching in a way that supports children's engagement in scientific investigations, to assess children's learning and introduce ideas for them to test. As Harlen (1997) puts it, pedagogical content knowledge enables teachers to use their subject knowledge in order to:

plan, knowing the progressive understanding they are aiming for; it enables them to recognise the seed of a scientific idea in what children say and write and work on this; it enables them to recognise misunderstandings and the possible reasons for them; it enables them to recognise "blind alleys" and re-direct children's activity along more fruitful lines; it enables them to put forward scientific ideas for children to consider (not as the "right answers", but to be tested against what is there); it enables them to assess pupils' progress and to involve children in assessing their own progress by communicating the directions of learning in the feedback they give to children. (p. 7)

Like with teachers' science subject knowledge, "big ideas" constructivists, draw on a *Piagetian constructivist view* of the learner to explain that children are *active* and *reflective* learners who bring their own ideas into the learning process. Sometimes these ideas are referred to as "small ideas of science" (Harlen, 2000, p. 13) because they are specific to an event that children describe or explain, whereas the "big ideas" of science explain a wide range of phenomena. Such small ideas of science are the product of children's "immature thinking and reasoning" (p. 57). Neverthe-less, their ideas are the product of reasoning and make sense to the children them-selves; they are viable in helping children to solve problems successfully. More-over, like scientific ideas, children's ideas are viable as long as there is evidence to support them. When children encounter a perturbation relative to some expected result, they may be actively induced to reconstruct their small ideas of science so as to re-establish a relative equilibrium between previous knowledge and the new experience. "Big ideas" constructivists, stress, however, that in order for children to reconstruct their small ideas of science towards a particular big idea of science they need to have developed *procedural knowledge* "to the point of being scien-tific", prior to the testing of their ideas; otherwise, their ideas "will not be properly tested and may be retained when they really do not fit the evidence" (p. 63).

Children's reconstruction of their everyday understanding can also take place as they interact with the ideas suggested to them by the classroom teacher. Harlen (2000), for example, argues that children should not be expected to acquire abstract scientific concepts by testing only their own ideas against evidence. If this were the case, "there would be a danger of recycling ideas from limited experience and not making the headway that an input of new ideas might make possible" (p. 80). She stresses, however, that any idea suggested to learners has to be put forward as an idea to be tested out by them so as to enable them to judge for themselves that the new idea is more viable in explaining their own experiences compared to their ex-isting understanding. Furthermore, she points out that any learner's interaction with the ideas of others should take place within that learner's *zone of proximal devel-opment*. Thus, for "big ideas" constructivism, the construction of knowledge re-mains an individual process of conceptual change. In this way, children acquire an increasingly more complex network of links between scientific ideas and experi-ence.

"Big ideas" constructivists appear to attribute to scientific knowledge a form of hierarchical structure in terms of various levels of perceived difficulty and status.

49

They argue, for example, that some of the scientific concepts included in the Curriculum are more easily understood by children than are others. From this point of view, it is essential that teachers possess adequate science subject knowledge in order to be able to select the understanding of a science concept that children of different ages and abilities can manage, and include it in their learning objectives.

Furthermore, "big ideas" constructivists argue that teachers' need to be able to select those activities that enable children to develop their procedural understanding and include this in their learning objectives. Here, too, they seem to argue that there is some kind of hierarchical structure in the processes and procedures that children of different ages are able to acquire understanding. Unlike "small range" constructivists however, who argue that teachers' conceptual objectives determine the knowledge that children ought to acquire and the sequence in which this knowledge is to be learned, for "big ideas" constructivists learning objectives determine at a general level what children are to learn, when and how. This is taken to mean that the teacher must be able to alter his/her learning objectives or practical activities to respond to children's suggestions. However, this does not imply that teachers ought to respond to all of the ideas suggested by the children. Some of these ideas may be beliefs that cannot be tested, or ideas that are not likely to lead children towards the development of a specific "big idea" of science that is included in the teacher's learning objectives. Therefore, teachers should be able to recognise children's everyday ideas, and make an appropriate selection of these for testing.

Nevertheless, "big ideas" constructivists stress that teachers need to be clear about the objectives of the lesson and the intended learning outcomes, and that they structure their lessons in a way that enables them to achieve their learning objectives. They argue, for example, that science lessons need to have a clear structure of phases in which different kinds of activities take place, such as introduction, discussion, practical work, and whole class discussion of outcomes which offers opportunities for reflection. In "big ideas" constructivist approach to teachers' pedagogical content knowledge there are no explicit references as to how the effectiveness of teaching should be evaluated. They do, however, suggest several methods by which children's learning can be assessed. These include the use of paper-and-pencil tests, concept maps, diagrams, etc. (Harlen & Qualter, 2004).

It follows, that an important aspect of the effective teaching of primary science is to *elicit* the starting point of children's understanding. Unlike "small range" constructivists who use *elicitation* in order to assess children's prior understanding against specific conceptual objectives, for "big ideas" constructivists a main purpose of elicitation is to help learners *reflect* on their own thinking, that is, to make it clear to themselves, and reconsider or modify it. This is achieved after children have been offered opportunities to get engaged in a practical task and *explore* a "new experience"; that is, an experience that is likely to be novel to them. This exploratory phase is fairly unstructured; children are not asked, for example, to systematically test their ideas. In doing so, any ideas elicited at the end of the practical task are more likely to be the outcome of children's thinking rather than ones made up on the spur of the moment. For example, at the beginning of a teaching session about the nature and properties of soil, the classroom teacher provided his nine and ten years old children with samples of three different types of soil: sandy, loamy, and clay soil, and asked the children to look at them. Thus, he organised the children in groups, offered them some hand-lenses, sieves, disposable gloves and some general instructions about what to do. Children were asked, for instance, to separate the different parts that each of the soils contains, to find out what is contained in the soils, to find out what is different in each soil and to think about how each of these differences might affect how well plants grow in the soils. During this exploratory phase, the teacher's role is to visit each group and listened to children's ideas.

After the children had completed the practical task, a whole class discussion took place during which the teacher collected findings and ideas from each of the different groups. The teacher focused the discussion on the "new experience" that children would explore during the session. Thus, the teacher explained to the children that they would test their ideas about which was the best soil for growing plants after they had found out more about the soils and the differences that might make one better than the other. He then asked the children to think of possible factors that plants need to grow.

"Big ideas" constructivists explain that primary teachers should encourage children to answer these questions by *making links* between the new experience and earlier experiences "through noticing some similarities of form, behaviour, reaction or names" (Harlen, 2000, p. 54). At the end of this process, children are expected to come up with an idea that may explain the new experience. This idea can be used to predict something about the new experience that has not so far been observed.

Of course, teachers should have already planned the ideas that children ought to test in order to develop their understanding of a particular scientific concept. Nevertheless, teachers must try to draw these ideas out from the children. In turn, if children do not mention some of the teacher's ideas, the teacher may decide to direct their thinking towards them. For example, during the previous classroom discussion children suggested that plants need water and fertilizer to grow but none of the children mentioned the presence of air in the soil, which was one of the ideas that the teacher wanted children to investigate. To help children consider the presence of air in the soil, the teacher asked the children to think about the difference between soil that was compressed and the same soil in a loose heap. In particular, he encouraged them to think about whether there was the same amount of air between the particles in each soil and whether this was likely to make a difference to how well plants would grow in it.

Furthermore, during such classroom discussions the teacher may decide to introduce scientific terms or analogies that might help children develop their understanding of the new experience. "Big ideas" constructivists, stress, however, that decisions about when to introduce a scientific term or analogy should be left to the classroom teacher, who may need to consider whether children have experience of the event or the phenomenon described by the term or represented by the analogy, whether the term or the analogy is needed at the time, and whether or not it is going to help them to link related ideas and experiences to each other. For example, during the previous classroom discussion, the idea of "fertilizer" led to a discussion of what this meant in terms of the soils children had looked at; and it was eventually related to the bits of leaves and decayed plant material that children had found in the loam. In this respect, "big ideas" view of pedagogical content knowledge differs from subject specific teaching knowledge in which scientific terms, analogies, metaphors and demonstrations are specified in detail prior to teaching.

Once the ideas that children should systematically test have been identified, the teacher is expected to engage them in practical activities. Such activities are carefully planned to enable children to collect accurate scientific evidence. In turn, it is the teacher's responsibility to ensure that children have adequate procedural understanding prior to teaching, although this understanding can be further developed through children's engagement in practical activities. Thus, teachers are advised to ask questions aimed at eliciting children's procedural understanding and provide explicit support if they judge that children do not have adequate understanding of it. It is worth noting here, that, unlike "small range" constructivists who stress teachers' use of technical equipment, for "big ideas" constructivists, both everyday and specialised equipment can be used in children's practical activities, depending on the topic.

Children should work on groups, and should be encouraged to discuss and reflect on their ideas, and keep records of their findings. Children should also prepare a report to the class in which they should include what they did, what they found, whether what they found was what they expected, and how they explained the differences they found. The teacher's role during this phase is to listen to children's findings and explanations and relate them to the scientific questions of the teaching session. By listening at what the children say, the teacher also forms an assessment of children's scientific understanding, especially in relation to how they progressed from their initial ideas towards a better scientific understanding. In this way, the collection of scientific evidence is expected to help children to develop their small ideas of science by making links between these ideas and scientific evidence. It is at this point that the teacher may decide to engage children in another practical activity during which children may ask to test an idea suggested by the teacher or by other children. As Harlen explains, if the evidence confirms the prediction as correct, children's ideas are made "a little bigger by explaining the new experience" (Harlen, 2000, p. 54). If there is no supporting evidence, another idea linked to the new experience may be tried. However, before children go on to set up another inquiry, the teacher should encourage children to reflect on their learning by asking them, for example, to think about the parts of their work that they had enjoyed most, and which they would do differently if they could start again.

Following on from this, for "big ideas" constructivists, the teacher's role can be best described as the *director* of children's construction of scientific knowledge, responsible for providing appropriate support to enable them to construct understanding of a particular scientific principle. This support may include the introduction of scientific ideas for the children to test, the use of specific questions which aim to help them clarify procedural issues, or to develop their ability to ask scientific questions. This kind of support is often described as *scaffolding*. As Harlen (2000) puts it: "scaffolding means supporting children in considering an idea that they have not proposed themselves but are capable of making "their own" (p. 80). The judgment of when this is likely to be possible has to be made by the teacher, who has to take into account children's zone of proximal development, their existing ideas and how far they are in taking the next step.

Questionable Assumptions about PCK for the "Big Ideas" Approach

As I mentioned earlier, in "big ideas" approach to primary teachers science pedagogical content knowledge learners are treated as active and reflective in the learning process. Indeed, a crucial aspect of a socio-constructivist approach to the teaching of science is the engagement of children in practical activities that offer them opportunities to reflect on their ideas, so as to reconsider the limitations of these ideas in explaining a new experience. However, in Piaget's account active learners not only use ideas to solve problems, but are also able to evaluate these ideas as solutions. Piaget describes this characteristic of knowledge as *operative* (see Piaget, 1970). It is knowledge of what to do to produce an answer. In other words, from a Piagetian perspective, to know that the air in the soil affects the growth of plants is only part of scientific understanding. It is important that children know why the testing of their prediction is necessary and how it would be possible. Following on from this, some constructivist researchers argue that children's ability to use a new scientific idea in explaining a novel problem is only part of scientific competency. To be a competent problem solver in science, children need to know what they are doing and why it is appropriate. This means that it is important for a teacher to draw children's attention to both the conceptual and procedural aspects of a problem, throughout teaching and not just if or when it is judged to be necessary. Indeed, it has been argued that within UK research on primary science education very little emphasis has been placed on the development of children's operative understanding (Murphy, et al., 2000).

Furthermore, in "big ideas" approach, it is the child's responsibility to *make the links* between familiar and unfamiliar problems. This is because, from a socio-constructivist perspective, learning remains an individual process of conceptual change. Social interaction only plays an external role in this process (see Lerman, 1994). Thus, although teachers are encouraged to scaffold children's learning, their support is restricted to making suggestions about conceptual and procedural aspects. Teachers are not expected, for example, to provide explicit guidance about how and why to carry out an investigation or how to link ideas with scientific evidence. In criticism of this, it has been suggested that children are seldom capable of making the connections between problems, and that explicit guidance in creating links needs to be provided by the classroom teacher (D'Andrade, 1981). Furthermore, it has been argued that the links between a familiar and a novel problem do not involve only the transfer of learners' conceptual understanding but also the transfer of procedural understanding about how to solve familiar problems.

This last point raises a more serious question about the central assumption of "big ideas" constructivism, that learners will reconstruct their small ideas of science through their engagement in practical activities and classroom discussion. As with "small ideas" constructivism, this assumption implies the existence of clearly structured physical phenomena, which can be easily identified and restructured inside the learner's head, with the help of classroom interaction. It is expected that the knowledge children acquire in this way should enable them to explain future problems associated with it. However, children do not perceive or interpret problems in the same way as their teachers. For instance, as I discussed in the previous section, not all the children suggested that air in the soil affects the growth of plants. Moreover, the systematic testing of their small ideas, will not necessarily replace learners' small ideas precisely because children will perceive and interpret problems differently on different occasions.

Thus, this approach, like the "small range" constructivists' approach, seems to underplay the way in which problems are often expressed within contexts that are complex and ambiguous. To solve such problems children may need to use a different way of thinking about solving problems than the one supported by "big ideas" constructivism, one which takes into account the ambiguous and contingent nature of knowledge and involves learners in reflecting on, discussing and reconsidering both their procedural and conceptual understanding, in their attempts to make sense of a problem. Thus, even if children's learning seems to have been modified towards a "big idea" of science this still leaves open the possibility that they may continue to use ideas on other occasions that are less appropriate.

The "big ideas" constructivist approach to the learning and teaching of science has implications for her notion of teachers' pedagogical content knowledge and how this should be used during teaching. Teachers are given greater control over their own teaching than in "small range" constructivists' approach. Whereas "small range" constructivists argue that the most appropriate means for representing scientific knowledge effectively to children can be prescribed prior to their teaching, for "big ideas" constructivists teachers are expected to make judgments about the appropriateness of such means on the basis of their understanding of how useful these means will be in promoting children's scientific learning on particular occasions. At the same time, for "big ideas" constructivists, pedagogical content knowledge enables teachers to use their abstract knowledge of science to support a highly specified approach to the teaching of science that works for all learners as long as teachers take into account their starting points. This knowledge enables teachers to recognise immediately children's everyday ideas and engage them in well-structured scientific investigations. It also enables them to respond effectively to children's ideas or questions for which the teacher does not know the answer by setting up an inquiry that will test such ideas against scientific evidence. However, this view of pedagogical content knowledge seems to undermine the complexity of classroom practice and the contingent and ambiguous nature of knowledge. It neglects the fact that it may not always be possible to retrieve the correct "big idea" of science, or to solve problems using highly specified procedures. Moreover, teachers' pedagogical content knowledge, for the "big ideas" of science is seen as largely decontextualised. It assumes that one model of effective learning and teaching might be appropriate for all children in all settings.

Thus, despite their differences both constructivist approaches treat teachers' pedagogical content knowledge as largely decontextualised, available for use independently of the contingent situations that may arise during teaching. Furthermore, if teachers' subject knowledge is seen as dynamic and situated, the very distinction between teachers' subject and pedagogical content knowledge is open to question. It is not surprising, then, that sociocultural approaches offer a different picture of the learner, the learning process and the teaching of science. These are discussed in the next sections.

SOCIOCULTURAL APPROACHES TO SCIENCE LEARNING AND TEACHING

As I discussed in chapter 2, like constructivist approaches sociocultural perspectives are also concerned with the development of children's scientific understanding. However, unlike constructivist approaches, which regard science knowledge as having an existence independent from the situation in which it was produced, sociocultural perspectives recognise the inseparable roles of concepts, theories, social activity, and individual efforts. Indeed, they stress the functional character of knowledge and argue that the essence of individuals' scientific understanding is their ability to make decisions about which cultural tools to use and how these can be employed to act successfully in problem solving situations that may be either well or ill-defined. Moreover, they treat scientific understanding as a *dynamic* process resulting from actions in situations and from negotiations with other members of the community.

As with teachers' science subject knowledge, sociocultural perspectives argue that children develop functional knowledge through a process of *enculturation* into the authentic activities of a particular scientific community. This process enables children to learn through *cognitive apprenticeship,* the discursive practices of that community. It should be noted here that the term *authentic activities* is used to refer to both *personal* and *cultural authenticity.* Personal authenticity means that in order for learning to occur, problems cannot be given to children by teachers but need to be conceived as problems or *dilemmas* by the novices (Roth, Tobin, & Ritchie, 2001).

Drawing on a view of science as practice, authentic activities in science classrooms frequently include engaging children in research projects that allow them to learn how to conduct whole research projects, to experience ambiguities and uncertainties and the social nature of scientific work and knowledge (e.g. Roth, 1995). In engaging learners in such activities, more capable participants guide the interaction with them until children are able to manage the activity on their own. Indeed, teaching within a sociocultural approach is sometimes conceived of as a *joint problem-solving event* in which an expert and a novice structure their interaction so as to help the novice appropriate new knowledge and skills. During this interaction several adaptations are made by the participants as the novice gains greater understanding of the problem and the expert evaluates the novice's readiness to take greater responsibility for solving problems independently. Such teaching is sometimes referred to as the *community-of-learners* teaching model. At its core is the assumption that both mature and less mature members of the community are *active*: "no role has all the responsibility for knowing and directing, and no role is by definition passive" (Rogoff, 1994, p. 213). Thus, the teacher and the children together structure their shared endeavours, with the teacher responsible for *guiding* the overall process but with the children able to participate in the management of their own learning and involvement. It is worth noting that, for some sociocultural theorists there is still some *asymmetry* in the teacher-learner relationship here. Indeed, as Rogoff notes, in any activity participants' roles are seldom equal: "they may be complementary or with some leading and others supporting or actively observing, and may involve disagreements about who is responsible for what aspects of the endeavor" (ibid.). Following on from this, it is argued that collaboration in joint activities is not limited to asymmetrical dyads. Rogoff (1990), for example, argues that children are likely to appropriate knowledge and skills when solving a problem with another partner whose knowledge and skills are "at a level *just* beyond that of the child" (p. 173, italics in the original). It has also been pointed out that collaborating with a partner equal in skill and knowledge, or even less advanced, also yields progress (Forman & Kraker, 1985; Light & Glahan, 1985).

Thus, for some sociocultural researchers, the *zone of proximal development* is defined as "the structure of joint activity in any context where there are participants who exercise differential responsibilities by virtue of differential expertise" (Cole, 1985, p. 155). Such researchers claim that the notion of differential expertise has particular implications for children's leaning in school classrooms, because it enables children to distribute the responsibilies of a task so that the whole responsibility in solving the problem does not fall on any one learner.

The role of the teacher in such joint activities is to scaffold children's performance, that is to structure their interaction by building on what the teacher knows the learners can do. Thus, scaffolding means closing the gap between the task requirements and the existing skills and knowledge of the learner, thereby enabling the learner to develop his/her knowledge and skills by accomplishing the particular task in hand (Greenfield, 1984). In this respect, scaffolding is different from the way it is used in "big ideas" constructivists in which it aims to help learners acquire commodity knowledge.

Certain methods have been identified which can be used by the classroom teacher or other participants in order to scaffold children's science learning. The metaphor of cognitive apprenticeship is often associated with the practices of situated *modeling*, *coaching* and *fading*, whereby the teacher first models the solution to a new problem by offering children extensive support and/or by making his/her reasoning explicit to the children (Brown & Palinscar, 1989). Then, the teacher supports and directs the children's attempts at implementing the strategies (coaching), and finally he/she leaves more and more room for the learner to work independently (fading). In particular, *modeling* aims to facilitate learners' appropriation of new knowledge and skills by making explicit to learners the *links* between their existing understanding of solving problems and the new problem. Rogoff and Gardner (1984), for example, argue that, when faced with a new problem, learners make use of the knowledge and skills that are familiar in the context of the new problem to produce a solution. Aspects of the particular problem context are important in facilitating or blocking the learner's application of knowledge and skills developed in other contexts. Therefore, children need to learn how to find or create similarity across contexts.

Unlike some of the "big ideas" constructivists who argue that learners are able to find the connections between problems by themselves, for sociocultural theorists an essential part of teacher-children interactions is the provision of explicit guidance in creating links between the context of a novel problem and more familiar ones, allowing in this way the application of available skills and information. Once the teacher models the solution to a novel problem, he/she then *coaches* the learners in their application of their understanding of the new knowledge and skills in solving similar problems. As learners become more competent performers, the teacher gradually withdraws his/her support. This can be a subtle process involving successive attempts by the participants to assess the novice's readiness for greater responsibility.

Wertsch and Stone (1979) describe this kind of teaching as *proleptic instruction.* In proleptic instruction the novice carries out simple aspects of the task as directed by the expert. In turn, by actually performing the task under expert guidance, the novice participates in creating the relevant contextual knowledge for the task and acquires some of the expert's understanding of the problem and its solution. Proleptic instruction contrasts with explanation, where the teacher tells about a new piece of knowledge rather than guides the child through the task. It also contrasts with demonstration, where the teacher carries out the task rather then involving the child in the action. Proleptic instruction, can also lead into joint inquiry when both the teacher and student engage in a problem that is novel to the teacher. The discourse is more evenly distributed and there is less teacher guidance than during the scaffolding phase.

Much of the mediation in joint activity is done by means of language. Drawing on Vygotsky's theory, sociocultural perspectives argue that what children learn first as they begin to participate in authentic activities is how to make sense of others' behaviour and to construct knowledge that enables them to carry out successfully these activities. In this endeavor, words (including scientific terms like *force*) become transparent means through which children make meaningful contact with their environment. When there are problems in this contact, this transparency disappears, and new meaning has to be developed through a process of *interpretation*. This process suggests that the child's understanding of specific terms is *negotiated* with other more knowledgeable participants and the new meaning is *coconstructed*, within the child's zone of proximal development (ZPD). Thus, as children interact with more knowledgeable participants (e.g. the classroom teacher) in joint activities within the ZPD, they appropriate knowledge and skills that were initially external to them. And, once cultural knowledge is appropriated, it can be used by the child to control his/her own actions.

As Tobin and McRobbie (1999) put it, in a school science community it is expected that learners would engage in ways such that "over a period of time, the discourse of a class would become more science-like" (p. 216). On such a view, the teaching of science focuses not on helping children acquire decontextualised knowledge, but on supporting learners to develop a dynamic network of links between concepts as tools of science and how they are used in specific situations. In turn, learners' misconceptions are not regarded as "wrong" understandings but as part of the argumentative discourse that guide their interactions. Thus, the elicitation of children's prior conceptions takes place in the context of a particular activity, in order to help the learners carry out successfully the particular activity.

It follows, that an important requirement for effective teaching is to organise school classrooms to resemble and operate as scientific communities. Roth (1993), for example, created a classroom environment which encouraged his students to select their own research questions about a particular scientific topic, to carry out their own scientific investigations using their own designs, to discuss and share their ideas about the design and the outcome of their investigations with other children in their groups. Not offering to students ready-made procedures has the implication that different groups may decide on varying experimental designs which may lead to the same or different results and claims. Indeed, three groups of children decided to investigate the relationship between the mass and the acceleration of falling bodies.

At the end of their investigation, the students were asked to justify their designs and findings to the other groups and to the classroom teacher. In order to do this they had to rely on their understanding of the concepts involved as well as on their procedural understanding of how they interpreted the problem and carried out the activity. Thus, by contrast with "big ideas" constructivism in which the role of scientific evidence is to prove or disprove a specific prediction, for this sociocultural teaching approach the role of evidence is to engage children in *reflective discourse,* where both their conceptual and procedural understanding as well as their uncertainties and ambiguities are employed in supporting a knowledge claim. In this way, learners develop their understanding of general strategies "for constructing an understanding of the problem as intended by its creator or strategies for negotiating the conventions of interpretation" (Roth, 1993, p.154). During classroom discourse, the teacher's role is to guide the overall discussion, and to scaffold learners' construction of scientific meaning by asking them appropriate questions or suggesting scientific ideas that could explain a particular aspect of the problem. The classroom teacher might decide to introduce and demonstrate to learners some key scientific concepts, as well as technical equipment that students may not have encountered before. Teachers might also decide to propose an investigation that could be carried out by the students when the need for it arises. Teachers' support should take place in an environment where the power constituted in the discourse is equitably distributed between the teacher and the children to enable the clarification of learners' knowledge claims.

Although encouraging students to select their own questions and carry out their own investigations is at the core of this sociocultural teaching approach, students are also encouraged to participate in other activities that may include solving text-book problems, reading scientific texts, producing concept maps or writing assignments in various scientific concepts. Moreover, given that from a sociocultural perspective knowledge is functional, the construction of scientific meaning does not necessarily take place only through classroom discourse. It can occur as students think and rethink a particular problem individually, or when they work with fellow students in small groups and when they interact with the teacher either one-to-one or within a group. It can sometimes occur independently from the course of the teaching.

Sociocultural Approaches and Science Pedagogical Content knowledge

As I indicated earlier, from a sociocultural perspective science teaching is seen as a joint-problem solving activity in which the teacher and the children structure their interaction so as to help the children appropriate new knowledge and skills and learn how to function successfully in the activities of their science classroom community. From this point of view, teachers' science subject knowledge plays a crucial role in effective practice. It enables teachers to organise their classrooms to resemble and operate as particular scientific communities, and to facilitate and support the development of children's scientific understanding. Thus, to be effective in structuring their interactions with the children, teachers need to know how to model, coach and fade their support, how to engage children in reflective discourse, how to regulate the complexity of the task, and how to assess children's readiness for taking greater responsibility over the task. Moreover, effective science teachers must also know how to re-present the scientific discourse in ways that makes it accessible to learners and in relation to actions and goals that are important to both teachers and the children in their class.

Following on from this, some sociocultural researchers argue that the science pedagogical content knowledge teachers need in order to promote the learning of their students might involve "knowledge of the subject matter, knowledge of the students and how they learn, and knowledge of the resources that can appropriately mediate learning" (Tobin & McRobbie, 1999, p. 217).

However, rather than seeing pedagogical content knowledge as separate from subject knowledge, sociocultural theorists draw our attention to the functional character of teachers' subject knowledge. Indeed, as argued in chapter 2, from a sociocultural perspective teachers' subject knowledge is itself a resource: a set of tools that teachers need to employ skilfully in order to act successfully in the activities of a particular community of practice. Moreover, to act as a teacher means making decisions about what science tools are most appropriate to use to respond to specific problem situations that arise from children's questions and ideas. And, because the situations that arise during teaching are variable and contingent, teachers need to be prepared to respond to actions and products that go beyond the already known, by using different knowledge and pedagogical tools that enable them to interpret the situations and facilitate children's learning. It can be suggested, therefore, that from a sociocultural perspective teachers' subject and pedagogical knowledge is an integrated and situated whole.

CONCLUSION

In this chapter, I have examined the attitudes of the two constructivist approaches to teachers' pedagogical content knowledge. Both see this as a separate kind of knowledge from knowledge of science itself, one that allows teachers to help children acquire abstract scientific understanding. However, as with teachers' subject knowledge, these constructivist approaches differ in the way in which they see children's scientific understanding as developing. Moreover, they differ in their interpretation of constructivist learning and teaching. In turn, such differences have particular implications for the form that teachers' pedagogical content knowledge should take.

The "small range" constructivists despite their constructivism adopt a passive view of the learner. They assume that children acquire understanding of a small range of science concepts and simple process skills by being explicitly told and shown the desired scientific concept. Moreover, their approach to the teaching of science parallels transmission teaching, and the teacher's role is best described as the deliverer of knowledge. From this point of view, subject specific teaching knowledge includes a list of separate components that specify in detail the science knowledge and skills that teachers need to acquire in order to deliver effectively to children their own understanding of a small range of scientific concepts and simple process skills.

By contrast, "big ideas" constructivist support a socio-constructivist view of the learning and teaching of science, according to which children construct understanding of broad scientific principles as they test their everyday ideas or ideas suggested to them by the classroom teacher against scientific evidence. Learners are treated as active and reflective in the learning process, responsible for making links between their scientific ideas and experience. Moreover, the conduct of highly structured scientific investigations is a central aspect of teaching. The teacher's role within this approach is to provide scaffolding, so as to help the children acquire commodity knowledge. For "big Ideas" constructivists, the notion of teachers' pedagogical content knowledge is employed as a broad framework that enables teachers to use their conceptual and procedural understanding of science to support this socio-constructivist learning and teaching approach.

However, despite these important differences, both approaches to teachers' pedagogical content knowledge suggest that, although dependent on teachers' subject knowledge, is separate from it. Moreover, they treat both as *acquired*, commodity-like knowledge that is essentially decontextualised and available to be used across classroom situations. There are however, a number of problems associated with this view. One relates to the fact that classroom situations are variable and contingent, and that in order to respond to such situations teachers may need to make decisions about what the situation is about and how best they can respond to it. Moreover, such decisions may require a different kind of thinking from the one supported in the two approaches to pedagogical content knowledge, one that takes into account the functional and situated nature of knowledge.

These criticisms derive from a sociocultural perspective which treats the learning of science as a process of enculturating children into the authentic activities of their classroom science community, so that children learn, through cognitive apprenticeship, how to use the tools of science in order to perform successfully in problem solving situations that can be either well or ill-defined. Here, teaching is seen as a joint problem-solving activity, where the teacher together with the children structure their interaction in order for the children to appropriate new tools. During these interactions teachers make decisions about which tools to use and how these tools should be employed in order to perform successfully in specific problem solving situations that arise from children's ideas and questions. From a sociocultural perspective, teachers' subject and pedagogical knowledge is integrated and situated, and is developed through teachers' participation in their science classroom communities.

There are several implications of this discussion about the pedagogical content knowledge requirement. The most obvious one is that it challenges the idea that the knowledge that teachers ought to possess in order to teach science effectively can be specified in detail prior to teaching, or that it includes the application of a highly defined pedagogical approach that works for all learners as long as teachers take into account their starting point. It also challenges the idea that pedagogical content knowledge is a separate kind of knowledge from subject knowledge. From a sociocultural perspective, scientific knowledge is functional, and one of its functions is its use in teaching.

NOTES

[1] The metaphor of scaffolding was originated by Wood, Bruner, and Ross (1976) to refer to the kind of teacher intervention that provides a supportive tool for the learner, which extends his or her knowledge and skills, thereby allowing the learner successfully to accomplish a task not otherwise possible.

PART B

METHODOLOGICAL IMPLICATIONS OF A SOCIOCULTURAL PERSPECTIVE FOR STUDYING TEACHER EXPERTISE

In the previous two chapters I used a sociocultural perspective to examine in detail the arguments supporting the current emphasis in UK research on the importance of subject knowledge. In the remainder of this book I want to apply this perspective to an empirical investigation of primary science expertise. Therefore, in this chapter I will begin by outlining some of the methodological implications of a sociocultural approach for studying teacher expertise in action. I will then discuss the qualitative case study that will be the focus of chapters 5, and 6.

There are two important methodological implications of a sociocultural approach to knowledge and learning, for my purposes here. The first is that this approach does not require a researcher to begin by defining science expertise on the basis of some normative theory of knowledge or learning. Rather, the researcher must study expertise as it is defined in action, by the relevant community of practice: its character is to be discovered empirically by studying the activities of those who are recognised as experts, or situations where novices are inducted into practice. Thus, the strategy I adopted in my research is to study in-depth the perspective and practice of one teacher who was locally, and more widely, recognised as an expert in primary science. In this, I am not claiming that she is representative of expert primary science teachers, only that she provides one exemplar, a *critical case*, of what could count as expertise in this field at the present time.

The second important methodological implication of a sociocultural approach, which in some ways follows on from the first, is that an exploratory or *qualitative* approach is a valuable way of investigating expertise. Of relevance here are the qualitative traditions that have been developed in anthropology and sociology, in which participant observation and/or in-depth interviewing are employed to understand what people do and how their perspectives on the world are implicated in their activities (see, for example, Denzin & Lincoln, 1994). These have been an important influence on many of those working in the sociocultural tradition (e.g. Aikenhead, 2001; McGinnis, Parker, & Graeber, 2004). A clear example is Lave's participant observation research on how knowledge, understanding and skill develop as apprentices learn to become tailors in Liberia (Lave, 1988). This is an approach which differs significantly from those that have typically been used in studying the role of subject knowledge in primary science teaching. I can illustrate this by looking at the methods employed by two of the main studies that have been carried out within UK research in primary science education on the relation between teachers' subject knowledge and classroom effectiveness. The first of these studies (Harlen & Holroyd, 1995, 1996) was a research project commissioned by The Scottish Office Education and Industry Department (SOEID) on the implications for primary teachers of implementing the National Guidelines for Environmental Studies. For science, these guidelines included the following areas: Living Things and the Processes of Life, Energy and Forces, and Earth and Space. The research was concerned with the difficulties teachers could encounter and the help that might be needed. It was carried out by independent researchers at the Scottish Council for Research in Education from March 1993 to February 1995. In relation to the science aspects of the guidelines, the project was framed by Harlen's view that the task of primary science teaching is to introduce children to broad scientific principles, and that doing this effectively requires that teachers have an adequate understanding of those ideas as well as of how scientific investigations are carried out (see the discussion in chapters 1, 2, and 3). Thus, her assumptions about the knowledge to be taught to primary school children, and the importance of teachers' own understanding of it, provided the basis for the research.

The project investigated teachers' understanding of the concepts of science in three main ways. Firstly, by means of a survey designed to explore their confidence in teaching science. Secondly, through semi-structured interviews aimed at assessing their understanding of the "Big Ideas" of Science. And, finally via discussions of structured records kept by teachers about topics and activities that they used in their teaching.[1] As this description indicates, the research was framed by a set of hypotheses about what counts as expertise in primary science, and it used methods that enabled the researchers to collect data that could help them to identify the extent to which the teachers studied had this expertise. The focus was, therefore, rather narrow; and the data collected were structured in terms of a prior notion of what constitutes primary science expertise.

The second study investigating the impact of teachers' subject knowledge on the teaching of science was an Economic and Social Research Council-funded project, aimed at examining "classroom influences on children's perceptions and learning in mathematics and science" (Osborne & Simon, 1996a, p. 119). One focus of the project was on the ways in which teachers' subject knowledge and associated pedagogic knowledge influences the selection and use of science activities in the classroom. And it was framed by the view that the relevant abstract scientific concepts should be introduced to the children prior to their engagement with practical activities, and that teachers' understanding of these concepts is the key requirement for effective primary science teaching. This project employed a case study method to illustrate the "nature of pedagogical problem generated by lack of subject knowledge" (Osborne & Simon, 1996b, p.1). As this description suggests, there was little attempt to *explore* the nature of primary science practice. Rather, the investigation was framed by the researchers' assumptions about this, and the data were used largely for illustrative purposes. Such a use of case study is at odds with the ways in which it is typically used by qualitative researchers.

THE USE OF QUALITATIVE CASE STUDY IN THIS STUDY

As I mentioned earlier in this chapter, my research approaches the study of teacher expertise in primary science from a sociocultural perspective: by identifying a teacher who is recognised in her local school environment as an *expert* primary science practitioner, and by investigating in detail the nature of her expertise. Unlike other research in the area of primary science, which studies teacher expertise by starting with a set of assumptions about the kind and role of subject knowledge and pedagogical content knowledge that defines expertise, my research is open-ended in character, to allow for the in-depth and detailed investigation of the ways in which a practitioner (Coral) displays her own expertise. It involves the study of her views about her own subject knowledge and its role in teaching, her beliefs about children's learning in science, and her pedagogy.[2]

From this point of view, my research aims to capture complexity, and in this respect it has similarities with Robert Stake's approach. He argues that case study is the "study of the particularity and complexity of a single case, coming to understand its activity within important circumstances" (Stake, 1995, p. xi). However, unlike Stake's work, my research does not aim to capture the complexity of the single case for its own sake. Instead, it aims to widen the debate and to question assumptions about the nature of subject knowledge, learning and pedagogy that appear to underlie constructivist approaches to expertise found in the literature of primary science education research (as discussed in chapters 1, 2, and 3).

Thus, I use the information collected from the case study to deepen my theoretical analysis of primary science expertise. The aim is to infer meaningful patterns and explanations from studying the features of the case studied, and the relationships among them, during a relatively long period of time. By exploring similar issues at different points in time, it is possible to develop sound generalisations within the case (Hammersley & Gomm, 2000) to try to ensure that the data represent the case adequately. However, explanations cannot be validated solely through the study of a single case or even through the study of a small number of cases. Thus, the patterns and explanations produced in this study do not claim to have universal validity. Rather they constitute hypotheses that need to be tested in future research (Gomm, Hammersley, & Foster, 2000).

It is also important to emphasise that Coral was not selected on the grounds that she was typical or representative of all expert teachers of primary science. Rather she was chosen on the grounds that she provides an exemplar, a *critical case*, of what is widely taken to count as such expertise at the present time by practitioners.[3]

CONTEXT OF THE STUDY

As noted earlier, some of the literature on sociocultural perspectives defines expertise in terms of recognition by relevant communities of practice. Coral met this requirement in several key respects. At the time when I began my research, she had been working as a primary teacher for seven years in a large inner city school in

Northern England. She was the class teacher of twenty eight Year 5 children (10—11 years old), many of who had English as their second language. She was also the science co-ordinator for her school, assisting other colleagues with aspects of their science teaching, especially those related to their understanding of scientific knowledge and procedures. Her qualifications included three Science A levels, some modules from an unfinished undergraduate physics degree, and an under-graduate teacher education (B.Ed honours) degree with a specialisation in science. Coral had published articles in a professional journal of primary science about the ways in which her own teaching was contributing to the development of children's science learning, indeed, she was a member of the editorial board of that journal. Furthermore, she had presented papers at science education conferences and acted as the science advisor in her Local Education Authority.

I first sent Coral a letter to explore the possibility of visiting her classroom, to discuss with her aspects of her work, and to find out about her views on teaching, learning and science education. Soon after that, I had a telephone conversation with her, in which she expressed her interest in participating in my research, since she considered that this would be an opportunity to reflect further on her own science teaching. We arranged for me to visit her class for a period of a half term (six weeks) starting immediately after the Easter break. During this telephone conversation we also discussed very briefly her plans for the term. Coral proposed to focus her teaching on the area of the Primary Science National Curriculum dealing with *forces*. She explained to me that the children had already been introduced to ideas about pulling and pushing in the previous year, and that she wanted to build on this understanding and develop it further.

I first visited Coral's class to observe her second lesson on forces which was about gravity and air resistance. At the beginning of that lesson, she provided me with the following brief outline of what took place in the initial lesson and the ac-tivities that children would be engaged in during the session I observed:

Initial session 7/4
Discussion of falling objects
Set of questions generated from children

Session 9/4
Recap of discussion
Task - to make paper fall as slowly as possible
May go on to making a 100g weight fall slower.

I was introduced to the class as "a visitor to see what we do in science". I first re-corded classroom observations in field notes, and a tape-recorder was also used to record the teacher's talk. During group work I joined in with a group of children and observed the ways in which they were getting involved in the practical activi-ties that Coral had set up for them. I talked to the children about what they were doing and I discussed some of these observations with Coral at the end of the les-son, when we had a brief interview about how she thought the lesson had gone.

I visited Coral's class again the following week to observe the lesson on *measuring pulling forces*. I worked in a similar way to previously, though this time I decided to video-record the second half of the session. This was because I found that field notes and audio recording had not captured some of the important classroom interactions that took place between the teacher and the children. Prior to my visit, I telephoned Coral to ask for her permission to use the video camera during this lesson, and explained to her the reasons why I wanted to do this. I also asked her how she thought the children in her class would react to it. At the beginning of our conversation Coral said that she was afraid that she would not be able to concentrate on her teaching with the presence of a video camera in her classroom. However, she did mention that her teaching had been video-recorded before, and that the children were used to the presence of a video camera. And, on that basis, she decided to agree to it.

During this second visit, I also interviewed Coral for about thirty minutes. The interview, which took place during her lunch break, was aimed at helping me develop my understanding of her general approach to teaching and learning science, and her views about her role as a teacher. I asked her broad questions about the role of science in primary education and the aim of science teaching, and for her views about how children learn science. I also asked her questions about the ways she planned her teaching, her beliefs about the role of practical work in promoting children's scientific understanding, her preferred ways of working with the children, and her views about her role as a teacher. Towards the end of the interview we talked more specifically about her aims for the particular session I had been observing. I asked her questions about her learning intentions for the session, the ways she assesses children's learning and how she organised her session in terms of what the children were to do, and what she did in order to help them develop their scientific understanding. The interview was tape-recorded and subsequently transcribed.

I arranged to visit Coral's class again the following week to observe a session on *friction*, which, once again, was video-recorded and subsequently transcribed. A few days before my third visit, I received an e-mail from Coral, in which she included a three-page piece of writing entitled "Year 5 work of forces–rationale for planning." Coral explained that she had decided to write down her thoughts about what took place during the three sessions on forces I had observed, so as to offer me a more detailed account of her teaching, and because she found it stressful to talk about her teaching in school time when there were frequent interruptions. She called this piece of writing her "class diary." It involved a description of and justification for how each of the three sessions had been planned, which included a discussion of the aims for each one, a description of what went on, the practical activities the children were asked to engage in, her understanding of how their learning progressed, and her dilemmas and concerns about her own teaching in helping children to develop their scientific understanding. She also included in that e-mail examples of children's questions and explanations in relation to aspects of forces, as an indication of their progression in science.

When I first started this research, I had not anticipated that e-mail communication could be used as a means for collecting data, so I was surprised when Coral initiated it. However, it proved to be a very useful way of collecting data because it enabled me to communicate quickly with her the issues about her teaching that needed further discussion, whilst at the same time it offered Coral more time to think about these issues than she would have had during a telephone conversation. Email also offered Coral the opportunity to initiate discussion about issues related to her teaching that she had not previously thought about. Moreover, I had not anticipated that Coral would provide a detailed written account of her own teaching. Yet I found this an important source of data and encouraged her to continue to send me similar pieces of writing.

I observed three more lessons on forces during that half term: a lesson on *pendula*, and two lessons on floating and sinking. After each lesson Coral e-mailed me a piece of writing similar to the one described earlier. During that half term she also sent me three separate e-mails with examples of children's explanations and questions about *friction, forces* and *floating and sinking*.

I fully transcribed my interviews with Coral and the teaching session on friction. I also transcribed parts of the other sessions. I then classified my field notes, observation and interview transcripts and Coral's own writing and email exchanges by identifying repeated words and phrases that seemed to be significant for her views concerning the role of science in primary education, her beliefs about her role as a teacher and about children's learning in science, and her approaches to science teaching. By examining these classifications I was able to identify relationships among them and I began the process of understanding these relationships by using a number of theoretical perspectives from the literature on primary science teacher expertise. Trying to make sense of the data also involved the identification of issues that needed further clarification to enable me to suggest that certain relationships hold firm in the case being examined. Moreover, in trying to understand the data collected, other issues emerged which my study had not given much attention to until that time. Such issues included some aspects of the teacher's understanding of science knowledge and its role in her teaching.

Given this, I contacted Coral again and asked her to discuss further with me issues related to her understanding of children's learning, her approaches to science teaching, and her understanding of science subject knowledge and its role in her teaching. We decided to carry out the interview at her home - she suggested this as the most convenient place for discussion. Like the previous interviews, it was unstructured, taking the form of a conversation, which lasted about an hour and a half and was tape-recorded and subsequently fully transcribed. Just before we started talking, Coral gave me a one-page piece of writing which included four paragraphs. Each of these paragraphs had a subheading to indicate that it tackled a specific issue associated with an aspect of subject knowledge. Thus, the first paragraph referred to the role of "subject knowledge in primary science teaching", the second one offered "an example of the complex issue of subject knowledge", the third paragraph discussed Coral's own "subject knowledge", and the last paragraph dealt with her "responsibility for science throughout the school". I started the interview by discussing the issues Coral included in that piece of writing, though soon after this other issues emerged, including her worries about other teachers' lack of science understanding; the ways in which she develops her own science understanding; the ways she plans her teaching of science; her concerns about balancing her approach with the demands of the Primary Science National Curriculum and the Science Assessment Tests (SATs) exams; and her beliefs about how children learn and progress in science and the ways in which she assesses their science understanding.

I transcribed the interview soon after it took place and I did some preliminary analysis, aiming to identify issues that needed further clarification. A few days later, I emailed Coral, and asked her to elaborate on some issues that arose from the interview. These included questions to do with her own understanding of science subject knowledge, and how she assesses it. In that e-mail I also asked whether I could visit her class again to observe another science lesson. The reason for observing her teaching again was to clarify some issues about my own understanding about her practice. She invited me to visit her class during a day in the summer term where she was teaching *balancing forces*.

One day before that final classroom observation, I received two email messages from Coral in which she responded to my questions regarding her own subject knowledge. In the first email, she talked briefly about the ways she forms an assessment of her own scientific understanding. In her second email, she described in more detail what she means by scientific understanding, how she develops this, and its role in her teaching. At the end of my final classroom visit, I carried out another interview with her, focused on content of her last emails and the lesson I had observed. The data collected were then reanalysed to produce the content of the following two chapters (chapters 5 and 6).

CONCLUSION

In the first part of this chapter I discussed some of the methodological implications of a sociocultural perspective for studying primary science teacher expertise. Drawing on the work of Jean Lave, I argued that teacher expertise needs to be explored in action, in the context of relevant communities of practice. This requires an in-depth investigation of practitioners who are recognised in their local environments as expert. Following on from this, I described the approach to qualitative case study that I employed in my research, with its aim of capturing the complexity of a single case and using the findings to interrogate the theoretical assumptions that underlie currently influential notions of primary science expertise. Finally, I outlined the nature of the data that I collected and how I set about analysing it.

[1] The project also used semi-structured interviews with college and local authority staff to gather information about initial and in-service primary teacher education in science and technology. This is because a further aim of the project was to assess the extent to which initial and in-service training were adequately providing for the development of primary teachers' understanding of science and technology.

[2] The name Coral is a pseudonym to protect the teacher's anonymity.

[3] I use the term critical case to refer to the selection of a case which offers evidence that could illuminate a set of theoretical ideas, and enable the researcher to come to a clearer judgment about them, without necessarily providing a clear-cut confirmation or refutation of such ideas (Martyn Hammersley, personal communication).

AN EXPERT PRIMARY SCIENCE PRACTITIONER'S PERSPECTIVE

In this chapter, I explore the ways in which one teacher of primary science, who was widely regarded as expert, discusses her own expertise. In the first part, I examine Coral's views about her science subject knowledge, the ways she assesses her own understanding of this and her beliefs about the role of her subject knowledge in her teaching. In the second section of this chapter I discuss Coral's views about the learner, the learning process, the teaching of science, and her role in supporting the development of children's scientific understanding.

The data I used in this chapter derive from unstructured interviews with Coral, her class diary about her teaching of *forces*, and email exchanges between Coral and myself. Coral taught forces to 28 ten to eleven year old children during a period of six weeks. She started her teaching of this area with the concepts of gravity and air resistance. She then moved on to teach measuring pulling forces, friction, pendula, and, finally, floating and sinking. In the English Primary Science National Curriculum, these aspects of forces should be taught at Key Stage 2 (7-11 years old) whereas the notion of a force as a push or a pull, and the idea that a force is needed to change the movement or the direction of an object should be taught at Key Stage 1 (5-7 years old).

CORAL'S PERSPECTIVE ON HER OWN SCIENCE SUBJECT KNOWLEDGE

Coral discusses her own scientific understanding in terms of a network of links between her "formal knowledge" of science and aspects of the experienced physical world. And she describes her understanding of science in dynamic terms, as generating a "wider picture":

> Linking bits of knowledge and experience in a meaningful way seems to be the key to conceptual development. This is what I mean by the development of a "wider picture". Thus, the wider picture changes all the time for me as I see new links between areas of knowledge.

Coral traces her formal knowledge of science back to her education, which included three Science "A" levels and some science modules from an unfinished physics degree. She sees this knowledge as tied to problems of the kinds that are often found in secondary science textbooks. These problems have a single right answer and therefore only required rules or simple algorithms to solve:

I went to a grammar school and all the teaching there was very formal . . . I knew facts to be able to do A level calculations about them.

What Coral refers to as making "meaningful" links between her formal knowledge of science and experience relates to her understanding of the process of explaining phenomena of the kinds that are addressed in primary school classrooms. She says that she developed this understanding further during the science education courses of her first degree. She explains that during these courses, she was offered opportunities to get engaged with problems associated with specific scientific concepts or phenomena which did not have an immediate clear answer (e.g. what makes the difference to the brightness of a bulb in an electric circuit?). To solve such problems, students had to redefine the problem in a form appropriate for investigation. In other words, students were encouraged to use their knowledge of science to ask questions that could be systematically tested, to form hypotheses and make predictions. They were then asked to carry out their own investigations in order to test their predictions, collect and interpret their data and discuss their interpretations with colleagues and other tutors.

For Coral, her involvement in such practical activities helped her to develop an understanding of how to ask scientific questions about aspects of the physical world, and to find answers to these questions by using both her formal knowledge of science and her procedural understanding: her understanding of how to do science. She compares this approach to solving problems with the discovery learning approach that underlay Nuffield secondary science. As I discussed in chapter 1, this approach involved encouraging learners to ask their own scientific questions, isolate a scientific problem and find its solution through careful investigation. Coral had briefly come across this approach during her secondary schooling, but she did not find it helpful. It was not until her college education that she began to appreciate this approach:

> [talking about her secondary school education] In chemistry we had the beginning of Nuffield science, which of course was completely not formal and we had textbooks that were all questions . . . It was completely hopeless for me . . . When I went to college I could see the value of this approach, that in doing science in that way you do actually learn something . . . All of a sudden I could look at really basic things like circuits with batteries and bulbs and could find out what was going on. I found that really nice.

Her Views about the Adequacy of her own Subject Knowledge

Coral believes that she has an adequate level of scientific knowledge: "good enough for Key Stage 2." She explains that she feels "comfortable with the science in the National Curriculum" and argues that she uses several means of assessing her own science knowledge. One of these is associated with her ability to explain adequately to other colleagues aspects of the scientific concepts that are included in the National Curriculum. This kind of assessment is further reinforced by the fact that other teachers often say to her that they find her support helpful:

I feel able to support colleagues with any difficulties. Other teachers have told me that I have helped them to understand things.

Another way that Coral uses to assess her science knowledge seems to relate to her ability to identify correctly instances as examples of particular scientific concepts. She argues, for example, that her knowledge of scientific concepts offers her "security" in distinguishing the aspects of scientific knowledge she understands from those which she does not:

I have a certain amount of security in terms of formal education (3 science "A" levels and some science in my first degree course). The main outcome of this is familiarity with basic concepts and a fairly clear idea of what I don't understand.

Coral goes on to explain that once she has identified "a patchy area" in her "science network" she is "keen to reinforce it". So, once she has realised that she does not know enough about a particular aspect of scientific knowledge to explain a particular scientific experience, she is willing to develop her knowledge of that aspect by reading up about it, for example, or by watching scientific programmes on the television. In this way, she widens her existing picture of science. Coral emphasises that she is able to do this because she knows that her "level of background understanding is good enough" to allow her "to assimilate new ideas". In this respect, her views about the development of her own scientific understanding suggest a metacognitive awareness of the organisation and synthesis of her scientific understanding: Coral seems able not only to identify the knowledge she lacks but also to reorganise and synthesise her existing picture of science (see Bruner, 1986). Following on from this, it seems clear that Coral believes that the foundation of knowledge that she acquired at A level and undergraduate level is important.

However, Coral also argues that her knowledge of science does not always enable her to identify situations as examples or non-examples of particular scientific concepts. She explains that during her science teaching she often come across situations that she cannot immediately understand, even if they relate to a concept she has taught before:

I will frequently come across things that I am suddenly aware that I don't really understand whilst I am talking to the children.

Coral describes an episode which followed work about forces acting on floating objects:

During a discussion following work with Newton meters and floating objects, I began to wonder about the situation of a person on a floating boat who was, from one perspective apparently weightless. This was not a helpful thought.

It seems that this situation of a person on a floating boat was interpreted by Coral as a problem that involves the concept of the balanced forces which exist between the weight of the floating object and the upthrust force of the water in which the object floats. So she was led to the possibility that the person would be weightless.

To explain this situation, Coral needed to interpret it as a problem which involves the balanced forces that exist between the weight of the person and the reaction force of the floor of a building on land. Although Coral had used this concept in other situations, her previous experience in using this particular concept was not sufficient to enable her to interpret the situation as effectively as in the previous ones. In other words, in this situation Coral has an abstract knowledge of the concept as taught to her and a situated knowledge of it in the contexts she has experienced it and taught it. The situation of the person on the boat was a new context, so she had to transfer her understanding to the new context. From a sociocultural perspective, situations like this indicate that an individual's understanding of a particular problem involves the individual's interpretation and perception of the problem depicted in it, a process which is contingent (see the discussion in chapter 2).

For Coral, such situations are "a real problem" for her and the children, because she gets confused, her teaching stops and she "loses momentum". Nevertheless, she argues that during her teaching she tries to resolve such confusing situations either by thinking about them alone or by sharing her confusion with the children. She explains that the way to deal with such situations is to ask "hard and searching questions" that aim to clarify the problem and broaden her own and the children's understanding of the same concept across problem situations. So, a solution to a scientific problem is sought, yet this simultaneously involves developing children's learning. It seems, therefore, that for Coral the ability to know how to make sense of experience, which she developed on her initial teacher education course, is as important as her formal scientific knowledge. It is this ability, as well as her approach to the teaching of science, that allows her to explain confusing situations that may appear during teaching. It also seems to allow her to widen her picture of science by forming new links between familiar concepts and new experiences. Indeed, she claims that only after she has taught a specific concept several times can she say that she has developed a better understanding of it:

> I develop my understanding all the time. When I've taught something for the third or fourth time running I think "all right" now I know what it means.

Following on from this, it can be suggested that Coral acknowledges the contingency of her scientific understanding, and has developed ways of coping with this when it emerges during problem-solving situations that arise during her teaching.

Her Views about the Role of Subject Knowledge in her Teaching

Coral argues that the aim of her science teaching is to help children become "really scientifically literate", and she explains that this means that what she wants the children to be able to do as a result of her science teaching is to look at things and say "I know what's happening there. I understand it". This kind of understanding seems to be similar to that which she developed during her initial teacher education course, and relates to children's metacognitive awareness: their ability to know how to make sense of physical experiences by using their scientific understanding. And, she seems to use evidence of children's metacognitive awareness to evaluate the success of her teaching. As she comments: "the thing that gives me pleasure is when they relate one thing to another, when they say: "that's like when.""

Coral describes her science lessons as "genuine processes of exploration", during which she helps the children to ask their own scientific questions about a particular experience and to develop their procedural and conceptual scientific understanding, so as to be able to provide adequate answers to these questions. Discussing the way she teaches the content of the primary Science National Curriculum, she stresses the interrelated nature of the concepts, procedures and processes of science:

> I am not doing lots of investigations that are just AT1 investigations which have not got any content. I wouldn't want to do that. I am interested in the content, so are the children. But the teaching of content does not necessarily take place at the expense of process.[1]

From this point of view, Coral argues that her own picture of science plays a significant part in her teaching. It enables her to have an understanding of what are the "interesting questions" about a particular aspect of the physical world, and of the concepts and processes that could be used in order to explore it. In turn, this understanding gives her "confidence" in her teaching; it helps her to organise her teaching in a way that encourages children to explore physical experiences. Coral compares her teaching of science with her teaching of geography. She argues that in geography her network of conceptual links is much smaller, and therefore her understanding of interesting questions is limited. This prevents her from organising her geography teaching in an exploratory way, so that she usually simply offers the children "facts". Commenting on her science and geography teaching Coral says:

> I find it difficult to give children neatly packaged, easy to understand facts which obscure the interesting questions in science. I don't find this at all difficult in geography because I don't know the interesting questions. I am a much more confident science teacher than geography teacher.

However, she also points out that her picture of science can cause problems in her teaching. In particular, she explains that quite often her broad understanding of links between knowledge and experience encourages her to push the children beyond their abilities to understand certain links:

> I push them as far as they can go and beyond all the time. I can see they know this bit and they know the other bit and I want them to put these bits together and I get so excited that I want to share this with them, and then I just lose them.

Coral seems to suggest that her understanding of scientific knowledge is important in assisting the children to address scientific questions. This knowledge enables her to identify "profitable lines of thought" in what the children say or do and link them together towards the understanding of a particular scientific concept:

> I often think: "If I didn't know the next fact, I wouldn't be interested in what that child says or does. I am only interested in that because I know it can lead to some other understanding of what I think might be an important concept."

She also argues that her knowledge of science helps her to "shape" what she says to the children. In particular, she says that she is able to select and introduce to the children appropriate scientific terms. She explains that, prior to her teaching, she forms an idea of which terms to use and how they can be defined and related to children's everyday language. She comments, however, that "over a period of two years there are relatively few terms that the children need to know". Moreover, she stresses that she does not necessarily associate children's scientific understanding with children's use of scientific language. She explains that she is more concerned with the thinking underlying children's responses rather than with the extent to which their responses conform to or deviate from certain specifications laid down by her at the beginning of a session.

To illustrate this point she refers to the use of particular tests (e.g. Standard Assessment Tasks, SATs) to evaluate children's learning in science. She points out that in these tests, children's science learning is associated with their ability to answer particular questions which are expressed in a decontextualised way. By contrast, when the evaluation of children's learning is more concerned with understanding children's thinking, their ability to use a scientific term is less important than their ability to explain a particular phenomenon using their own language:

> In a SAT paper we did last week there was a question about burning candles saying that when a candle burns a liquid is formed. What is this liquid called? That's a hard question. It's too technical. Some children did know the name of course. And then the next question was "What is the name of the process by which this liquid is formed?" And if you say to the children "what do we say is happening here", they'll say "it's melting". They know it is melting except that some of them will say "it's burning" because we are talking about the candle is burning.

Furthermore, Coral says that her scientific understanding helps her to simplify complicated scientific ideas and draw a "sequence of learning objectives in my mind". Such objectives also include the scientific skills and procedures (e.g. how to construct a graph or how to carry out a fair test) that she is expecting the children to learn during a teaching session. However, she does not produce written detailed descriptions of the learning objectives of her sessions.

Moreover, for Coral such learning objectives are only used to determine at a general level what the children are to learn and to guide her in the choice of scientific terms, explanations, activities and resources that she may need to provide in order to help the children develop their scientific understanding. She disagrees with the idea that knowledge within a specific area of science can be broken down into smaller bits and taught according to their degree of difficulty, expecting the children to construct their understanding following the same kind of logical relationship that the teacher has drawn between concepts in her objectives:

I don't believe that you can put things in order, that you have to learn this first and this second and this last. Learning science does not come in nice neat little packages that can be taught in a nice neat way and fit together afterwards.

Nevertheless, she points out that certain areas of science (e.g. forces) include complicated concepts and explanations that cannot easily relate to children's everyday experiences:

Well some areas are quite complicated. The teaching of forces is very difficult. The ideas are very sophisticated and maybe are not appropriate for ten year olds. It's very hard to teach forces and it's very difficult for children to understand.

Furthermore, the structure of a session or a series of sessions is based partly on what Coral thinks is the order that children will find easier to follow, and partly on her formative assessment of the children's current understanding. So, her teaching does not follow a fixed course. As she explains, she decided to start her teaching of the topic of forces with a session on falling objects because it is an everyday phenomenon that all children have experienced, and about which they are likely to have developed a number of different conceptions. When the children had shown evidence in their understanding that they "could expect things to fall at the same speed", Coral moved on to discuss the concept of air resistance, hoping that the children would find this phenomenon interesting to explore since it is closely associated to gravity and the speed by which different objects fall:

I now assumed that the children knew that they could expect things to fall at the same rate, and that they would, therefore, find air resistance an interesting phenomenon.

I will discuss the role of learning objectives in Coral's teaching again in the next sections.

CORAL'S VIEWS ABOUT THE NATURE OF CHILDREN'S SCIENCE LEARNING

Coral argues that children bring their own ideas to the science classroom which are the outcome of their attempts to solve problems that they encounter in their everyday interactions with the physical world. Talking about children's everyday ideas of forces, for example, she says:

After all, from the time a baby drops something out of the pram and looks down and not up, he or she is developing concepts about forces.

Coral assumes that children's everyday ideas of a scientific concept or phenomenon are likely to be different from the one held by scientists. This is because children's ideas are the product of their mundane thinking about the world, which is different from "the logical thinking" that scientists employ to explore particular scientific phenomena. "Logical thinking" refers to the processes and procedures that scientists use to produce a body of scientific propositions that explains aspects of the physical world. Thus, for Coral scientific understanding requires evidence, and this in turn, requires procedural capability. Coral states that in her science teaching she aims to help the children to think about their experiences of everyday scientific phenomena in a way similar to the one employed by scientists. As she puts it: "in science children find out about things that are obvious in everyday life but they haven't thought of in this way before". For instance, referring to her session on gravity and air resistance she explains that although children had their own ideas about falling objects, they had not "thought about it like Galileo or Newton thought". Thus, encouraging the children to think "logically through it, they were surprised when they found that things fall at the same speed". In this respect, her views about the learner seem to draw on Piagetian constructivist accounts of the learner, according to which learners are regarded as intelligent problem solvers motivated to initiate and complete acts, and to construct conceptual structures which enable them to make sense of aspects of the physical world that are related to what "has been experienced by individuals" (Murphy, et al., 2000, p. 12).

Coral emphasises the tacit character of children's everyday ideas. She says, for example, that children's ideas are often "implicit and difficult to access", and argues that her role during elicitation is to help them "articulate their thinking". Coral stresses that the elicitation of children's ideas is used as a "tool" for the children and as a "tool" for herself. As she comments, children do not "know what they know and what they think unless they are asked to articulate their thoughts". This comment indicates Coral's concern with the development of children's metacognitive awareness, which appears to be central in her view about how scientific understanding develops. In her teaching the elicitation of children's ideas is achieved by encouraging the children, during whole class discussions or smaller conversations, to "relate their ideas to everyday experiences and real contexts". For example, in order to find out children's ideas about gravity, weight (as a force) and air resistance, Coral presented the children with three objects of different size and weight. She then dropped the three objects in a situation with minimal air resistance and asked the children to predict the results. She reports that the children expressed a range of ideas such as "the heavy one would fall first because it was the heaviest; the lightest one would fall first because it was little and would drop quickly; the heavy one would fall slower because it was bigger".

As I mentioned earlier, as a teacher, Coral is "particularly interested" in eliciting and identifying children's everyday ideas about aspects of the physical world. She explains that eliciting children's ideas helps her to assess their understanding in relation to the scientific knowledge that she has included in her learning objectives. It also informs her about the range of children's everyday ideas on a specific topic, so as to incorporate some of them in her teaching. As she puts it, eliciting children's ideas helps her to "find out what the children already knew in terms of school learning, and in terms of their own conclusions".

Sometimes Coral uses the context of a practical task to elicit both children's conceptual and procedural understanding. She explains that during such activities she offers children one way of testing a particular idea and then invites them to suggest ways of modifying or extending the task. For Coral, children's attempts to modify or extend a task offer her a "good opportunity to gain access to their thinking". And, she comments:

> It rapidly becomes clear if they have not grasped the essential experimental technique or rationale, or, on the other hand, if they can enrich the activity in a meaningful way.

Quite often, Coral elicits children's ideas through writing. She comments that classroom discussions are not appropriate for all the children in her classroom because "not every child is involved in these discussions". Therefore, Coral decided to use writing to help the children make explicit their understanding of a topic; that is, to "articulate their thoughts about what they know and what they think". Coral explains that, either at the beginning or towards the end of a session on a topic, and after having discussed their ideas in the classroom, she asks the children to write on a piece of paper their current understandings of the topic under discussion. She calls this "Any Answers" type of writing.

In a similar way, she also often asks the children to write on a piece of paper any scientific questions that they would like to find an answer to ("Any Questions?" type of writing). This is because she places particular emphasis on helping children develop not only their ability to articulate their thoughts but also their ability to ask scientific questions. She argues, however, that some children are better than others at asking scientific questions, and she believes that, overall, it is hard to encourage the children to think of scientific questions. She gives the children a time limit and asks them to think of questions which could be tested in the classroom, or answered by thought experiments or by looking at a science book, or questions which may be too hard to be dealt with at the moment:

> Well, I say to them may be there will be questions that we have already answered or may be there will be questions that we could do some experiments to find out the answer or there might be questions we just have to think about or look at books or there might be questions which we will have to leave on one side because they are too hard.

Furthermore, in order to help the children develop further their ability to provide explanations and ask scientific questions, Coral selects those of the children's explanations and questions that include elements of a scientific way of thinking and displays and discusses them in the classroom.[2] It seems that by making children's developing understanding available to them, Coral aims to frame their new learning. In other words, she helps them to tackle new topics with some organised understanding of what counts as a scientific explanation or a scientific question. Moreover, although she argues that these methods are not "the best for all the children", they can, nevertheless, provide valuable information to her about children's developing understanding of science.

Coral's interest in eliciting children's ideas is further illustrated in her continuing search for finding better or more profitable methods for eliciting children's thinking. For instance, she argues that recently she has tried to access their ideas by talking to the children whilst they are working together in small groups to solve a particular problem. Nevertheless, she argues that she is "still left with the problem of not being able to talk enough with each group to thoroughly access their thinking".

Coral believes that not all of the ideas expressed by the children during classroom discussion or in writing are "firm or deeply held beliefs" and so resistant to modification. Some are ideas that they think of for the first time when asked, or that do not have any link with their experience. She argues that such ideas can be more easily changed. Thus, although eliciting children's ideas, especially at the beginning of a new science topic (e.g. forces), "encourages children's interest and produces some real thinking", it also has the "disadvantage of introducing all sorts of untidy ideas and diffuse theories". From this point of view, Coral argues that it is not necessary to incorporate in her teaching all of the children's ideas. In fact, she stresses that "it is also pointless because the children's ideas will have already changed and developed as they relate them to experience and rethink them". For Coral, finding out about children's existing understanding is useful as "an overview of pre-existing ideas" so as to enable her to assess children's learning during further work. From this point of view, eliciting children's ideas also helps her to consolidate prior learning and set the scene for future learning.

Her Views about how Children Learn Science

Coral seems to believe that children develop their scientific understanding as they participate in practical activities which offer them opportunities to reflect on the viability of their existing understanding and to begin to reconsider and develop this understanding towards the desired scientific one. Such reflection and reconsideration occurs as children use their everyday ideas to resolve what they find problematic within the world of their own experience:

> Children remember what they have done practically. They learn by actually having an ice balloon or using the electricity equipment and trying to figure out what is happening.

Coral stresses that the more opportunities children are offered to reconsider their own understanding, the more likely it is that they will modify this understanding towards the desired scientific one:

> the more working out for themselves they do the more conceptual development takes place in a way.

In order to help children to reconsider their existing understanding Coral engages children with practical activities that relate to a specific physical experience (e.g. floating and sinking), and offers children opportunities to use their existing understanding to explain those aspects of this experience that interest them. This is because she believes that learning occurs when children are intrinsically motivated, that is when they become "genuinely curious" about the aspects of the topic under study. And this is achieved when they are offered opportunities to pursue their own interests. Discussing children's practical work, Coral points out that such explorations are similar to young children's play:

> [Involvement in practical activities] It is not superficial messing about, it is real play like small children do when they are completely involved in what they are doing.

In this respect, Coral's views of how children learn seem to have similarities with Piagetian staged views of the learner, which argue that in order to encourage children's learning, the problem that they are to investigate needs to be generated by the children, and not to be given to them by the classroom teacher.

However, Coral also points out that she does not necessarily expect the children to discover scientific concepts through their engagement with practical activities. For her, participation in such activities simply provides the basis upon which scientific knowledge is built. In this respect, Coral's views of how children learn science seems to have similarities with Piagetian constructivist accounts of the learner, according to which the learner is regarded as an active constructor of meaning, responsible for organising, structuring and restructuring experience in the light of existing conceptual structures, and for determining the value of a conceptual structure by judging how well it fits with experience (see for example, Driver, 1984, 1989). She argues that her beliefs about how children learn and of the learning process were developed during her initial teacher education course, which was influenced by constructivist approaches to the learning and teaching of science:

> [discussing her experiences during her initial teacher education course] It was the fashionable thing then. You know, all this about Driver and children's ideas about science.

Coral emphasises that if learning science is concerned with understanding, scientific knowledge should be presented to children after they have been offered opportunities to get involved in practical activities, to reconsider and problematise their existing understanding of a particular scientific concept). By contrast, Coral argues that if the children are not offered opportunities to rethink their own science understanding but are instead presented with abstract scientific knowledge, then the learning that takes place is likely to be superficial "rote" learning:

> I don't think you can do that [introducing a science concept] unless they have practice with it first. Unless they use the stuff first unless they play with it. If you don't have that there is nothing to build on. And children do not remember or they might remember things superficially. They memorise sentences but these they do not mean anything to them. They cannot build on it and learn more with understanding.

Coral explains that in her teaching a new scientific idea is introduced to the children so as to build upon their developing understanding, so as to help them link successfully in their explanations of particular physical experiences their existing understanding with the new knowledge. This is achieved during classroom discussions where Coral tries to identify those of the children's ideas that are closer to the desired scientific one, and to represent these ideas to the children using appropriate scientific terms:

> And then you can [after children had been involved in practical activities], I hope, build on that [children's developing understanding] rather more formally and draw what I feel I can draw out of it, so they've got some real real science out of it.

From this point of view, it seems that for Coral children's engagement in practical activities offers them opportunities to get an initial understanding of a problem, and she also uses this to form an assessment of children's current point of development. In turn, this assessment enables her to judge how far children's thinking can be developed towards a particular scientific concept, making appropriate links between children's point of development and scientific understanding. As she comments, during teaching her role is to "lead the children along as far as they can towards developing their own understanding". In this respect, her views about the learning process seem to draw on Vygotskian accounts, which argue that learning takes place within learners' zones of proximal development (see for example, Harlen, & Qualter, 2004; Rogoff & Gardner, 1984).

For Coral the key to what scientific understanding children are going to develop depends on "the experiences they have had". Thus, she seems to suggest that the interaction between scientific knowledge and children's prior understanding and experience may produce knowledge which either consolidates the latter, complexifies it or deconstructs it (see Pépin, 1998). For example, according to Coral, children's writing that followed teaching of gravity and air resistance showed that most children had deconstructed their prior conceptions about the falling of objects and constructed understanding that objects fall at the same speed. A few children, however, seemed to maintain their previous conceptions. In the second session of floating and sinking, Coral wanted the children to begin to use the "weighty for size" concept in their explanations of flotation. She says that as the "Any Answers" type of writing showed, many children appeared to complexify their current understanding by incorporating this concept into their existing knowledge. However, she stresses that only one child seemed to understand the relation between the "weighty for size" concept and the floating of objects:

> Unfortunately, he was the only one.

Coral suggests that children are capable of developing each other's scientific thinking when they are working in pairs because "they talk about what they are doing and they get more out of it". However, she does not believe that encouraging children to work in groups bigger than two necessarily promotes science learning. This is because children at this age (nine and ten years-old) are still "socially egocentric"; that is, they do not seem to have skills of collaboration. Therefore, when they are working together in a large group, they find it difficult to listen to and discuss each other's ideas. To support her view, Coral gives an example from classroom discussions. She says that children quite often offer responses to a question that she asked earlier in the session, despite the fact that the theme of the current discussion has changed:

> I don't particularly like big groups. Threes I tolerate. But bigger than that, children are not involved. I think children are pretty egocentric at this age, nine or ten. They will come with an answer to the question or to the idea that occurred to them five minutes before and they will say *that* regardless of what has gone on since. And I think they are like that with each other as well. They are very much into their own track.

Thus, Coral does not usually promote group discussions. Instead, most of the discussions in her class take place between Coral and the whole class, with her organising the discussion and regulating the exchanges of ideas between the children and among the children and herself. In this way she is able to help children develop each other's ideas. She describes the outcome of such discussions in terms of "shared thinking", and argues that this often occurs implicitly, as children participate together with the teacher in classroom discussions:

> Most of the learning that takes place in my science teaching is the result of shared thinking. Children do develop other children's ideas, without even realising it sometimes. Sometimes, I say "this was my idea" and they will say "no that was my idea" and it was, but the two things were so linked.

She also suggests that children's development of scientific understanding can happen independently from the structure of the session. It occurs when "the moment is right and the interest is there". She also points out that children's construction of their picture of science is often not as continuous or smooth as she would like it to be:

> It doesn't build up a nice picture, a nice neat jigsaw that's in my mind.

Quite often children forget or misunderstand what was discussed during teaching until they "gradually build one thing on another and things come together for them". Here, Coral's views about children's construction of science knowledge seems to have similarities with di Sessa's (1988) view that an individual's learning in science should be seen in terms of discontinuous changes in a collection of belief fragments which have arisen from everyday experience.

Furthermore, Coral also believes that learning science can occur indirectly, when meanings are not explicitly negotiated between the teacher and the children. She argues, for example, that it is possible for the children to build up their "picture of science" when experiencing situations outside the school classroom:

> Things probably come together for them with absolutely nothing to do with me directly; just because of what they are experiencing and what they are doing and things fit together from the outside too. Things they see on the television or read or just see outside. They may fit all things in gradually building up a more useful picture.

A similar view is expressed by Bauersfeld (1988). Discussing the learning of mathematics, he argues that learning can be seen as a process of often implicit negotiations in which subtle shifts and slides of meaning occur outside the participants' awareness. During teaching, students learn when to do what, and how to do it. However, "the core part of mathematics enculturation comes into effect on the meta-level and it is learned indirectly" (in Cobb, 1994, p. 15; see also Roth, Tobin, & Ritchie, 2001).

CORAL'S VIEWS ABOUT HER TEACHING OF SCIENCE

Coral argues that in her teaching she does not use a set of teaching strategies "ready to direct a session to a preconceived conclusion". Nevertheless, she tries to exercise a certain degree of control over what is to be learned, when and how, by keeping the children "working along the same lines". This is taken to mean that she organises her teaching in a way that it engages the children in the same practical activities which aim to fulfil her own learning objectives. This is because Coral believes that all the children in her classroom should be offered the same learning opportunities to develop their understanding of those aspects of scientific concepts which she regards as significant for explaining adequately particular physical experiences. She gives as an example how, during the second session on gravity and air resistance, she asked the children to investigate a range of model parachutes made of different materials because she wanted them to begin to develop their understanding of the relation between "air resistance, surface area, density and rate of fall". For Coral, this understanding is important for explaining experiences associated with the rate of fall of different objects. Commenting on the importance of the fulfilment of her own objectives, she wrote that she probably considers it more significant than the fulfilment of children's own interests:

> I think that my learning objectives for them are important, and I suppose I feel that *their* learning objectives are secondary.

To some extent this is encouraged by her belief that although many children are able to develop their conceptual understanding with less guidance by her, some other children are unable to do so and, therefore, she needs to exercise some control over their learning:

> There are some children whom I feel I can't trust to have the development of a conceptual framework as a primary aim. The most straightforward way of making sure that these children use their time effectively is to control what they are doing by giving them instructions by which they cannot vary unless I agree.

Nevertheless, during practical activities Coral offers the children a certain degree of autonomy to modify a specific task by pursuing their own ideas. Indeed, these activities are organised in a "fairly unstructured way". As she comments, a situation where all the children in the classroom perform the same activity in exactly the same way is "pointless" because it is associated with pretending to be discovering something interesting. She tries, however, to encourage the children to pursue those of their ideas which seem to be closer to her own objectives. This enables her to maintain control over what can be learned by bringing together at the end of the practical activity those of the children's learning outcomes which seem to be closer to her own intended ones:

> I encourage original thoughts and directions but I know that I can draw them all together into one conversation at the end. If they want to pursue interests which will fulfil my own criteria then I am delighted but I don't want them to substitute their own criteria.

Thus, it seems that in Coral's teaching what the children are to learn is determined at a general level beforehand, by her choice of learning opportunity, and at a more specific level by the children during the session as they respond within an appropriate degree of freedom. For example, during the first session on gravity and air resistance, children were given two templates for spinners and asked to investigate how to make paper fall as slowly as possible. One child found out that a piece of paper the same size with no cutting or folding fell more slowly than either spinner. Coral regarded the child's finding as "interesting" and decided to ask her to repeat the test in front of the class, thinking that it could lead to a discussion about the rate of fall and surface area, which was one of her learning objectives for that session.

However, Coral argues that she is not always able to explore further all of the children's ideas that relate to her learning objectives. This is because there is never enough time to develop children's thinking, "even in terms of planning for next time". Children think "too much, too fast" she says, and, therefore, some of their ideas are ignored even if they are relevant to her own learning objectives. For instance, during the same session on gravity and air resistance, one child asked a question about the direction of air resistance, which was not discussed further, although according to Coral "it could have led to an interesting discussion about directional forces, and air resistance opposing movement rather than gravity". Not being able to explore further all of the children's questions seems to be a problem for Coral, because she thinks that on one hand she professes interest in children's ideas and on the other hand she "ignores almost all of them".

On some occasions, children may begin to explain adequately a particular phenomenon (e.g. the rate of fall of parachutes), drawing on different concepts from the ones included in Coral's learning objectives. To some extent she encourages this, especially in relation to "the more able and creative children" in her classroom. However, the decision about whether to explore further such ideas seems to be based on what the teacher thinks is an appropriate line of development for the majority of the children in the class. For example, as mentioned earlier, during the session on gravity and air resistance, Coral wanted the children to begin to develop their understanding of the relation between "air resistance, surface area, density and rate of fall". To achieve this aim, she asked the children to design their own parachutes according to their own criteria. Two children who were working together seemed to be thinking of the effect of shape on the falling of parachutes and appeared to favour a round shape for their own design. Coral did not know about their theory until the following session but she argued that even if she had done she would not have used it, because she did not believe shape was a suitable idea for the majority of the children in her class:

> Shape was not a fruitful variable on my agenda - I wanted them to think about surface area and density. Also, round is a difficult shape - we don't know how to calculate the area of a circle and we are not very good at using compasses. Using shape as an independent variable would have been very difficult mathematically in terms of keeping the area constant. It would have led us into aerodynamics rather than surface area and density.

As we can see, in her teaching Coral tries to balance her beliefs of how children learn science with her concern to help all the children develop appropriate scientific understanding. One way to achieve this is by creating a learning environment where simple and more complex tasks are ongoing and discussed in parallel.

Her Role in Supporting Children's Development of Scientific Understanding

Coral describes her task in supporting the development of children's scientific understanding as mainly involving "talking to them". Such talking takes place within the context of children's scientific activity and the problems which such activity gives rise to. She explains that in her teaching she "looks for opportunities" in what the children say or do which may lead to the development of some aspects of their scientific understanding. Following on from this, she comments that she thinks on her feet, she gets the next idea as she talks to the children:

> I don't do any planning. I'm doing what I'm doing. I've got the next idea whilst I'm talking to the children.

For instance, during the session on floating and sinking some of the children seemed to begin to think that a possible explanation for the floating of an object is a combination of the size, the shape and the material an object is made of. However, their ideas could not be applied with consistency to explain the flotation of a range of different objects. Thus, as a signal to the children that their explanations for flotation (size, shape, material) are scientifically inconsistent, Coral decided to introduce "weight" as an idea which was intended to have the explanatory power to overcome these inconsistencies:

> I decided to introduce the idea of weight at this stage as we had already considered size, shape and material and seemed to be getting nowhere.

It seems that in introducing *weight* Coral wanted to help the children to incorporate the weight variable into their understanding of the relation between the size and the material an object is made of, so that they begin to explain flotation in terms of the "weight for size" concept (that is the difference in space occupied by two objects of the same weight made of different materials).[3] She explains that to work towards this aim she asked the children to compare the space that is occupied by a small candle and a candle shaped piece of plasticine of the same weight. The children could see that the plasticine was smaller and sank but "they were puzzled about why the candle took up more space for the same weight". At this point, in order to help the children make the link between weight and size, she reminded them of the discussion that had taken place earlier in the year about the expansion of freezing water. Coral comments that this reference to previous learning helped some children to make the link between volume and material and how this affects the floating of objects:

> One child immediately understood, "If you weighed a balloon full of water that size it would spread out more. The ice is more spread out and the candle is more spread out, that's why the candle floats".

Thus, Coral's role in her teaching is to try to scaffold children's thinking so that it becomes increasingly compatible with that of the established scientific community and yet remains personally meaningful to them. From this point of view, the choice of practical activities seems to be based on their contribution to helping the evolution of children's thinking towards particular scientific ways of knowing. This final decision seems to be made by Coral's reflection on her understanding of the current point of development of the children (the choice of activity may have been different if some children had already begun to use a combination of weight and size in their explanations for flotation).

DISCUSSION

In this chapter, I have discussed the ways in which Coral understands her own subject knowledge and its role in her teaching, and examined her views about the learner and her approach to science teaching.

I argued that Coral conceives her science understanding as a network of links between the concepts of science, as these were taught to her as a secondary school student and a physics undergraduate, and her concrete experience of the world. Central to her ability to create connections between scientific knowledge and experience is her problem-solving procedural understanding. Coral developed this understanding during her initial teacher education courses, and it enables her to find solutions to problems that may be well or ill defined. Her network of links is conceived in dynamic terms: as evolving all the time, as she sees new links between areas of knowledge and experience. In this respect, her view about the development of her own scientific understanding is perhaps closest to a sociocultural view of knowledge.

Although Coral values her knowledge of abstract scientific concepts she defines adequacy not in terms of commodity knowledge in the manner of "small range" and "big ideas" constructivism, but in a way that links to performance. For example, she uses her experience as a successful mentor for her colleagues as a measure of the adequacy of her scientific understanding. It is possible then to argue that Coral understands her expertise in a way similar to sociocultural perspectives. She also associates her own understanding with metacognitive awareness. She is capable of assessing her own understanding about a specific area of science, developing it further, and reorganising her picture of science accordingly. Furthermore, she seems to recognise the contingency of her scientific understanding, by arguing that providing explanations for situations that arise during teaching and relating them to scientific concepts that she has taught previously is not a straight-forward process. To respond to such situations, she often engages the children in the process of asking questions that aim to interpret and clarify the situation. In this respect, too, her expertise is perhaps closest to sociocultural perspectives.

At the same time, like "big ideas" constructivism for Coral the task of science teaching is to help the children ask scientific questions about a particular physical experience and seek answers to these questions in order to develop their understanding of abstract scientific concepts. Following on from this, she argues that her scientific understanding plays an important role in her teaching. It helps her to recognise scientific questions and organise her teaching in a way that encourages the development of children's ability to ask questions and seek answers to these questions. It also enables her to recognise children's everyday ideas that are different from scientific understanding, to decide on appropriate scientific terms and practical activities, and to simplify scientific concepts. Furthermore, it helps her to plan a set of learning objectives in her mind which determine at a general level what the children are to learn, when and how in terms of procedural and conceptual understanding. As with her own scientific understanding, for Coral children's scientific understanding is recognised in terms of metacognitive awareness. Unlike "small range" constructivism in which the effectiveness of teaching is determined according to children's responses to tests and/or interview questions, Coral uses children's evidence of metacognitive awareness to determine the success of her teaching.

In line with "big ideas" constructivism, Coral believes that children are active and reflective learners who bring their own ideas to the situation. These ideas are recognised as being different from scientific understanding, which requires evidence, and therefore procedural capability. Thus, the elicitation of children's ideas as well as their procedural understanding plays an important role in her teaching. It is used as a tool for developing the children's metacognitive awareness and in her own assessment of their learning.

Coral's views about the learner also seem to draw on aspects of Piagetian staged learning. She believes, for example, that children need to get intrinsically motivated to tackle the task in hand, which, in turn, is achieved as they are involved in unstructured practical activities and are offered opportunities to ask their own questions. However, for Coral, children's participation in such activities also serves other goals in the learning process: it offers children opportunities to reflect on their ideas and to explore the limitations of these in explaining a particular physical experience. In this respect, her views about the learning process also draw on Piagetian constructivist learning, and on parallel "big ideas" constructivist perspectives of how children learn.

Although, for Coral, children's engagement in practical activities plays a crucial role in the learning process, she sees their participation in the classroom discussions that follow these practical activities as equally crucial in the development of children's scientific understanding. During such discussions, she tries to identify those of the children's ideas that are closer to the scientific ones, and then to reformulate and represent these ideas to the children. Here, Coral's views about the learning process have similarities with sociocultural perspectives on learning, which are characterized by a particular concern to work within the children's zone of proximal development, and to offer explicit guidance to them about making connections between their ideas and scientific evidence. In this way, she helps the children develop understanding according to their own abilities and experiences and not according to a set of conceptual objectives set out by the classroom teacher at the beginning of a lesson, as in "small range" constructivism. Moreover, she stresses that scientific understanding can be developed independently from the structure of the lesson and indeed from her teaching. Nevertheless, although she values discussion, she does not seem to believe in group discussions – probably because her views about the learner draw on Piagetian staged learning.

Coral, describes her role in supporting the development of children's scientific understanding as mainly involving talking to them. This is taken to mean that in her teaching she looks for opportunities in what the children say or do to scaffold their thinking so that it becomes increasingly compatible with that of the established scientific community. At the same time, Coral argues that in her teaching she does not use a set of specific strategies that aim to help the children arrive at the same endpoint, nor does her teaching follow a fixed course. Indeed, she stresses that she often decides on what to do next on the spot, whilst she is talking to the children. Nevertheless, she stresses that in her teaching she tries to exercise a certain level of control over what is learned, when, and how by creating a learning environment in which both simpler and more complex tasks are ongoing and discussed. For Coral, such an environment enables the children to develop understanding of her own objectives yet simultaneously allows them to pursue their own interests. In this respect, her approach to teaching differs from both of the constructivist approaches to teacher expertise discussed here.

NOTES

[1] AT1 refers to Attainment Target 1 of the English Primary Science National Curriculum, which deals with scientific inquiry.
[2] The selection of the children's ideas which are to be discussed in the classroom also depends on Coral's learning objectives.
[3] The children had explored this concept earlier in the year in relation to the difference in space occupied by two identical balloons one of which was full of water and the other one full of ice.

AN EXAMPLE OF EXPERT PRIMARY SCIENCE PRACTICE

In this chapter I am going to focus in detail on one teaching lesson, as a sample of Coral's teaching. The aim is to discuss the ways in which Coral enacts her science expertise. The lesson is about *friction*. Coral had specific learning objectives in mind, which, in her class diary described in the following way:

> I wanted the children to learn: that friction was something that happened between two surfaces and that it opposed movement; that the force of friction varied according to the surface; that lubricants can be used to reduce friction; that friction could be useful to prevent slipping; that friction produced heat; that discrete data can be represented on a bar chart. I wanted them to begin to think about a friction-free environment; the mechanism of friction; the relationship between friction and/or surface area. I can offer these ideas to all the children by keeping them working along the same lines.

As I discussed in chapter 4, I visited Coral over a period of six weeks when she was teaching forces. The lesson on friction was the fourth in the series. Her first lesson focused on gravity and air resistance. It involved a series of practical activities on making paper spinners fall as slowly as possible and investigating some factors that affect the rate of fall of parachutes. At the end of this first lesson on forces, the children in Coral's class were asked to write down their ideas and questions about the factors that affect the fall of objects. In her class diary, Coral commented that children's writing indicate their developing understanding about forces in opposition. And she used this evidence to plan her lesson about friction. Prior to this lesson though, Coral taught the children how to measure forces by constructing their own pull meters. At the end of that lesson, the children were introduced to the use of Newton meters as a more accurate instrument for measuring forces. They also discussed possible reasons which could stop objects moving, including friction.

In her class diary, Coral provides the following justification for her planning of the session on friction:

> As an idea about forces in opposition was developing I thought we would have a look at friction. To do this we would need to be able to measure the force of a pull. Much discussion brought us to elastic bands and the children

designed their own "pull measurers". The principal difficulty was measuring the stretch and this brought us neatly to proper Newton meters. We talked about what stops things moving. We left it at the point where we knew that something happens between two surfaces and this something is called friction.

This is the point at which the teaching session I describe here began. Based on Coral's writing about the session and my own observations I have divided the session into the following six interrelated phases:

First Phase: Introduction. This phase aimed to establish continuity with previous learning, to introduce a propositional definition of friction, and to make clear to the children the learning objectives for the lesson;

Second Phase: Generating children's interest in investigating friction. The aim of this phase was to elicit children's everyday ideas about friction and generate interest in investigating aspects of it; *elicitation*

Third Phase: Investigating friction. This phase involved a structured practical task aimed at helping children to systematically test their ideas about the friction of different surfaces. This led to a secondary investigation that focused around two specific questions about the effects of friction.

Fourth Phase: Discussing findings of children's investigations about friction. This phase focused on the discussion of children's findings of their investigations with the aim to use these findings to develop further their scientific understanding of friction;

Fifth Phase: Investigating lubricants. The aim of this phase was to engage children in systematic investigation about the effects of lubricants in reducing the friction between surfaces.

Sixth Phase: Discussing the findings of children's investigations about lubricants. This phase focused on children's findings of their investigations about the use of lubricants, and was aimed at using these findings to develop further their scientific understanding of lubricants. It also aimed to draw the lesson to a conclusion in relation to children's learning about the aspects of friction included in Coral's learning objectives for the session.

FIRST PHASE: INTRODUCTION

In her introduction to her lesson, Coral aims to establish continuity between the previous session and the present one, to introduce a propositional definition for friction, and to set the scene for the lesson in terms of an investigation of friction. In order to achieve these aims, Coral uses two bridging pedagogical strategies: posing to the children an everyday problem, and asking questions about the problem to remind them about what they have learned about friction in the previous session:

Coral	We've talked about what stops things moving if we are pulling them along. Now I want you to imagine that you've got to pull something along that it's really heavy and it hasn't got any wheels, no wheels, no prams, no pushchairs, no truck. Nothing with wheels on . . . you've just got to pull it. And it's quite hard work. So what's hard work about it? What stops something moving when we're pulling it along? We've talked about it . . . Adele.
Adele	It's heavy.
Coral	It's heavy . . . Graham.
Graham	It grips.
Coral	It grips on something. You're pulling it and the thing you are pulling is gripping onto the ground and that gripping on force that stops it from moving is called something . . .
Simon	Gravity.
Coral	No. It is not called gravity. It's another force . . . Rosie. [Some children raise their hands saying "friction", "push", "fraction"].
Rosie	Friction.
Coral	Friction. The force that stops things sliding across each other [Coral slides her hands across each other] and makes them rub on to each other and not move very well is called friction. And that's what we are going to try and investigate today. We are going to try to find out how much friction there is between different surfaces. What do you think . . . what do you think has got lots of friction? What do you think has got less friction? What sort of things? Paul.

As we can see, Coral begins her lesson by presenting children with an everyday problem with the intention to focus their thought on a limited range of experiences that can be explained using a particular scientific concept. The description of the problem finishes with Coral posing two questions: "What's hard work about it?" "What stops things from moving them along?". Her comment "we've talked about it", which follows the two questions, is used to remind the children of what was said about a similar situation during the previous session on pulling forces. What can be inferred from the transcript is that Coral is searching for the answer "friction". In asking the two questions and adding the comment "we've talked about it", she implies that the children should be able to recall what was said at the end of the previous session, when the term "friction" was introduced.

However, despite this, the children's responses seem to be based on their everyday language. This is perhaps to be expected. A question takes its meaning from the context in which it occurs and a response depends on the respondent's understanding of this context (Hammersley, 1977). Here the context is an everyday problem. Coral's comment "we've talked about it" is not picked up on by the children. Adele says "it's heavy". Coral accepts her answer but she does not evaluate it or at least does so only implicitly. She repeats Adele's response and then turns her attention to Graham who gives a different answer, "it grips". Both answers to the question are valid in the context of an everyday problem, something can be hard to pull along because it is heavy, or because it grips on something. However, Graham's response "it grips" is recognised by Coral as a key point. At this point, she decides to use the "gripping" analogy to relate everyday experiences to school science. Perhaps she is aware that the "gripping" analogy is close to one of the scientific theories for explaining friction, the "surface roughness theory of friction" (Bowden & Tabor, 1973). According to this theory, when two surfaces are placed together, one against the other, it looks as if the roughness of one is getting into the roughness of the other; they somehow interlock with each other.

Coral is still searching for the answer "friction" but the context of the discussion has changed. The initial question "What is stopping something moving when we're pulling it along?" is now reformulated to "What is the name of the gripping force that is stopping something from moving?". The use of the word "force" seems to function as a clue which helps children to begin to respond in terms of scientific language, and one of them provides the answer "gravity". This is rejected with the clue that another force is required. Rosie's recall of the word "friction" is accepted as the "right" answer. Coral then gives a propositional definition of friction as a force which opposes movement, and an explanatory account of friction as a force which "makes things rub on to each other". Children very often associate friction with rubbing, particularly the rubbing of two solid surfaces (see Osborne, Schollum & Hill, 1981; Stead & Osborne, 1980). Thus, it can be suggested that in choosing to explain friction as "rubbing", Coral is aiming to help the children to make links between their everyday ideas about friction and the scientific language about *friction*.

As we can see, during this phase of her teaching Coral uses close questioning to assess children's knowledge about what stops objects from moving easily. Furthermore, her abstract knowledge of friction as gripping and rubbing enables her to look for opportunities in children's responses that are closest to this knowledge. And, she introduces friction as a rubbing force only after some children have suggested the ideas of gripping and rubbing. This indicates her Vygotskian concern that the introduction of a scientific concept should take place within the children's zone of proximal development, and that the teacher's role is to offer explicit scaffolding so as to help the children make connections between their everyday ideas and those of the school science (see for example, Rogoff & Gardner, 1984; Osborne, 1999).

SECOND PHASE: GENERATING CHILDREN'S INTEREST IN INVESTIGATING FRICTION

As Coral indicated in her class diary, this phase aims to generate children's interest in investigating friction. She achieves this by encouraging the children to offer their own explanations and ideas about friction in their responses to the following questions that were posed by her:

> What do you think has got lots of friction? What do you think has got less friction? What sort of things?.

Some of the children's responses are offered as a tentative outcome of a practical test which was thought up and immediately carried out by the children. For example, one child (Paul), pushes his rubber across his table and reports his observation to Coral:

Paul	When I push the rubber across the table it is difficult. [Paul is actually pushing the rubber across this table].
Coral	If you pick up a rubber . . . [Coral picks up a rubber and she asks Paul if the particular rubber is okay for her to use. She then pushes it across the table surface which is at the front of the class]. It is very hard to push it across the table . . . so you can say that there is a lot of friction there.

Paul does not seem to be certain whether what he has observed is an example of something that has got a lot of friction. He waits for Coral's response to his observation. At the same time, Coral does not appear to have a ready answer. Her answer develops as she increases her own understanding of what the child has observed. Thus, she repeats the practical test herself and she decides that pushing the rubber across the table can be an example of something that has got a lot of friction.

Although Coral has now given an answer to Paul's observation, this practical test generates a lot of discussion. Some of the children try to explain why there is a lot of friction between the rubber and the table. These explanations are not responses to a question asked by Coral. Rather, they are initiatives which aim to elaborate Coral's answer; "there is a lot of friction because . . .". Children's explanations appear to be based on their everyday experiences of how specific objects and materials behave (for example rubber, plastic table, fabric):

Graham	Miss . . . it's the same material . . . it's like Paul says . . . it's rubber and it's plastic on the table and plastic is like rubber and there is a lot of friction.
Coral	So you think if two things are the same that will make a lot of friction. So what do you think will make less friction?
Graham	Something like a fabric.
Coral	Something like a fabric . . . Sharleen.

Coral accepts Graham's explanation about the effect of having two similar materials upon the amount of friction between them, but she does not evaluate his idea. She seems to want to explore the pupil's idea further and for this reason she repeats the question "what do you think will make less friction?". An interpretation of Coral's decision to find out more about Graham's thinking is that she is not entirely convinced that his idea is plausible.

During this time, some of the children in the classroom appear to repeat Paul's practical task (pushing their rubbers across the table) and one child in particular reports to Coral that her result is different from Paul's. This child (Sharleen) claims that it is easy to push the rubber across the table. Coral recognises a conflict between the children's observations and she decides to resolve it. She repeats the practical test and this time agrees with Sharleen's observation. At the same time another child (Kathleen) expresses the view that two objects that are made of similar materials do not have a lot of friction between them. Coral then turns to Graham and presents him with the evidence from Sharleen's observation, her own understanding, and Kathleen's idea about the effect of two similar materials upon the amount of friction. It is left to Graham (and to the rest of the children) to decide whether to accept the evidence provided or not. In this respect, her approach to learning has similarities with the Piagetian notion of operative knowledge, the idea that the learner is not only able to initiate and complete acts but also to evaluate them (see Murphy et al., 2000). It is not clear why Coral decided to agree with Sharleen's observation. An interpretation of her response could be that Coral's ideas developed as the discussion about the effect of two similar materials upon the amount of friction developed or clarified.

The opening questions asked by Coral thus led to a discussion of a problem which was initiated by a child. The discussion, which involved many of the children in the classroom, led Coral to modify her initial response to the Paul's problem. Both the teacher and the children seemed to co-construct their understanding of the problem through their participation in the same activity. In turn, the problem shares some of the features of what is called within a sociocultural view of learning a "dilemma", in that it is perceived by learners as a problem which has no unique solution (see Lave, 1988). The children's willingness to extend the discussion suggests that the problem is personally meaningful to them because it is related to their experiences. Furthermore, the ways in which they participate in the discussion, by repeating the practical test and by offering their ideas and explanations, suggest that they are aware of how to make progress towards solving the problem. Coral's role is to accept and explore the different sorts of evidence and explanations offered until a tentative answer is found, even though it does not resolve all the conflicts (Graham, for example, is still left to sort out his views). Coral maintains her role as an authority in the classroom, in the sense that she is recognised by the children as the one who is expected to be the knowledgeable adult. Children respond to her and not to the particular children who ask the questions or offer explanations, and they expect Coral to give the final answer.

The outcome of the discussion concerns the effect of different materials on the amount of friction between surfaces. This emerged in relation to specific materials and in a specific context. During this time, only one child (Graham) seems to have been using the term "friction". The other children do not use the term in their explanations or observations, although Coral herself keeps using the term.

At this point, Coral asks again the initial question "what things do you think have got less friction?" The question generates a number of responses which seem to represent children's everyday understanding:

Coral	Now what things do you think have got less friction? Simon.
Simon	Ice. [Other children say 'ice' at the same time].
Coral	Right ice. Simon what do you think about ice then?
Simon	Miss, it's easy to move.
Coral	Right. Paul.
Paul	You can't test it like card or other solids because when it slides along it gets water on it.
Coral	However cold it is as soon as you have it out it starts melting. Well there is another reason you can't test ice today and that is we haven't got any.

As we can see, Coral accepts the children's responses about ice and she uses an additional question to explore their understanding; "what do you think about ice then?". The first response seems to be a confirmation of the idea that ice has got very little friction. The second response is procedural; it says that it is difficult to compare ice with solid materials because ice melts. Both responses are accepted as valid by Coral. Following this, a hypothesis is offered by a child (Graham) based on a practical test which the child is carrying out in the classroom:

Graham	If you push something really rough like my shoe it doesn't slide but on this floor it slides very easily.
Laura	Miss, it's the floor, it's because it's a bit dirty that's why it's slippy. [several children talk together]
Coral	So if it's covered by little bits of dirt they act like ball bearings. Sharleen.

Graham notices that it is easy to slide his shoe across the classroom floor. However, he seems surprised by this because his understanding is that something "rough" like his shoe should not slide easily. Before Coral replies to his idea another child (Laura) offers an explanation. Coral accepts and reformulates this explanation to make a scientific point. She uses a ball bearings analogy to explain how the use of particular materials helps to reduce the friction between different surfaces.

Next, Paul is pushing a piece a paper on his table and he observes that the paper slides along and then flips up:

Paul	Miss when I push this paper on the table, the paper slides along

	and there isn't much friction.
Coral	Come and do it on the floor. Paul is just going to push a piece of paper. He says that the paper slides very easily. It can't have enough friction.
	[Paul pushes the piece of paper the paper slides along the floor and it flips up]
Coral	What's happening there?
Rosie	Is it gravity?
Coral	So what's getting in the way of that paper?
Sam	The air is getting in the way.
Coral	Well I think that's what's happening to Paul. The air is getting in the way. So, if you've got air resistance it doesn't push up. It only pushes up when things are moving down if you've got something moving that way the air resistance pushes it back that way.
	[Coral shows the direction of the air resistance when things are moving horizontally]

In this extract, Paul is employing his developing understanding that friction is a force which opposes movement and that the less friction there is between two surfaces the easier it is for an object to slide, to explain his observation about the sliding of the paper on the table. This is the second time during the session that the term "friction" is used by children in their explanations. Coral accepts Paul's observation but she decides to explore it further. She asks Paul to repeat the practical test in the front of the classroom. The paper slides along the floor and flips up. The "flipping up" of the paper is the result of the force of air resistance, which depends on the surface area and the shape of the object. The concept of air resistance was discussed in detail in the first session on forces in the context of falling objects. Coral decides that Paul's observation is an opportunity to consolidate children's learning about air resistance. She then asks the children to explain what is happening.

It is clear from the transcript that Coral is searching for the "right" answer here. One child says "is it gravity?" but her response is not validated. Coral gives another clue which aims to help the children recall the information she is looking for; "what is getting in the way of that paper?". A child (Sam) offers the right answer. Coral then explains how the force of air resistance acts upon objects which move horizontally.

In this situation, Coral responds in a way similar to the one she used in the introduction to the session when she was searching for "friction". Unlike the problem posed by the same child earlier (pushing the rubber across the table), which generated a lot of discussion, this problem does not appear to initiate a large number of responses from the other children.

Furthermore, the kind of responses offered by the children in each case is different. During the discussion of the first problem children's responses seem to represent their everyday ideas and experience. During the discussion of the second problem, children appear to be trying to recall the correct scientific term (for example, "is it gravity?"). This is perhaps related to the way in which Coral deals with each problem. When Coral and the children were discussing the friction between the rubber and the table, Coral kept the discussion in the context of children's experience and her final response was the result of shared understanding between her and the children in the classroom. Indeed, in that situation, she did not appear to know the answer in terms of a straightforward application of a specific scientific concept. In the second case, the questions asked and the exchanges between the children and the teacher suggest that Coral knows the answer, and, this is provided by her, expressed in scientific language.

The discussion about air resistance could not have been planned beforehand. It emerged from a child's practical experience. Coral's understanding of the forces involved when objects move horizontally enables her to recognise an appropriate context to discuss this.

Coral's expertise is enacted in a different way during the following episode. Sue is asking a question about the friction between a ball and the ground. This question (or problem) is a response to Coral's question about "what things have got less friction":

Sue	Miss . . . when you kick a ball there is friction there.
Coral	Friction from what? On the ground you mean?
Sue	Yes.
Coral	Let's think about it. Let's think of a ball just an ordinary ball a tennis ball.
	[several children say "a tennis ball"]
	You are talking about kicking a ball and it is going across the ground like that. [Coral rolls a tennis ball across the table in the front of the class]
Paul	Rolling miss.
Coral	Friction is the force which stops things from moving. So the ball is moving and friction is stopping it.
Sue	It's like a wheel.
Coral	It is like a wheel. So what is the difference between a ball and a wheel and something that slides across?
Paul	It rolls.
Coral	So the difference is something to do with . . .
Adele	Roundness.
Coral	Yes, the fact that it has got all different bits on the ground all the time. Every little tiny bit it moves it's got a different bit of it on the ground [Coral rolls the ball across her arm] so it hasn't got force for a certain sort of time. So the rolling ball will never get off the friction I don't think.
Paul	Miss can you put it on our table?
Coral	Yes. [Coral takes the tennis ball to Paul's table]

Sue asks a question about the friction between a ball and the ground. Coral's response, "let's think about it", invites the children to offer their explanations. At the same time her response is inventive and resourceful. She picks up a tennis ball and rolls it across the table at the front of the class. Some children begin to describe the situation ("it rolls", "it's like a wheel"). Coral then uses her scientific understanding that friction is a force which opposes movement to explain a new situation, the rolling of the ball. She asks the children to think about the difference between rolling and sliding, and one child says "roundness". Coral accepts this answer and reformulates it to involve the concept of friction as a force which opposes movement. In this way, she relates children's everyday ideas to her own subject knowledge and produces a tentative answer. At the same time she seems to develop her own understanding at least to the extent that this is applied to the context created by Sue's question.

Coral's response to Sue's question differs from the way she responded earlier when she was encouraging children to offer their explanations. One interpretation of this is that it arises from Coral's personal interest in understanding the question. By making her thinking explicit to the children she offers the children a way to make connections between the scientific discourse and everyday situations. Paul's request to have the tennis ball on his table suggests that he wanted to repeat the experience for himself, which is an indication that the problem of the tennis ball is meaningful to him.

THIRD PHASE: INVESTIGATING FRICTION

Coral indicates the end of the second phase of her teaching by emphasising to the children what they are going to do next:

Coral	Now. You are going to do a bit of investigating into what does have a lot of friction and what does help things move smoothly. And you are going to do that with a pretend "you" if you like or a pretend weight . . . [Coral is standing at the front of the classroom and presents children with 1kg weight and a piece of cloth]. And we are going to pretend this is you or your little sister and you've got to pull your sister along. And she has clothes on so we are going to dress her [Coral wraps the weight in a piece of cloth and uses an elastic band to tie it]. Now this is your little sister or whatever. Now you need to pull it so you can measure. the pull . . . how do we measure the pull?
Several Children	A Newton meter.
Coral	A Newton meter. The perfect thing. You need to pull it to see how well it moves so you can measure its pull. You can give it a pull with the Newton meter and if you do it quite gently . . . [Coral pretends that she is pulling the weight across an imagi-

nary surface].

So you pull gently until it just starts moving . . . you'll see how much force it needs to just move it over that surface . . . if you pull it hard then you won't be able to tell anything . . . just pull it really gently . . . you will be able to tell how much force you need to pull it over that surface . . . now you are going to hook a paper clip on the cloth and attach the Newton meter on the paper clip...[Coral shows the children how to attach the Newton meter on the paper clip and she then rests the wrapped weight with the attached Newton meter on the front table].

Sharleen	Miss we could use elastic bands to pull the weight.
Coral	We could but it's hard to use the elastic band. We've tried it before. It's hard . . . it doesn't measure the pull.
Simon	Why are you pulling it with the Newton meter?
Coral	Somebody tell him. [Several children raise their hands] Charley.
Charley	To measure the pull.
Coral	Right. To measure the pull. Simon, come and do it. [Simon goes to the front of the class where Coral stands and he pulls the weight which rests on the front table].

Coral begins this part of her teaching by asking the children to "investigate" "what does have a lot of friction" and "what does help things move smoothly". These two questions are similar to the ones she asked at the beginning of the second phase of the session, when she invited the children to express their ideas about the things they think have got less or a lot of friction. However, Coral's use of the term "investigation" is an indication that now Coral wants the children to explore the concept of friction in a systematic way, before they offer their responses to these questions. Thus, although there appears to be a continuation between the two phases of the session in terms of the content of the discussion, the use of the term "investigation" signals to the children a different way of working in science.

As we can see, Coral sets a practical task and describes a method which children ought to follow in finding answers to the two questions she asked. Thus, she presents the children with a 1kg weight which she wraps in a piece of cloth. Coral explains that children "need to pull it to measure the pull". She then asks them to think "how do we measure pulls?". Here she is searching for the answer "Newton meter". Several children offer the correct answer. Coral accepts the children's answers and incorporates them into her talk.

As I mentioned at the beginning of this chapter, Coral introduced the use of the Newton meter at the end of the session on pulling forces as a more accurate instrument for measuring forces compared to the elastic bands they had used for the same purpose. Thus, this interaction indicates Coral's attempt to establish some continuity between an already introduced idea and the task in hand and to assess children's procedural understanding. The use of the Newton meters for measurement is an important part of this session's practical task, probably because Coral wants to offer to the children further opportunities to develop their understanding of the use of this particular instrument. The format of the interaction is similar to the interaction that took place at the introduction to the session, when Coral is searching for the answer "friction", and during the second phase of her teaching when she was searching for the answer "air resistance".

Coral then emphasises that children need to pull the Newton meter very gently, until "it just starts moving", to be able to read the measurement. Her expression "you need to pull it to see how well it moves" provides the children with a conceptual simplification of the measurement of frictional force. This equates the pulling force children are asked to measure under the conditions the task has prescribed with the degree of difficulty in pulling the same weight over different surfaces. This also indicates Coral's conceptual understanding about frictional forces. In other words, she seems to be aware that when a force is exerted on a weight which rests on a table surface attempting to pull it along that surface, a frictional force arises. This frictional force matches the magnitude of the force that has been applied on the weight. While the weight remains at rest and the applied force is gradually increased, the frictional force also increases until it reaches its maximum value, opposing the motion of the block. At a certain instant the magnitude of the applied force increases further to such a value that the weight can no longer maintain its stationary position, it "breaks away" and it starts sliding in the direction of the applied force. At the moment the weight "just starts moving" the value of the applied force just exceeds the value of the frictional force (Haliday, Resnick & Walker, 1993). When the weight begins to slide, it accelerates fast, the frictional force decreases and the magnitude of the pulling force decreases at the same time.

Thus, in asking the children to measure the force that is needed to pull 1kg weight until it just starts moving, Coral also implies that this measurement is a close approximation to the magnitude of the frictional force that opposes motion. If the weight is pulled too hard then it will accelerate fast and the Newton meter will not be able to measure the frictional force. This relationship between the measurement of the pulling force and the measurement of the frictional force is not made explicit to the children. Indeed, as we can see, Coral emphasises the procedural consistency and the accuracy of the measurement rather than the conceptual understanding that lies behind it. Thus, although the questions posed by Coral at the beginning of this phase of the session are associated with the measurement of friction, the children are presented here with a method for measuring pulling forces and some implicit conceptual knowledge associated with this.

It is apparent that Coral regulates this exchange. However, this sequence of teacher question followed by the children's responses breaks down when some of the children appear to question Coral's suggestion about the use of the Newton meter by offering an alternative suggestion or by expressing their lack of understanding about or justification for the use of that instrument. One child (Sharleen) says that an elastic band could be used for the measurement of forces. Although Coral does not reject the child's answer, she emphasises that a Newton meter is a more accurate instrument for the measurement of forces. Another child (Simon) does not seem certain about the reasons for using the Newton meter. Simon asks the teacher "why do we use Newton meters?". Coral asks the children to respond to his question probably thereby checking the other children's ideas about it. The answer, "it measures the pull", is accepted by Coral as an appropriate response to Simon's question. Thus, although in this part of her teaching Coral regulates the exchanges between herself and the children, children's questions about the use of Newton meters is an indication of the learning environment that Coral has created in her classroom, where children are treated as knowleadgeable; as having their own ideas which are respected by the teacher, and as being free to question the authority of the teacher (see Roth, Tobin, & Ritchie, 2001; Tobin & McRobbie, 1999). .

So far, Coral appears to be using her procedural expertise to describe several of the important elements which are necessary to carry out an investigation (Harlen & Qualter, 2004). Thus, Coral introduces the 1kg weight as the controlled variable of the practical task. The use of the same weight in all the measurements that children are going to carry out is important for the test to be fair, to make measurements by different pupils comparable with each other. Furthermore, most of the Newton meters available in the classroom can measure the force up to ten Newtons. A bigger weight than the chosen one could have led to some difficulties regarding the resulting measurements. Thus, 1k Weight appears to be a sensible value for the resulting measurements to be meaningful. The use of the Newton meter as the appropriate instrument to measure the pulling force, the way it should be attached to the weight and the way the weight should be pulled along the surface are also important elements which are standardised for conducting the practical task.

A demonstration of the suggested method follows Coral's description of it and aims to consolidate the method introduced. She asks Simon, the child who seemed uncertain about the role of the Newton meter, to carry out the test, helping him in this way to develop his own understanding of the value of using the Newton meter:

Coral	Now. If you just did it once you might make a mistake or it might be a lump on the table or all sorts of things might go wrong. So how many times do you have to do it to have a fair result?
Nicole	Four.
Brian	Five.
Coral	Four or five is quite good . . . or even three . . . but one is not enough let's try again see what happens [the same child who did the demonstration before tries again. The result is the same]. He must be doing it really accurate then.
Coral	So, you're going to do it more than once . . . two times . . . three times. Whatever you think is fair. Now . . . that is the pull you need to measure on the table.

Coral does not immediately validate the initial result of the demonstration. The reason for this appears to be associated with her decision to use the result to discuss the concept of repeatability. This concept refers to the understanding that "the inherent variability in any physical measurement requires a consideration for the need of repeats, if necessary, to give reliable data" (Gott and Mashiter, 1995, p. 31).

Thus, Coral gives possible reasons which could make it necessary to repeat the measurement and she then asks the children to think how many times they should repeat the test to get fair results. The context of the question suggests that Coral expects the children to give a different answer to "once", and to display in this way their procedural understanding. The children respond to the Coral's expectations by offering a range of numbers other than one, which is an indication of their procedural understanding.

Coral, then, emphasises that a result is fair when it is repeated more than once, and she leaves to the children to decide the number of times that they think it is necessary to repeat the measurement. The implied meaning of "fair" in this context appears to be associated with the application of a judgement of the consistency of the measurements. If the same or very similar measurements are made for any particular test on two or three occasions, that would suffice. If there were more variation, then more measurements could be judged to be necessary. This is the first time during this part of her teaching that Coral gives children some autonomy in their involvement with the practical task. The control which pupils are being asked to exercise is that of the number of repetitions of measurement which could count as "fair". This involves not only the differences, if any, between the measurements, but a sense of how big the differences could be in relation to the number of repetitions that could be appropriate. The bigger the differences, the larger the number of repetitions required.

Coral next presents children with a range of materials to be the independent variables in the practical task. The different materials create the different surfaces on which children are going to measure the different amounts of friction:

Coral	So, you're going to do it more than once . . . two times . . . three times. Whatever you think is fair. Now . . . that is the pull you need to measure on the table. I've got some other things for you to try to pull the weight on. I've got this piece of carbon paper and I've brought you these boards of sandpaper. [Coral presents children with square pieces of each material. Picking up one piece of sandpaper she asks Simon to feel it and then she says]. How does it feel Simon?
Simon	Not very smooth. [Simon is still standing at the front of the class]. [At the same time some other children are going to the front of the class to feel the sandpaper].
Several children	It's smooth.
Coral	Right sit down. Yes it is pretty smooth.

Sara	Miss, can I feel the sandpaper?
Coral	Yes.

[Coral does not give the piece of sandpaper to Sara. Instead she goes to the back of the class and picks up some other pieces of sandpaper. She then shows them to the children].

Sandpaper has these little rough things on for rubbing down wood or other things all right? It's designed to rub things off so if you try it on you to see how rough it is, it's going to rub it off you so *don't*.

Now this sort . . . [showing to the children a particular piece of sandpaper] says "180". Each paper has a number at the back which reminds you how smooth it is. Anyway, the bigger the number the smoother the paper.

I've also got some fabric which you could try and some felt and you need to write down as soon as you've done it what the measurements are on what you're trying.

As we can see, Coral asks Simon to feel a particular type of sandpaper. The main purpose in asking this question seems to be associated with Coral's aim to raise some safety issues related to the use of the different types of sandpaper. The children's responses to Coral's question are immediately accepted by her.

The discussion about the practical work then focuses on the recording of the results. Coral is asking children to think about how they are going to present the data in their books:

Coral	So how are you going to organise that in your books?
	[Several children raise their hands or talk].
	Cindy.
Cindy	We'll make a chart.
Coral	Right a chart. A table of results. So you could put the name of the thing here . . . um . . . surface and then you are going to put the pulling force.
	[Coral makes a table on the board which includes the surface to be tested and the pulling force]. And you are going to write the name of the surface here like table top and then you write the pulling force. Simon, what pulling force did you get first time?
Simon	Two Newtons.
Coral	Right. Two Newtons. What pulling force did you get the second time?
Simon	Two Newtons.
Coral	Right. Two Newtons again. It doesn't matter if it is the same. Still write it down two or three times so you can remember how many times you did it. Another problem is that when you try to put the weight on something and you are trying to pull it, the paper comes with it [Coral shows to the children what happens

107

in this case]. So you could try to hold the paper with your hand or you could stick it down with the Sellotape.

Now then first of all . . . you need to write down the table of results on your books and the date so you know what you are doing.

Simon's response is immediately accepted by Coral and is linked to the specific idea of the "table of results". Coral then draws on the board a table which includes the two variables, the pulling force and the surface. Coral is asking Simon to repeat the test and she then writes both measurements on the board. She anticipates a discussion about the results of the test and she wants the children to be able to remember the different measurements. Coral also writes on the board the materials that the children are asked to explore, though she says to them that they can test other surfaces.

Before the distribution of the different materials, Coral clarifies another aspect of the concept of fair testing which is associated with the control of the necessary variables. She says that the children may be faced with a situation where the surface slides along with the weight. Coral implies that this will not lead to fair results because the identity of the independent variable will change; and she suggests a remedy for this - that the children should either hold the surface or stick it on the table with the Sellotape.

Coral then asks two children to help her with the distribution of the notebooks, the different materials, and the Newton meters. The children are sitting in tables of five or six and they seem to feel free to go from one table to another, to work on their own, or in two's or three's. Each table is given a range of each material and a number of Newton meters.

During this phase, Coral's role is to provide all the children in her classroom with a structure for what they are asked to do, and to offer them some autonomy to pursue their own interests. And she achieves this by regulating the difficulty of the procedures involved in carrying out the investigation. For example, she demonstrates a way of measuring friction and asks a child to repeat it. Once she has evidence of children's competence to carry out the task she gradually withdraws her support. This kind of teacher-learner interaction is often found in sociocultural approaches to teaching, in which the teacher's role is to model the solution to a novel problem, coach learners in the application of their understanding, and gradually withdraw support as learners are judged ready to carry out the task independently (see, for example, Roth, 1995).

Furthermore, Coral invites the children to think of other surfaces to test and she leaves it up to the children to decide which hypotheses they are going to test, although she has already provided them with a lot of support for this, during the second phase of her teaching. To this extent, her expertise appears to be closer to Piagetian staged perspectives, which argue that in order to encourage children's learning, the problem they are to investigate needs to be generated by the children, and not to be given to them by the teacher (see Murphy et al., 2000).

The children begin to work on the practical task by writing down in their note-books the table of results which the teacher has written on the board. They then begin to work in pairs or threes. Coral goes from one table to another and responds to the children's questions about procedural matters. She also sometimes helps them with the measurement.

At some point, just before the end of the morning session, Coral writes on the board the following questions, and she asks the children to explore them:

If you want to stop something from slipping what surface would you use to make the most friction?

If you want something to slip easily what surface could you use to make the least friction?

In her class diary that followed teaching this session, Coral explains that although she had planned for the children to investigate next the friction on different shoes, children's degree of involvement in the investigations led her modify her initial plans, and instead offer the children to investigate the above two questions.

The children break for lunch and when they come back they carry on with the practical task. At the beginning of the afternoon session, Coral introduces more materials for the children to test (bubble wrap plastic, foil, sand tray, mirror).

FOURTH PHASE: DISCUSSING FINDINGS ABOUT THE FRICTION ON DIFFERENT SURFACES

In the middle of the afternoon, Coral asks the children to stop their practical work and begins a discussion about their findings. The discussion focuses on the question "What interesting things have you found?" Most of the children reply by re-ferring to a comparison they made between two surfaces or between the measure-ments of the same surface.

One child (Sharleen) replies to Coral with a hypothesis about the effect of dust on the amount of friction between two surfaces. Sharleen says that she sanded down a wooden board using the coarse sand paper and that she thinks it is slippier to pull the weight along the board now that there is sanding dust on it:

Sharleen   Miss when I used the coarse sand paper to sand down this [holding the wooden board] most of the bits left and went on the table but I think it is slippier with the bits on.

Coral   So have you got any of those bits left on the board now?
Sharleen   Yes.
Coral   So what do you think will happen if you dust all those off?
Sharleen   I think it's slippier with the sanding dust on it.
Coral   Dust it off carefully. [Coral is giving Sharleen a piece of paper].

> Try to do the test again. Do it again so that you can show
> what's happening there.

Sharleen's attempt to try to make a surface smoother by sanding it down probably derives from her everyday understanding that smooth surfaces create less friction. The appearance of the sanding dust on the surface led her to form a hypothesis about the effect of dust on the amount of friction. During the second part of Coral's teaching, one child (Graham) expressed the idea that the floor gets slippier when there is dirt on it. Coral represented his idea by saying that "the little bits of dirt act like ball bearings" and therefore facilitate movement. It is possible, therefore, that Sharleen has linked that discussion with her observation about the appearance of the sanding dust on the wooden board, along with her everyday ideas that loose material can make surfaces slippery, to form her hypothesis. Sharleen's involvement in the sanding down of the wooden board has not been initiated by Coral (a wooden board is not one of the surfaces that Coral has suggested to the children to test). The child's decision to test a different surface is, however, an indication of the children's freedom to modify the practical task set, as well as of the children's understanding of the relationship with Coral and of the classroom culture.

Sharleen's reply is accepted by Coral who decides to ask her to test it. Coral asks Sharleen to say if there is any dust left on the board and to predict what will happen to the amount of friction between the surface and the weight when there is no dust left on the surface. These two questions aim to direct the child's attention to the important aspects of the task she is asked to carry out. Thus, in order to test her hypothesis, Sharleen needs to compare the measurement of the surface with the sanding dust on with the measurement of the surface without the sanding dust on. The outcome of this comparison will test the child's hypothesis. As we can see, Coral tells Sharleen to dust off the surface, conduct the test again and report her findings to the class.

In this interaction Coral's pedagogical technique seems to be similar to what sociocultural researchers refer to as *coaching*, which serves to "direct students" attention to a previously unnoticed aspect of the task or simply to remind the student of some aspect of the task that is known but has been temporarily forgotten"(Collins, Brown and Newman, 1989, p. 481). The type of questions the teacher asks here are known in science education literature as "action questions" (Feasey, 1998; Harlen, 1992), which entail simple experimentation that is intended to guide children's thinking in forming a relationship between their predictions and the results of a practical test.

Coral does not wait for Sharleen to carry out the test. The child's reference to the coarse sandpaper is used by Coral as a cue to initiate a discussion about it:

Coral	What results have other people got with the coarse sand paper. How many Newtons?
Several children	Ten.Ten. Fifteen. Sixteen. Ten. Ten.
Peter	Miss. When we put our weight on the bubble wrap we got seven Newtons the first time and then we did it again and

	we got four Newtons.
Coral	Can you explain that?
Peter	I don't know miss. We've got to try it again.
Simon	Oh I know miss . . . some of the bubbles have popped and that made it easier to pull.
Coral	Right. [holding a piece of bubble wrap].
	So it was hard to pull but then some of the bubbles popped and that made it easier to pull . . . Right what other interesting things did you find out? Sharon.

As we can see, a number of children almost simultaneously report their results about the coarse sandpaper. Immediately after that, another child (Peter) appears to respond to the question Coral had asked earlier ("what interesting things have you found out?"). Peter says that he tested the bubble wrap plastic twice and that the Newton meter showed a different measurement each time. Thus, for Peter an "interesting thing" to report to the teacher seems to be the difference between two measurements of friction of the same material. Peter's response indicates uncertainty as to how to interpret his data. It also seems to suggest that he expects Coral to offer a solution to or an explanation of his problem. Coral decides to focus the discussion on this child's problem rather than on the children's findings about the sandpaper. An interpretation for this is that she suspects a possible reason for the difference in the measurement and decides that a discussion about it may lead to the idea of the effect of the surface roughness on the amount of friction between two surfaces (Haliday & Resnick, 1981).

Again, Coral does not immediately offer a solution to or an explanation of the problem. Instead, she asks Peter to offer any possible interpretations of his data. Peter's suggestion that a third measurement is needed could be taken to mean that he attributes the difference in his measurements to the way he carried out the test. It also indicates his awareness of the need for repeats to give reliable data, which has been reported in the literature as being a difficult concept for primary school children (Foulds et al., 1992). His suggestion is reasonable: a third measurement could show which of the previous two was more accurate. Before Coral replies, another child (Simon) takes the initiative and offers an explanation (the two children have worked together in the testing of the bubble wrap). Simon uses his everyday ideas about the relation between the friction and the roughness of a surface and his observation about the bubbles, that some had popped during the test, to interpret the data.[1] Coral accepts Simon's explanation and redescribes it in a way which emphasises the effect of the surface roughness on the amount of friction between two surfaces. Here, Coral offers explicit scaffolding by introducing a scientific idea, which is nevertheless expressed in everyday language.

This type of interaction has similarities with what Cobb, et al (1997) call *reflective discourse*, in which what the pupils and the teacher do in action becomes an explicit focus of discussion. Coral's role in this interaction is to offer opportunities to the children to step back and reflect on what they have done so far. The children's explanations can be seen as examples of the development of their scientific

111

understanding through their participation in a discussion which offers them opportunities to reflect on their previous actions.

The teacher repeats the question "what other interesting things have you found out?". Most of the children reply to this question by referring to comparisons between different surfaces.

One child (Sharon) reports that she tested sand and washing up liquid and she found that the washing up liquid is slippier:

Sharon	Miss I found out that if you put liquid on the tray it will move more easily than like on little pieces of the sand.
Coral	So . . . [holding a tray] you've tried washing up liquid on the tray.
	[Turning to the whole class]. What do you think will happen if you try to pull it along on washing up liquid?

For Sharon, the difference in the amount of friction between the sand and the washing up liquid is an interesting finding either because she was expecting a different result or because she had no experience of pulling objects over liquids.

As we can see, although Coral acknowledges Sharon's reply that she tested the washing up liquid, Coral does not discuss this finding. Instead, she picks up the tray with the washing up liquid and asks the children in the class to predict what will happen if the weight is pulled along that surface:

Coral	So . . . [holding a tray] you've tried washing up liquid on the tray.
	[Turning to the whole class]. What do you think will happen if you try to pull it along on washing up liquid?
Kathleen	Miss it will slip dead easily.
Coral	So do you think that's just about as easy as you can get?
Several children	No miss . . . ice will be the best.
Coral	Right. Ice will be very good. I wanted to bring you some pieces of ice but it proved to be difficult.
	Right. That was good [the washing up liquid]. That was pretty slippy . . .
	What else do people try to do to make the surface as slippy as possible?

Coral's decision to ask the children to predict the behaviour of a material which has already been tested is probably related to her awareness that not all of the children in the class had time to test that material or to explore the question she posed at the end of the morning session ("if you want something to slip easily what surface could you use to make the least friction?"). Thus, in asking the children to make predictions, she is asking them to express their everyday ideas. In this way, she encourages more children to participate in a discussion about materials that produce less friction, which is a recurrent theme in this part of Coral's teaching.

One child (Kathleen), says that the weight will slip "dead easily" on the washing up liquid. Coral asks another question, which appears to have the effect of adding significance to the particular response offered by Kathleen, in suggesting that it could be the one which represents the minimum measurement of friction. At the same time, this question aims to challenge the children's ideas about the material which creates the least friction. A number of children suggest that ice "will be the best". Their response is accepted by Coral as a good prediction. Her response implies that the children's response about the ice is inadequate, because ice has not been tested.

Coral decides that this is probably a good opportunity to introduce a new practical task that she has planned for the children: the testing of a range of materials which, placed on a surface, reduce the friction. Thus, Coral relates the outcome of the discussion about the behaviour of the washing up liquid to her next question, "that was good [the washing up liquid] that was pretty slippery. What else do people try to do to make the surface as slippy as possible?". The reference to the washing up liquid aims to function as a clue for the children to think about materials which, placed on a given surface, reduce the friction:

Rosie	Glass.
Coral	Right. A piece of glass.
Coral	What does this [holding the tray with the washing up liquid] take to pull the weight on it?
Sharon	One Newton.
Coral	Right. One Newton. This is a mirror. [picking up the mirror from the front table where a group of children was working with it]. Which is a proper glass. What did you find?
Rosie	Two Newtons.
Coral	Right. Two Newtons. And you've tried it?
Rosie	Three times.
Coral	And each time you got two Newtons?
Rosie	Yes.
Coral	Right. So far washing up liquid is the slippiest but this is pretty slippy . . . what else have you tried?

Rosie's response is accepted by Coral, who realising that the child has tested a mirror, decides to focus the discussion on these findings and to leave the introduction of the practical task for later. This change in the discussion is another example of Coral's ability to modify and adapt her teaching plans according to the ways in which the children respond to her suggestions or questions and capitalize on what appears to be a potentially worthwhile line of discussion.

Coral turns to the child (Sharon) who has tested the washing up liquid and asks her to report her measurement. Sharon, says one Newton and then her measurement is compared with the child's measurement using the mirror. In eliciting and comparing the two measurements, Coral emphasises that in order to assert which material creates the least friction relevant measurements are needed. Coral summarises the outcome of the comparison and establishes which material has so far been shown to create the least friction.

The transcript also shows that Coral asks the children who tested the mirror how many times they repeated the test. Coral's role is to validate children's evidence, *coaching* them to think about the validity of evidence and reinforcing understanding that the difference in measurements is related to the force of friction. In this way, she *models* to the rest of the class the processes that are required to accomplish a task scientifically.

Coral then asks the children to report what else they have tried. Matthew replies:

Matthew	Miss. I put sand on a board and that was pretty slippy.
Coral	Now. You did the sand for this one [pointing at the board to the question "if you want to stop something from slipping what surface would you could you use to make the most frictions?"].
	What did you find out?
Matthew	I thought that the little pieces of sand would get stuck and stop the weight from moving.
Coral	You thought it would stop the weight . . . how many Newtons compared with other things?
	How many Newtons did it take to pull it on the fabric or on something like that?
Matthew	The sand was two Newtons and the sand paper was higher something like five Newtons.

Here, Coral asks Matthew to report his findings, and he replies by saying that he thought that the sand particles would prevent the weight from moving. This idea is associated with the effect of "surface roughness" on the amount of friction, a notion which was discussed earlier in this part of Coral's teaching in the context of a difference in measurement using the bubble wrap plastic. Coral accepts his statement and she reformulates her previous question. Thus, she asks Graham to report his measurement and to compare it with the measurements he got when he tested a different material. In asking this question, Coral reinforces her previous statement that in order to establish which material creates less friction, relevant measurements are needed.

As I said earlier, Coral has created in her classroom a situation where the children are expected to form hypotheses and carry out tests which aim to confirm or falsify those hypotheses. The conditions for learning are created jointly by Coral who chooses the materials that the children could test and by the children who choose which of these materials to test. Matthew's falsification of his initial theory is an example of this. The modification of his theory becomes explicit when he discusses his findings with the teacher:

Coral	So the sand is much easier than the sand paper. Why is that? What is the difference?

Matthew	The sand moves whereas the sandpaper doesn't.
Adele	Sandpaper is hard and the sand is soft.
Coral	Is it? Have you ever got any stuck between your toes? It is not very soft then.
Adele	[She gets the piece of sand paper that she used in her testing and takes it to the front of the classroom where the teacher is and where the sand tray is placed. Then she invites Coral to compare the two materials].
Coral	Actually the sand does feel pretty soft . . . it's so fine . . . it's very little sand [then picking up the piece of the sand-paper] actually it's not sand on here at all [holding the piece of sandpaper].
Graham	What is it?
Coral	Aluminium . . . I think.

Matthew expresses the idea that the sand is slippery because the particles can move, whereas the particles on the sandpaper do not move and therefore they create a lot of friction. His idea about the movement of the sand seems to be a modification of his earlier theory, and indicates effective learning in Coral's classroom. The movement of the sand particles means that they do not get in the way of movement but they function as wheels. His everyday ideas suggest that wheels facilitate movement, an idea which was also discussed during the second phase of the session (see discussion about "ball bearings"). It can be said that Matthew's new theory is plausible: it captures the main reason why objects move on sand better than sand paper. Another child (Adele) offers a different explanation: the sand is soft and this is why it is slippery. Instead of commenting on Matthew's idea, Coral decides to get into a discussion about whether the sand is soft or hard and whether sand paper is actually made of sand. Coral's own everyday experience suggests that sand is not soft. Adele goes to the front of the classroom where the sand tray is and challenges the teacher's assertion by asking her to feel the sand. Coral accepts the counter evidence. This is an example of the extent to which Coral has encouraged the children to use evidence to justify their thinking. Adele is confident to do this even in the face of the authority or status of the teacher.

Coral's decision to follow up Adele's idea instead of Matthew's theory is an indication of the potential risks that this kind of teaching involves. Matthew's theory could have led to a discussion about the surface roughness theory of friction. The discussion about the hardness or softness of sand has not led anywhere. Fruitful opportunities may be missed and dead ends that are misleading pursued.

The discussion about the sand and the sandpaper leads to a discussion about surfaces which create the most friction:

Coral	What do you think would create the most friction? Peter.
Peter	The woollen jacket.
Coral	Right. The woollen jacket. What have you got?
Peter	Six Newtons.

Coral	Right. Six Newtons. This would create a lot of friction. [Coral picks up the woollen jacket]. And it's a fair bit six Newtons, isn't it? But not so much as the sandpaper.
	Right. What other things have you found?
	What about those who went outside? Paul.
Paul	Sand and uhm . . . grass are the same.
Coral	How many Newtons did it take to pull the weight on the grass and on the sand?
Paul	Thirteen Newtons on the sand and thirteen Newtons on the grass and then ten Newtons and ten Newtons and then thirteen Newtons and thirteen Newtons.
Coral	Who else did the sand and the grass?
Matthew	Miss . . . when we did it with this Newton meter [showing to the teacher the Newton meter which measures up to ten Newtons] is smaller and we had to change it and use a bigger one.
Coral	Now this is an interesting thing. They used a Newton meter that they hadn't used before. Why did you have to swap to the others?
Matthew	We couldn't tell the pull miss.
Coral	The ones that went up to ten Newtons couldn't tell whether you needed more pull or that you just got to the end so you had to swap to these ones which have more Newtons on up to twenty five or fifty Newtons. The ones that aren't so small are better for more pull you can tell more easily what the pull is you only need a really strong pull and you can read it. Yes.

This type of teacher-children interaction is similar to the one that took place in the fourth phase of Coral's teaching ("discussion of findings") when Coral asked the children to report their findings about materials which create less friction. Thus, the children here are asked to compare their data, decide which material has created the most friction and communicate their findings to the teacher and to one another. As we can see, some children have tested materials which had not been suggested by Coral. A few children went to the playground and measured the friction that is created between the weight and the grass and the weight and the sand.

Coral starts a discussion about the second question she asked the children to explore at the end of the morning session, "what if you want to make something slip as much as possible?". This question has already been discussed in the second and fourth phases of the session, when the main ideas under consideration were to do with materials that create less friction. I mentioned earlier that it seemed that Coral thought that such a discussion offered a good opportunity for the introduction of a new practical task. At that point, however, Coral decided not to present it to the children. Coral's return to the same question indicates that she wants to create an appropriate context for discussion, which will lead to the presentation of the practical task:

Coral	What about the other question. What if you want to make something slip as much as possible? Sharon.
Sharon	Sand miss.
Coral	Sand can be quite slippery. What was the slippiest thing we tried today?
Celia	Miss . . . the fairy liquid.
Coral	The washing up liquid is the slippiest thing we've tried today. Anyone tried to pull something with less than one Newton?
Several children	No
Coral	Can you think of anything else that might make it easier to slip? Yes.

In asking the children to report which material can create the least friction, Coral appears to expect the children to recall the discussion which took place earlier in the session about the washing up liquid. Coral accepts Sharon's reply as an example of a material which is quite slippery. She then reformulates her previous question to remind the children of the whole class discussion about the washing up liquid. Celia gives that answer, Coral accepts it, and asks the children to say if they have tried to "pull something with less than one Newton". In asking this question, she invites the children to check their data again and communicate to her any findings which could falsify the conclusion about the material that was found to create the least friction. Having established which material has been shown so far to create the least friction, Coral asks the children to suggest other materials that make a surface easier to slip.

In this interaction, Coral attempts to establish some continuity between what has already been discussed earlier in the session and the new task she plans to introduce to the children. She checks the children's conceptual understanding of "the slippiest" material and their procedural understanding of how to know that a material creates less friction. Coral takes up the examples the children offer in their responses and uses them to pursue her pedagogic goals. Thus, she asks a new question "can you think of anything else that might make it easier to slip" which aims to elicit the children's everyday ideas about lubricants.

FIFTH PHASE: INVESTIGATING LUBRICANTS

Coral	Can you think of anything else that might make it easier to slip? Yes.
Paul	Soap.
Coral	Fairy liquid is soap really . . . you mean . . .

Paul	Bath soap.
Michael	Miss what about Sellotape?
Coral	Sellotape. It might be slippery. We've got to try and find out. Karen.
Karen	Water miss. Water in a tray and then put the weight on a piece of wood.
Coral	Yes. Water in a tray.
	Right. Now we are going to do one more thing. You said many interesting things and all your ideas will be interesting to test. I'd like you to test your Sellotape Michael [looking at Michael].
	I'd like somebody to test the water in this tray . . . who likes water? Right you can try the water in this tray [pointing at a group of children]. What else . . . I don't know if anybody has seen anyone at home trying to fix a sticky drawer. What do they do?

The children respond to Coral's question by suggesting a number of materials which can make a surface easier to slip. Their responses are accepted by Coral who invites the children to test their own ideas and suggests a way of organising the practical task. Coral then asks a further question; "I don't know if anybody has seen anyone at home trying to fix a sticky drawer, what do they do?". As I mentioned at the beginning of this chapter, one of Coral's learning objectives for this session is to help the children "to learn that lubricants could be used to reduce friction", and in order to carry out this objective, she has planned for the children to test a number of these materials. Thus, in asking this question, Coral is hoping that the children will find the context that is incorporated into the question familiar, and that they will use their everyday ideas to respond to it. Furthermore, their responses should include some of the materials Coral wants them to explore:

Natalie	They use oil.
Coral	Yes oil can make some things to slip easier, but I have seen people using something else to make drawers slip easier . . . yes.
Laura	Glue.
Coral	Glue to make it slippery?
Laura	Banana skin.
Coral	Yes banana skin can be slippery. Just a minute. Put your hands down. There are two other things I've got in mind because I've seen people do it to make drawers run more easily. So I'd like some people to test it to see if it's really true. I've seen people run a candle along the runners of the doors.

Natalie's response about the oil is accepted by Coral who is asking the children again to think of other materials which people use to make a drawer easier to run.

Laura's idea about the glue is rejected by Coral, but her second idea about the banana skin is accepted as an example of a material which creates less friction. However, none of Laura's responses is the one that Coral is searching for. Thus, she decides to stop the discussion and offer to the children two materials that can be applied to reduce the friction of a sticky drawer:

Coral	Yes banana skin can be slippery. Just a minute. Put your hands down. There are two other things I've got in mind because I've seen people do it to make drawers run more easily. So I'd like some people to test it to see if it's really true. I've seen people run a candle along the runners of the doors.
Several children	Miss . . . wax.
Coral	Yes. And I want some of you to test it. And the other thing I've seen people do is run a pencil along the drawer. What's a pencil inside is made of?
Several children	Lead, graphite, graphite.
Coral	What happens to the graphite when you run it along the paper?
Several children	It makes it smooth. It's coming off.
Coral	It is coming off. Yes. And I've seen people to do that so they are drawing really on the edge of the drawer and the graphite is coming off and there is graphite on the drawer and they say that makes it slip. Now we've got lots of ideas here . . . we've got water, we've got oil, we've got fairy liquid, we've got a candle, we've got graphite. What we want to find out is how many Newtons it takes to pull this one kilogram weight in this material. [showing the weight wrapped in a piece of material] why is it important you all stick on that?
Clare	To make the test fair.
Coral	Somebody wraps up four weights . . . what's wrong with that?
Several children	It won't be fair.
Coral	Right. You've changed something else. You still have the same material but the weight is different so stick to one kilogram weight.

Coral's reference to the candle initiates a number of responses about the material that it is made of. Coral says to the children that she wants them to test the candle and she then suggests that a pencil can be also used to reduce the friction of a sticky drawer. She then asks the children to say what the pencil is made of. Some of the children say "lead" whereas some other children say "graphite". Coral incorporates the last reply into her talk implying that it is the correct one, and she then asks the children to think what happens to "graphite" when it is run along a piece of paper. The children offer a number of different responses. Coral chooses to include in her talk the response which appears to be more appropriate for what she wants to explain to the children; that is that when graphite is run along a sticky drawer, that makes it slide better coming off.

In this interaction, Coral uses the children's responses to foster the transfer of their understanding of an everyday situation (running graphite along a piece of paper) to a new situation (running graphite along a sticky drawer). From a sociocultural view of learning, the building of bridges between the known and the new is assumed to be predominately supported through adult-child interactions. Parallels between two situations are drawn or highlighted to help the transfer of the relevant skills and information (see Rogoff, & Gardner, 1984). Here, Coral emphasises to the children that the way graphite runs along a sticky drawer is similar to the way that it is run along a piece of paper, in both situations graphite is "coming off". Coral explains in this way that certain materials when applied to particular surfaces stay on those surfaces, and this phenomenon can reduce the friction. The new knowledge is appropriated by the children who offer to Coral the following responses:

Kathleen	Miss you could use a bar of soap to make a drawer run easier.
Coral	Right. We've got three things, graphite, a candle and a bar of soap.
Paul	Miss what about fairy liquid?
Coral	Why won't you want to put washing up liquid to your drawer runner?
Sara	It'll go sticky.

As we can see, the children suggest more materials that can be used to make a drawer run easier. Their suggestions can be taken as an example of their developing understanding about the use of lubricants. Thus, they seem to apply their understanding about materials that can be slippery such as the bar of soap and the fairy liquid to a new context.

The discussion moves on to procedural matters. Coral is asking the children to suggest ways of organising the practical task:

Coral	Right. Can you just listen for a minute. We've got all these ideas everyone wants to try them and we've got a limited amount of time left. Can anybody suggest a sensible way of organising this. So we have more ideas tested without absolute chaos. Sin.
Sin	Test one at the time.
Coral	That will take us up to Christmas. No, we've got up to half past three.

	Right. I think I've got a better idea We've got soap . . . we've got water . . . we've got oil . . . we've got candle . . . graphite . . . Sellotape. [Coral writes on the board the materials that the children are going to test]. Allison.
Allison	Shiny paper.
Coral	Have we got any?
Allison	Yes.
Coral	Right. Shiny paper. I think we've got enough. [Coral then puts the children into groups. Each group will test one material].

Because there is not much time left for the practical task, Coral decides to divide the children into groups and to ask each group to explore a specific material.

The children are given some time to work on the practical task. Coral then asks the children to stop the practical work and begins a discussion about their results.

SIXTH PHASE: DISCUSSING CHILDREN'S FINDINGS ABOUT THE USE OF LUBRICANTS

Coral starts off this phase of her teaching by explaining to the children that "we are looking for the smallest amount of Newtons to pull that wrapped up kilogram weight" and asks the children to report "the smallest number of Newton" they found:

Coral	Right. We are looking for the smallest number of Newtons to pull that wrapped up kilogram weight and we call that the slippiest thing. So what's the smallest number of Newton you found Isaac?
Isaac	One Newton the washing up liquid. [Several other children offer their results].
Coral	Let me write these numbers on the board otherwise I will forget. I don't want you to write them down now we'll do that tomorrow. What did we say about the soap?
Several children	One point five Newtons. One point one Newton.
Coral	Right. [She writes one point one Newton on the board above the word soap]. What about the water?
John	Three Newtons
Coral	Right. Three Newtons. Oil?
Adele	Zero point five Newton.
Coral	Right. Zero point five Newton. Graphite?
Kelly	Zero point two Newton.
Coral	Right. Candle?

Paul	Three point five Newtons.
Coral	Three point five Newtons? So much for that!
	I thought it's going to be a really really good one. My mother used to run that on drawer runners. Sellotape?
Ros	Three point five Newtons.
	[Children report their results about different materials].
Coral	Right. So if you want to slide something or if you want to slide something really really well what are you going to do about it?
Several children	Graphite!

The children report their measurements to Coral who writes them on the board. When two measurements are suggested, she chooses to write on the board the smallest of the two. As we can see, Coral expresses her surprise at some of the results, such as the testing of the candle. She then asks the children to decide which material appears to have created the least friction. As Coral explains in her class diary, although she was surprised by the results of the testing of the graphite, she and the children agreed that "graphite won".

As we can see, Coral does not compare the results the children got with some set of "right" answers, which could possibly be found in some form within the body of scientific knowledge. Furthermore, she does not compare the varying results offered by different children. One interpretation for this is that Coral wants to emphasise to the children the importance of empirical tests and a respect for the outcome of such tests.

As I mentioned in the introduction to this chapter, one of Coral's learning objectives for this session was to help the children to develop their conceptual understanding about the use of lubricants in reducing the friction between two surfaces. To achieve this objective, Coral designed a practical task in which the children were invited to test a number of specific materials (candle and graphite). The same task also involved the testing of other materials that were suggested by the children. Some of those materials could also be used as lubricants (such as the soap and the oil) whereas other materials were less appropriate (such as water).

Coral here tries to reconcile two goals. The first goal is to help the children develop their conceptual understanding about lubricants and the second goal is to encourage the children to be investigative. In suggesting the testing of the candle and graphite, the teacher was anticipating that there would be results which will enable the children to achieve her learning objective. In allowing the children to investigate materials such as water, Coral may have expected that there would be practical problems, caused by the water being absorbed by the fabric, which might prevent the children from getting results which would be relevant to the achievement of her conceptual objective. Therefore, had that learning objective been the only one in her mind, she would have rejected the children's suggestion to test water. In accepting the suggestion, Coral is expecting that it will be a way in which the children can develop investigative abilities associated with her second goal. A procedural aim entails certain pedagogical actions which involve decisions such as these.

Coral probably based the design of the practical task, which aimed to achieve a particular learning objective, on her own everyday ideas about materials that can be used as lubricants. Coral anticipated that the candle would have produced better results than it actually did. Her surprise at the result of the test using the candle is made explicit to the children. From a sociocultural perspective, which places emphasis on the complex interdependence of knowledge and action, knowledge as organised for a particular task can never be sufficiently detailed, sufficiently precise, to anticipate exactly the conditions of actions (Keller & Keller, 1993).

Thus, it can be suggested that Coral, by taking part in the activity, develops her own understanding about the use of lubricants in reducing the friction between surfaces. Her developing understanding becomes explicit to the children in the concluding part of the session:

| Coral | Now then. I want you to keep all these ideas in mind all the things you've done today all the things you've learned because tomorrow I am going to ask you some of those ideas, some new questions perhaps that you've still got. Because I've still got lots of questions about friction because things I thought they are going to happen didn't happen. I'm really disappointed about candle and I thought the wet things would slide much easier. The oil was quite good, but the water wasn't, because the fabric soaked up the water and maybe that made a difference. I don't know. So, maybe, |
| Coral | we'll have to think of another experiment that didn't have fabric in it and that might be better. I'm not sure. But certainly graphite has done extremely well. |

At the end of the lesson, Coral here makes her own thinking about the practical work that the children carried out explicit to them. She talks about her own disappointment in the amount of friction created by materials such as the candle and water and draws the children's attention on the method used to test water. Coral, by evaluating the results of their investigations, encourages the ongoing development of the conceptual task. By making her thinking explicit to the children she *models* part of the scientific process, which the children could follow in thinking of their own questions and explanations about friction.

DISCUSSION

I have described in detail here, the ways in which, through a series of six interrelated phases, Coral enacts her expertise to guide children's development of scientific understanding.

In her introduction to the session (first phase), Coral started her teaching by using two bridging pedagogical strategies aimed at establishing continuity with children's previous learning about friction, and thereby assessing their current understanding. Her knowledge about friction enabled her to identify those of the children's responses that were closer to her desired definition of friction and link these responses with that definition within the children's zone of proximal development.

Next, Coral engaged the children in discussion about friction (second phase). This phase has similarities with the elicitation stage in the "big ideas" constructivist approach to teacher expertise, in that it aimed to probe children's current understanding of friction and to generate interest in investigating friction on different surfaces. There are, however, some important differences, notably in relation to the organization of this phase and the kind of interactions that take place between Coral and the children. More specifically, in "big ideas" constructivism the elicitation of children's ideas takes place at the end of an unstructured practical activity set up by the classroom teacher. The teacher's role is to facilitate the discussion by helping the learners to explain and clarify their ideas about the specific practical activity, justify their answers, and consider different explanations of what is happening. In Coral's teaching, the elicitation of children's ideas, and the generation of their interest in investigating friction, took place during classroom discussion that focused on a range of practical activities or questions which were generated by the children, as a response to Coral's initial request to think about things that have less friction and things that have a lot of friction.

In this respect, Coral's expertise suggests a Piagetian staged view about the learner: in order to encourage children's learning, the problem that they are to investigate needs to be generated by the children, and not to be given to them by the teacher. It also seems to relate to the sociocultural idea that in order for learning to be effective, the children need to be engaged in activities that are personally meaningful to them. It is indicative of the learning environment that Coral has created in her classroom that soon after she asked the initial questions about friction, one child suggested and immediately carried out a practical investigation into the friction between a rubber and a table, which, in turn, initiated other children's interest in the problem, or generated other problems and questions.

During this phase, Coral looked for opportunities in what the children said or did that could increase their interest in frictional phenomena and help them articulate their thinking about such phenomena. Her expertise enabled her to do this effectively. However, Coral enacted her expertise according to her judgment of learning opportunity. In the problem about the friction between the rubber and the table, she acted as a member of a community of learners that were trying to solve a problem which did not have an immediately obvious solution. Thus, her role was to explore together with the children evidence and possible explanations, until a tentative answer to the problem was found which, nevertheless, did not resolve all the conflicts. Moreover, during this discussion, Coral made her own uncertainties explicit to the children, offering them in this way, opportunities to experience the uncertain nature of scientific inquiry. Later on during this phase, a child's question about the friction between the ground and the sand was interpreted by Coral as an opportunity to make a scientific point about friction. And, to achieve this, she used the ball bearing analogy to draw similarities between the ways in which the pieces of sand move against the ground.

The use of analogies and metaphors is particularly encouraged by the "small range" constructivist perspective to teacher expertise. However, these are seen as means that are specified prior to teaching, whereas in Coral's practice the use of analogies depends on her choice of learning opportunity. Later on during this phase of her teaching, one child asked Coral a question about the friction between a ball and the ground. Coral decided to respond to that child's question despite the fact that rolling friction was not part of her learning objectives or part of the primary Science National Curriculum. Her response was inventive and resourceful. She picked up a tennis ball, engaged children in discussion and used her own experiences about rolling friction, and children's experiences about wheels, to produce a tentative explanation. In doing this she appeared to develop to some extent her own understanding of rolling friction together with the children.

Later on during the same phase of her teaching, another child's idea about the "flipping-up" of a paper was recognised by Coral as an opportunity to consolidate children's learning of air resistance. In this instance, her choice of pedagogical strategies was closer to "small range" constructivist teaching, and similar to the ones she used in the introduction to the session. Here, she asked closed questions that aimed to assess children's understanding against a specific definition of the scientific concept of air resistance. However, unlike "small range" constructivism in which such opportunities are specified prior to teaching, in Coral's teaching these opportunities emerge out of children's responses and questions.

In line with "big ideas" constructivism, Coral's aim for the third phase of her teaching was to engage all the children in systematic investigations about friction on different surfaces. However, unlike this form of constructivism, which suggests that the teacher should only offer procedural guidance if he/she judges that it is needed, Coral uses her expertise to model to the children how to test a 1kg weight along a surface and record the results. She also regulated the procedural support she offered to the children, by demonstrating to them one way of investigating friction and then asking a child to repeat the demonstration for the rest of the class. In this respect, her teaching parallels the coaching and scaffolding techniques that are supported by sociocultural perspectives. Once Coral assessed that the children had a clear understanding of what was required procedurally to carry out their investigations, she left them alone to choose their own hypotheses to test. She also offered them a range of surfaces to test, and clarified safety issues. To this extent, her expertise appears to draw on Piagetian constructivist learning: in order to encourage children's learning, the problem that they are to investigate needs to be generated by the children, and not to be given to them by the teacher.

During children's engagement in the practical task, Coral visited each group in order to assess their progress and provide support with procedural issues. Her Vygotskian concerns to work within the children's zone of proximal development enabled her to introduce new materials for the children to investigate, relevant to children's current point of development. Moreover, based on her assessment of their progress and interest in the task, she decided to modify her initial plans for the lesson, and offer to the children two more questions to investigate that arose out of her discussions with them. Unlike "small range" constructivists' view of expertise in which teaching proceeds according to a set of prespecified learning objectives, Coral's teaching is flexible and adaptive to children's emerging needs.

The fourth phase of Coral's teaching involved the discussion of children's work. Again, at a general level this phase has similarities with "big ideas" constructivist teaching, in that it aims to use children's findings as the means for further developing their scientific understanding. However, there are some important differences, notably in relation to the kind of support that Coral offers to the children. In a "big-ideas" constructivist approach, during this stage the teacher collects children's findings in relation to a specific question that they were asked to investigate. The teacher does not comment on the findings, but presents them to the class with the aim of leaving the children alone to make the links between the findings and their initial hypotheses. At this stage, if the findings are not adequate the teacher may decide to introduce a new idea for the children to investigate within the children's zone of proximal development (see the discussion in chapter 3). Yet in this phase of her teaching Coral looked for opportunities in children's findings that could be used explicitly by her to build further their scientific understanding. As with the second phase of her teaching, she did not start the discussion with a question about the results of the testing of a specific surface. Instead, she asked the children to report interesting findings. Coral used her expertise to identify those elements in the children's responses that could be developed further, and offered explicit guidance to them. Indeed, her role in this phase seems to be close to sociocultural perspectives on adult guidance in child-adult interactions. Thus, her guidance involved scaffolding techniques such as coaching and modelling that aimed to draw children's attention to aspects of the task that they had not noticed before, or to engage them in reflective discourse that helped them to step back from the task and think about their findings. Whilst she was offering this kind of support, she encouraged the rest of the class to contribute to the discussion, by repeating from time to time her initial question. Towards the end of this phase of her teaching, Coral directed the discussion towards the children's results for the last question. The aim was to establish continuity between the children's findings and the fifth phase of her teaching.

The main aim of the fifth phase of Coral's teaching was to engage children in an investigation about the use of lubricants in reducing the friction between surfaces. This was the last of Coral's objectives for the session. She used this phase to assess children's conceptual understanding of aspects of friction and their ability to interpret evidence. As in previous phases, Coral pursues her pedagogic goals by using the examples offered by the children in their responses. She suggested two materials for them to test (graphite and candle), and encouraged the children to test other materials. Furthermore, because she was running out of time, she explicitly organized the children into groups. She then used the evidence of their investigations to develop further their understanding of lubricants (sixth phase). In the discussion that followed the children's investigations about lubricants, Coral made her own surprise about some of the results explicit to the children.

In general, in Coral's teaching when new scientific ideas are discussed, her own scientific understanding is presented to the children as tentative and linked with everyday use and language or scientific evidence. Moreover, the children are treated as knowledgeable; as having their own ideas which are respected by the teacher.

The session ended with Coral making her thinking about the findings of the investigation on lubricants explicit to the children. In this way, she modelled part of the scientific process that the children could follow in thinking about their own questions and explanations.

NOTES

[1] Coral has not asked the other children to take part in the discussion. In Coral's teaching, very often the children assume that they are expected to offer their suggestions and explanations even when the teacher's question is not directed to them.

CONCLUSION: PRIMARY SCIENCE EXPERTISE-IN-ACTION

In the early chapters of this book, I examined the influential idea that, in order to be effective, primary teachers need to possess adequate subject knowledge and pedagogical content knowledge. Much of my discussion involved contrasting two constructivist lines of thinking that have been used within UK research to support this idea, with the rather different perspective provided by sociocultural theory. In later chapters, I examined in considerable depth the thinking and practice of a teacher who was regarded locally, and to some extent more widely, as an expert primary science practitioner. This was designed to provide the basis for further assessment of ideas about the role of subject knowledge in primary science expertise. My aim in this final chapter is to summarise the overall argument of the book, and to consider its implications for practice.

THE GROWTH OF EMPHASIS ON SUBJECT KNOWLEDGE

The kind and depth of primary teachers' science subject knowledge required for effective teaching has been a perennial topic for debate, both in the context of research and of policy; and not only in the UK but also in many other countries. There are several reasons for this, relating to changing ideas within psychology and other relevant disciplines, and to do with the wider context of educational policy and practice.

Piaget's theoretical ideas about child development have been a major influence on primary pedagogy over the past forty years. In particular, various interpretations of it have lent support to particular views about the learning and teaching of science, and these have informed conceptions of primary science expertise and the kind of professional development required by primary teachers (see Koch, 2006).

For much of the 1960s and 1970s, Piaget's staged theory influenced research and curriculum development, supporting the view that children learn *about science* by *doing science*. Within UK primary science education research, this became known as the *process approach*. It treated science teaching as a process of inquiry through which children acquire *useful* knowledge - that is, knowledge which can be established through practical work and applied to solve problems that are significant to the children's needs, interests and abilities, rather than consisting of abstract concepts and scientific principles alone. It was argued that, to teach science effectively, teachers needed to have an understanding of the process of inquiry and of developmental psychology, along with sufficient knowledge of science to be able to guide children's inquiries.

During the 1980s there was a significant shift. The emergence of Piagetian constructivism lent support to a view of primary science teaching which stressed the importance of children's prior conceptions in the learning process, and the need to challenge these directly during teaching. Unlike the process approach, in which practical activities are initiated by children's own questions and interests, Piagetian constructivism argues that practical activities need to be selected so as to provide the necessary evidence that will induce conceptual change in children's prior conceptions. Within this picture of science teaching, particular emphasis came to be placed on teachers' understanding of the theoretical constructs of science, since this was regarded as an essential prerequisite: both for eliciting and identifying children's ideas; and for providing appropriate learning experiences that would help learners to test their ideas against evidence and to use the evidence to modify these, so as to arrive at specific abstract scientific principles.

Since the 1990s, emphasis on subject knowledge has become a major consideration in research on teacher effectiveness. In many countries, the findings of constructivist research have raised questions about whether most primary teachers have the necessary level of science subject knowledge. And this has led to proposals about the kind of professional development that is required in order to develop both primary science practitioners' ability and their confidence.

Another intellectual source reinforcing ideas about the role of subject knowledge in effective science teaching has been the work of Lee Shulman, especially his notions of subject knowledge and pedagogical content knowledge. Over the past twenty years, much research, especially in the United States and Australia, has focused on the identification of the main dimensions of science pedagogical content knowledge, with the aim of producing a model of teacher cognition which could be used for the purposes of teacher training.

Within UK research on primary science education, the notions of subject knowledge and pedagogical content knowledge influenced the development of two influential approaches to primary science expertise that I have examined in this book: "small range" and "big ideas" constructivism. For "small range" constructivists, the effective teaching of primary science relies on teachers' adequate understanding of a small number of science concepts and of a set of pre-specified pedagogical skills (teachers' subject-specific knowledge) that enables teachers to transfer to children their own understanding of relevant science concepts. Moreover, effective pedagogy is also seen as depending on teachers' understanding of the practical implications of this particular interpretation of constructivism, which stresses the importance of introducing children to abstract scientific concepts *before* their engagement in practical activities.

By contrast, "big ideas" constructivism supports the view that the effective teaching of primary science depends on teachers' adequate understanding of a range of broad scientific principles, and of a particular orientation to scientific inquiry. Following on from this, for "big ideas" constructivists, pedagogical content knowledge is employed as a broad framework that enables teachers to use their subject knowledge to support a *socio-constructivist* learning and teaching process, through which children construct understanding of abstract scientific principles.

These two different approaches to primary science expertise reflect, to some extent, broader developments in ideas about the learning and teaching of science, as well as criticisms of Piagetian constructivism. For example, the view that all that is beneficial in constructivist pedagogy is the elicitation of children's prior conceptions has helped "small range" constructivists to argue that conceptual change occurs through telling and showing children the scientific view before their participation in structured practical activities.

The growing influence of Vygotskian perspectives on learning in the literature of science education research, especially their emphasis on the role of language and communication in the development of children's scientific understanding, has also shaped ideas about effective learning and teaching. Thus, many constructivist researchers, although they continue to support the view that the learning of science is an individual process which involves conceptual change, now argue that the modification of children's understanding can also be induced through directed processes of social interaction (see Koch, 2006). This has been particularly true for "big ideas" constructivists, who currently claim that children reconstruct their everyday ideas as they test both these ideas and those suggested to them by more knowledgeable adults against scientific evidence; at least where this operates within the children's zone of proximal development.

Like Piaget's work, Vygotsky's ideas have also been interpreted in various ways. Thus, not only constructivism but also the sociocultural perspectives that I used in my work has been strongly influenced by Vygotsky. Unlike even socio-constructivist theories, which treat social interaction as an external factor in the construction of an individual's scientific understanding, sociocultural perspectives regard language as intrinsic to processes of social coordination and adaptation. Moreover, they view knowledge and learning as necessarily situated within the activities of particular communities of practice. In this way, they raise new questions about the nature of teachers' science subject knowledge and their pedagogical expertise. Nevertheless, their current influence on research concerned with primary science teacher expertise remains limited.

Alongside developments in ideas about the learning and teaching of primary science, and about the education of primary teachers, the last twenty years have also been characterised by the introduction of standards-driven curricula for the initial preparation of primary teachers, high-stake assessment of children's learning, and a general climate of demands for transparent accountability. This is evident not only in England, which has also experienced the effects of various revisions of the Science National Curriculum, but also in other English-speaking countries. Such government-led interventions have often been at odds with the findings of research on science education, while also serving to increase the demands regarding what primary teachers ought to know and the prescriptions about how they ought to teach primary science.

ASSESSING CONSTRUCTIVIST APPROACHES TO PRIMARY SCIENCE TEACHER EXPERTISE

In evaluating the two main constructivist lines of thinking that have been influential within UK research on primary science expertise, I have argued that there are some important differences between them. These concern their interpretation of the relationship between conceptual and procedural knowledge, and of the role that social interaction plays in the construction of teachers' scientific understanding. In turn, these differences determine the kind and level of scientific understanding that primary teachers are judged to be capable of acquiring, and hence the foundation for their classroom expertise.

For "small range" constructivists, teachers' knowledge of science develops in a sequential manner: the concepts, facts and practical problem skills (lower functions of cognition) are basic in teachers' knowledge and exist as prerequisites for learning higher-order functions of cognition, such as complex concepts and problem-solving procedural knowledge. Following on from this, "small range" constructivists argue that teachers' subject knowledge needs to consist of a quite limited range of science concepts and practical problem skills, and that these should be introduced to teachers during professional development courses.

By contrast, "big ideas" constructivists support a socio-constructivist view of knowledge and learning, arguing that teachers are capable of developing an understanding of broad scientific principles when they are offered opportunities to test and discuss both their own prior conceptions and the ideas of more knowledgeable others against scientific evidence. Moreover, they stress that teachers' subject knowledge consists of a network of links between scientific concepts and experience, which can be extended as teachers make new connections between scientific concepts and ways of acting and interpreting evidence. In other words, for "big ideas" constructivists, knowledge of how to do science develops interactively with knowledge of the concepts of science. As a result, this approach to teachers' subject knowledge places particular emphasis on the importance of problem-solving aspects of procedural knowledge, those that in the other constructivist approach would be considered "higher order". From this point of view, teachers' subject knowledge involves a range of scientific principles and a particular approach to doing science, and these are linked to the processes of observation, asking questions, predicting and hypothesising, and carrying out investigations. In line with this, "big ideas" constructivists argue that the education of primary teachers should offer them opportunities to develop adequate understanding of the inquiry process, not only because it helps teachers to extend their own understanding of science but also because it is central to children's learning of science.

Despite the important differences between them, from the point of view of sociocultural theory, both "small range" and "big ideas" constructivism underestimate the complexity of classroom practice. They assume a universalistic view of scientific knowledge: the idea that the concepts of science are abstract, precise entities which can be internalised by the individual teacher, and also by children. They further treat this as *acquired*, commodity-like knowledge that is essentially decontextualised and available to be used across situations. This is evident in their approaches to assessing the adequacy of teachers' subject knowledge, which is judged according to teachers' ability to retrieve, or collaboratively achieve, the correct scientific knowledge; and to apply it in their explanations of well-defined situations that are included in interviews and/or questionnaires. Thus, both "small range" and "big ideas" constructivists assume that once teachers acquire adequate understanding, of either a set of simple concepts or a range of broad scientific principles, they will be able to apply it relatively straightforwardly in future classroom situations.

By contrast, sociocultural perspectives argue that knowledge is tied to action, and they emphasise the idea that understanding is often messy and contingent. It depends upon processes of interpretation and negotiation, in which both the problem at hand and decisions about which cultural tool to use are recurrently reformulated. From a sociocultural perspective, teachers develop their understanding of science in the process of being enculturated into the practices of a particular scientific community. In the course of this, they learn through cognitive apprenticeship the relevant language, and other cultural patterns of communication, as well as how to make decisions about which conceptual and procedural tools to employ in order to solve well- and ill-defined problems. Thus, teachers' science subject knowledge is expected to include not just their grip on the concepts, processes and procedures of science, but also an understanding of how to go about solving problems that may not always be well defined: how to work up problems, framing them in ways that are amenable to investigation.

Like constructivists, sociocultural theorists emphasise the crucial role that knowledge plays in practice. However, they also recognise the essential and inseparable roles of cultural tools, social activity and individual interpretations. And they argue that assessment of individuals' knowledge should be based on how they perform, rather than on what they say about their own performance or on what they can do in artificial situations. On this view, teachers' subject knowledge is a resource whose adequacy is determined by functionality; it must be judged in terms of teachers' ability to employ tools skilfully, in order to achieve specific goals that emerge as they participate in the activities of the various communities of practice in which they are involved, especially those that develop in classrooms.

It is important to note here that a sociocultural perspective does not imply complete rejection of the methods used by constructivist research in assessing the adequacy of primary teachers' scientific understanding. However, it does suggest that the findings from this kind of research need to be treated with great caution, and that they should be supplemented by in-depth study of teachers' use of cultural tools in particular contexts, the problems they face in their practice, and how these relate to the practical communities in which they participate.

If we apply this sociocultural perspective to the learning and teaching of science, by both teachers and children, it raises some fundamental questions about the two forms of constructivism that have been most influential in the field of UK primary science research. For one thing, it implies that no fixed distinction can be drawn between subject knowledge and pedagogical content knowledge, since all knowledge is functional in character: it is tied to its contexts of use. Thus, from a sociocultural perspective, teachers' subject and pedagogical knowledge is integrated and situated, and is developed as teachers transform their identities through participation in the activities of their science classroom communities. Above all, however, a sociocultural perspective implies that what counts as primary science expertise can only be judged in the context of local communities of practice, not laid down in abstract terms on the basis of research concerned with assessing scientific knowledge through tests or interviews. The two constructivist approaches to teacher expertise adopt this latter position, even though they employ slightly different research strategies that reflect different views of learners and teachers "Small range" constructivists treat both learners and teachers as passive, and the resulting concept of effective teaching of science parallels the transmission model. "Big ideas" constructivists consider learners and teachers as active in the learning process, and suggest a socio-constructivist approach to the teaching and learning of science. However, both support the view that teachers should acquire commodity-like subject and pedagogical content knowledge which can then be applied in the classroom, so that children can acquire well-established scientific concepts and ideas. By contrast with both these forms of constructivism, a sociocultural perspective argues that in order to understand expertise we need to place emphasis on the perspectives and actions of those who are recognised as expert practitioners by their local communities.

UNDERSTANDING CORAL'S EXPERTISE

In the second half of this book, I sought to apply a sociocultural approach in investigating primary science expertise. This involved a qualitative case study of the perspective and practice of a teacher who is recognised locally and to some extent more widely as an expert practitioner of primary science. I explored her views about her own subject knowledge and her beliefs about the learning and teaching of science. I also described in detail an episode of her teaching in order to discuss the ways in which, through a series of six interrelated phases, Coral enacts her expertise.

Perhaps the key finding concerning Coral's perspective on her own expertise and her practice is the *eclectic* character of her approach. As I have shown, in some respects she draws on Piagetian ideas about how children learn. She believes, for example, that children need to be intrinsically motivated to handle the task in hand. Thus, in her practice, especially at the beginning of a new science topic, she engages children in unstructured problem-solving situations which stem from their own questions and interests. However, her practice is also influenced by ideas from more recent forms of constructivism. Indeed, for Coral, children's participation in practical activities serves other goals in the learning process: it offers them opportunities to reflect on their everyday ideas and to recognise the limitations of these in explaining particular physical events. It also offers her opportunities to assess the children's current point of scientific development; in other words it helps her to elicit their ideas as well as their procedural understanding. Moreover, because she believes that scientific understanding involves procedural capability, enabling links to be drawn between scientific knowledge and experience, the systematic testing of children's ideas occupies a central part in her teaching.

At the same time, Coral also seems to draw on socio-constructivist and sociocultural views of learning and teaching. She strongly believes, for example, that discussion plays a crucial role in the development of children's scientific understanding, and throughout her teaching she engages children in that. The kind of guidance she employs, however, during such discussions, is closer to what is encouraged by a sociocultural perspective. Indeed, she shows a particular concern to work within children's zone of proximal development, constantly looking for opportunities in children's suggestions, and findings that could be used explicitly to build further their scientific understanding. Thus, in her practice her guidance often involves scaffolding techniques, such as coaching and modelling. These are aimed at developing specific aspects of children's procedural understanding, or drawing children's attention to aspects of the task that they had not noticed before, so as to engage them in reflective discourse that will enable them to step back from the task, think about their findings, and use these to make a scientific point. Where she judges it appropriate, she uses children's ideas that are closer to her desired scientific one and then reformulates and re-presents these ideas to the children. In this way, she helps the children in her class to develop metacognitive awareness and to develop their scientific understanding, so that it increasingly becomes compatible with that of the established scientific community.

Like advocates of sociocultural perspectives, Coral stresses that the development of children's scientific understanding is not easy to bring about, and that it can happen independently from the course of her teaching. As I indicated during my discussion of Coral's teaching about friction, there is evidence of the difficulties that the children in her class experience at appropriating the term "friction" in their explanations, though at the same time it is clear that they are developing a good understanding of the processes of scientific inquiry, along with respect for using evidence in supporting their arguments during classroom discussions. Nevertheless, unlike supporters of socio-constructivist and sociocultural approaches to learning and teaching, Coral does not promote group discussions, possibly because her beliefs about children's ability to engage in social interaction with each other are tied to Piagetian staged views. However, what is involved here is not a confused mixture but a dynamic blending that is guided by a pragmatic orientation. It reflects, in part, Coral's responsiveness to the contingencies of the classroom process.

An important feature of teaching is its *practical* character, in the sense that it involves making judgments, almost moment by moment, about what is happening and what is needed in order to further children's learning. The practical character of teaching has been emphasized in the work of many philosophers, psychologists and sociologists, where the contrast is often drawn with technical activities that are governed by instrumental rules (Olson, 1992; Schwab, 1969). The practical character of teaching means that it requires a distinctive orientation, involving an ability to make rapid assessments of where events are leading and what can be done to guide them in productive directions. Coral's teaching is characterized by judgments about what is happening and reformulation of her plans, often on the spot, in order to respond to opportunities and problems that arise from children's ideas or questions, and thereby to facilitate their learning. These opportunities and problems are variable and contingent, and open to different interpretations. Thus, her teaching involves choices, which cannot be easily codified or made entirely explicit. Indeed, the *tacit* character of practical knowledge has been emphasized by many authors who argue that professional knowledge is always to some degree implicit (see, for instance, Polanyi's account of science as relying on tacit knowledge, Polanyi 1959).

Coral's subject knowledge helps her to interpret and function successfully in these situations. She claims to have a good scientific understanding, which enables her to recognise scientific questions and organise her teaching in a way that encourages the development of children's ability to ask questions and seek answers to these questions. It also helps her to recognise children's ideas that are different from current scientific understandings, to simplify scientific concepts and decide on appropriate scientific terms and practical activities. However, the knowledge that she enacts does not take the form of commodity knowledge available to be used across situations. Rather, it is a resource that she employs skilfully according to the task that she has to achieve, or her assessment of the learning opportunities available. During her practice, it unfolds as she and the children raise issues and questions in relation to the task at hand. It is also integrated with her understanding of the children's current point of development and her choice of pedagogical strategies. For example, at the beginning of her lesson on friction, her knowledge enabled her to identify those of the children's responses that were closer to her desired definition of friction and to link these responses with this definition. She uses her scientific understanding of air resistance, and close questioning, to respond to a problem that she interprets as an opportunity to consolidate children's prior learning of this concept. On other occasions, her scientific understanding of friction is combined with an analogy in order to help the children to develop further their thinking about friction, as this is expressed in a specific context. Her understanding of the uncertain nature of scientific inquiry enables her to engage with the children in problem-solving situations (e.g. the problem of the friction between the rubber and the table) that do not have an immediately obvious solution, developing in this way her own understanding of the problem together with the children. Her procedural understanding of science and her pedagogical strategy of coaching allow her to offer explicit guidance to a child in formulating a hypothesis, or to allow the children to reflect on the available evidence, and to draw their attention to aspects of the task that they had not noticed before.

Thus, her expertise has a number of dimensions each of which can only be understood "relative to and against unfolding conversations and against the physical, social, historical and cultural settings within which these conversations occur" (Roth, Tobin, & Ritchie, 2001, p. 277). Above all, her science expertise is constantly evolving. As Coral argues, she learns all the time as she talks to the children, as she tries to provide scientific explanations for situations that arise during teaching and realises that there is not a straight-forward process for doing this, even if these situations relate to scientific areas that she has taught before. This is because, as Osborne (1996) puts it, during teaching "knowing and learning are inextricably connected because in teaching the actions enabled by "knowing" are problematic" (1996, p.1).

Coral's expertise is guided by a set of core beliefs about the learning and teaching of science that allow her to orchestrate her practice in a specific way. These beliefs, which she had developed over the years as she participated in various communities of practice, including her own science classroom community, include the assumptions that teaching science is a process of exploration through which children must be encouraged to ask their own scientific questions and seek answers to these questions; that children are knowledgeable and their ideas should be respected even if they are recognised as being different from scientific understanding; that scientific understanding involves procedural capability, enabling links to be drawn between knowledge and areas of experience; that her role as the teacher is to look for opportunities in what the children say or do that could help them reflect on the evidence and use their ideas to further their scientific understanding.

Coral's expertise also includes rules that enable her to organise her practice in a specific way. As we saw in chapter 6, at a general level her teaching sequence has similarities with "big ideas" constructivist teaching approach: it involves an elicitation stage, and proceeds with the systematic testing of children's ideas, and the discussion of their findings.

Moreover, Coral's teaching is guided by her value commitments about the aim of science teaching. This aim involves helping the children develop understanding of school science, as well as understanding of a model of what scientific thinking involves which includes respect for evidence and experience of the uncertain nature of scientific inquiry. In her teaching, she tries to balance these values, as well as to cope with the demands of the primary Science National Curriculum and of the preparation of children for formal testing. Thus, quite often she engages in thinking about scientific problems that do not have an obvious answer, and may not relate explicitly to her objectives for the session. On other occasions, she focuses classroom discussion on the consolidation of children's learning about school science. She recognises that her teaching does not follow a fixed course, she often decides on what to do next on the spot, whilst she is talking to the children. At the same time, she also stresses that in her teaching she tries to exercise a certain level of control over what is learned, when, and how, by creating a learning environment in which both simpler and more complex tasks are ongoing and discussed. Such an environment may enable children to develop understanding of subject knowledge yet simultaneously allow them to pursue their own interests and even to question the authority of the teacher.

This set of values, rules and beliefs not only allows Coral to orchestrate her teaching in a particular way, but it also helps her to reflect on her own practice: to evaluate her actions and use these evaluations to develop her teaching further. As I discussed in chapter 4, in her class diary she explains the aims for each lesson; discusses why and how each session progressed, drawing on her own beliefs about effective teaching and learning, and appealing to evidence from what the children said, wrote or did; illustrates how she used her assessment of children's progress to plan the following session, or modify activities within the same session; and expresses concerns and dilemmas about her own role in helping children to develop scientific understanding, and how this could alter in order to improve her teaching. This process of reflection is one of the reasons that Coral's beliefs are not static; they evolve as she employs them in the classroom, re-considers them herself, and discusses them with colleagues.

However, the core of Coral's expertise lies in her ability to perform successfully in the contingent situations that arise during her teaching by integrating her selection of scientific resources with her knowledge of the children and her choice of appropriate pedagogical strategies. In this way, she develops a repertoire of ways of dealing with science classroom situations. Her subject knowledge, past experiences as a learner and teacher of science, and her beliefs and value commitments about the teaching and learning of science all play a significant role in shaping the ways that she responds to children's questions and suggestions. They help her to see situations as similar to and yet also as different from others in her repertoire.

In light of this, one way of thinking about Coral's expertise is in terms of the notion of the *reflective practitioner*. This idea is associated with Schön's work, in which he depicts practice as messy, ambiguous, value laden and open to different interpretations and actions (Schön, 1983, 1987). He introduces the concepts of *reflection-in-action* and *reflection-on-action* as a way to describe how professional knowledge is used in the process of decision-making. The former amounts to "thinking on one's feet". It involves drawing on past experience to build new understandings that will inform actions in the situation that is unfolding:

> the practitioner allows himself to experience surprise, puzzlement, or confusion in a situation which he finds uncertain or unique. He reflects on the phenomenon before him, and on the prior understandings which have been implicit in his behaviour. He carries out an experiment which serves to generate both a new understanding of the phenomenon and a change in the situation. (Schön 1983, p. 68)

Here, interpretations are tested in action, tentatively, and this allows development of further responses and moves. This is necessary because every case is unique, though of course it is always possible to draw on what has gone before. In this process, practitioners bring prior knowledge, examples, values and actions to bear on the invention of new frames. By contrast, reflection-on-action always occurs after the action, when a practitioner critically reflects about it. Practitioners may write about key experiences, talk things through with others, and so on. The act of reflecting-on-action enables them to spend time exploring why they acted in the way they did, what was happening in a situation, why, and so on. In so doing practitioners develop sets of questions and ideas about their activities that can then be drawn on in future reflection-in-action.

Coral's orientation in the classroom, in which she openly engages with contingency and uncertainty, fits closely with the notion of reflection-in-action. Equally, there was considerable evidence of her engaging in reflection-on-action, in writing about her work, as well as in interviews and email communications. And her orientation as a reflective practitioner is sharply different from the two constructivist approaches to teacher expertise which tend to offer a technical view of teaching: treating it as a practice that can be pre-programmed so as to produce specified outcomes. This orientation is particularly evident in the "small range" constructivist approach, which treats teachers as passive learners, and measures the effectiveness of teaching in terms of specific learning outcomes. However, even the "big ideas" constructivist approach to teacher expertise, while it does not explicitly measure effectiveness, also assumes that teaching proceeds by the application of a standard set of pedagogical rules whose effective employment depends on the teacher's possession of commodity-like subject and pedagogical content knowledge.

Coral's approach as a reflective practitioner has closer similarities with sociocultural perspectives on learning and teaching. Indeed, some sociocultural theorists (Roth, 1995) argue that it is possible to integrate Schön's notion of the reflective practitioner into a sociocultural model of teaching and learning. This model argues that students and teachers engage together in an "authentic" activity, during which the teacher models the type of inquiry and reflection on it that they want students to appropriate within the zone of proximal development created by the collaboration. Such a setting provides the ideal context in which teacher and student can search for the convergence of their respective meanings by using the available resources.

However, such models also tend to assume that there is one specific approach to the teaching of science, whereas as we have seen Coral's expertise is eclectic in character. Moreover, they tend to compare the teacher-as-reflective practitioner with the practice of scientists, by arguing that the teacher in the classroom acts merely as the representative of canonical science whose role is to engage learners in authentic activities that model a particular approach to scientific practice.

This points to a significant difference between the character of Coral's expertise and the image of expertise presented by sociocultural perspectives, deriving from the nature and context of the teacher's work. Practising scientists do not have to respond to questions or suggestions from children "on the hoof" without advance warning, nor are they responsible for identifying or creating opportunities to facilitate children's learning. Moreover, Coral deals with a whole class of children not with individuals, which heightens the need for contextual judgment, both in terms of the choice of scientific concepts or procedures and pedagogical strategies. In other words, teaching is characterised by constantly dealing not just with instances of knowing but also with instances of non-knowing, which is not necessarily true in science (see Osborne, 1999).

Following on from this, another way of thinking about the practical, and eclectic, character of Coral's orientation towards primary science practice is to draw an analogy with the notion of *bricolage*, as developed by the anthropologist Claude Levi-Strauss (1966) and later writers (see for example, Nelson, Grossberg, & Treichler, 1992; Denzin & Lincoln, 1994). Here, a bricoleur is defined as using whatever resources are to hand in order to do the best work that is possible under the circumstances. This matches the way in which Coral's teaching requires invention of solutions to problems, often on the spot, drawing solely on cognitive and other resources that are currently available. Thus, she may pick up a tennis ball to develop, together with the children, their understanding of rolling friction; at other times she may ask close questions to consolidate children's prior learning; on other occasions she will offer explicit guidance as to how to test specific hypotheses, introduce analogies to make specific scientific points, or make her own uncertainties about a specific problem or surprise about the results of a practical activity explicit to the children.

The practical character of Coral's expertise also raises questions about the relation between research knowledge and practice. The two constructivist perspectives on teacher expertise seem to suggest that research knowledge feeds directly into practice, or ought to do so. This is most obvious in the case of the "small range" constructivist approach, which implies that it is the responsibility of researchers to develop the subject and pedagogical content knowledge that is necessary for the effective teaching of primary science, with teachers then transferring this directly to the classroom. And much the same direct model of the relationship between research and practice is also implicit in the "big ideas" constructivist approach, which assumes that since it is itself based on research evidence it will, if applied, ensure the effective teaching of primary science. By contrast, a view of teaching as a practical activity suggests that it cannot be based directly on research knowledge in this way. Instead, practice is seen as necessarily depending on experience, wisdom, local knowledge and judgment (see Hammersley, 1997). This does not mean that research has no contribution to make to practice. As we have seen, Coral's expertise is informed by her understanding of science, and by her knowledge of research about the learning and teaching of science. This expertise was developed during her participation in various communities of practice, including those she engaged with as a student. However, these are not standard views, they evolved as they were used in practice and informed by developments in the field. In these terms, what educational research provides can only be a resource that the teacher must use, deciding what will work, or what has worked, for the children, for particular purposes, on specific occasions.

It is significant to note, in this context, that there are some important differences between the ways in which the notions of subject knowledge and pedagogical content knowledge have been used in UK primary science education research, and how they were originally conceived in Shulman's "knowledge-base" model. As I indicated in chapter 1, this model was produced with the aim of capturing the practical knowledge of teachers. Shulman recognises the circumstantial nature of knowledge in arguing that "the knowledge-base approach does not produce an overly technical image of teaching, a scientific enterprise that has lost its soul" (Shulman, 1986; p. 20). However, at least as it has come to be applied, Shulman's approach does not capture the complexity of teaching, or address the close interdependence of subject knowledge, pedagogy and the practical and contingent nature of teaching. It is misleading to assume that teachers' subject knowledge can be separated from their pedagogy or practical ways of teaching.

IMPLICATIONS FOR THE PROFESSIONAL DEVELOPMENT OF TEACHERS

Recommendations for the professional development of primary teachers can only be tentative at this stage, given that further research needs to be done in this area, particularly looking at further examples of expertise-in-action. However, a first point that arises from my work is that rather than discussing teacher expertise in primary science in terms of a dualistic account of subject knowledge and peda-gogical content knowledge, it is more appropriate to focus attention on the ways in which teachers enact their expertise to function successfully in a range of different situations. As I argued earlier, teachers' science subject knowledge must not be treated as commodity-like, in other words available for use across all situations. Rather, science subject knowledge is always a resource, a set of tools that take their meaning from the contexts of application. Using science subject knowledge as a resource means that teachers need to decide which ideas or tools are most appro-priate to use in order to function successfully in a particular situation. And the situations in which teachers operate are variable and contingent. Furthermore, they require development of the teacher's own understanding of science both as a body of knowledge and as a way of thinking about how to solve scientific problems, as well as that of the children. Following on from this, I would argue that while teach-ers' subject knowledge plays an important part in their teaching, it cannot be sepa-rated from their understanding of children, pedagogy, or from their practical meth-ods of teaching. Subject knowledge assists teachers in identifying what is relevant in children's experiences, and how to use this to develop their learning so that it becomes increasingly compatible with that of the established scientific community. However, such identification involves judgments, often made on the spot, which are not easily codified or made explicit.

My work suggests that what is involved in the education of teachers is their de-velopment of a way of thinking about science as a resource: as a set of tools that need to be used skilfully in order to make sense of new situations. This is an itera-tive process that helps teachers to develop their own scientific understanding and to employ it in classroom situations. This can be achieved by introducing teachers to a range of well- and ill-defined scientific investigations related to some of the fun-damental scientific ideas included in the primary school curricula, so as to help them to learn how to ask scientific questions and seek answers to these questions.

At the same time, it is important in preparing teachers for work in primary sci-ence to engage them in inquiries into children's learning of science, and to encour-age them to think carefully about the role of their own scientific understanding and pedagogical practices in this. This requires explication of their own views about the learning and teaching of science as well as their exposure to learning theories, re-search on the learning and teaching of science, and teaching approaches, so that they begin to develop a clearer sense of the kind of teacher they want to become. It also involves tutors working with clusters of student teachers, or practising teach-ers in their classrooms, so as to help them discuss the ways in which they employ science and pedagogical resources to deal with the contingencies of their classroom practice. The main emphasis in such discussions must be to encourage them to de-

velop the skills of the bricoleur and the reflective practitioner, the ability to be reflective in and about their teaching, and to look for new or different ways of im-
proving their science understanding and their practice.

In terms of assessing teachers' adequacy of their subject knowledge, my study
suggests that this is a complicated issue which involves evaluating teachers' use,
and the limitations of their use, of cultural tools in relation to particular tasks in
particular contexts. As I have argued, this does not mean that interviews and questionnaires have no place in the assessment of teachers' scientific understanding.
However, findings from these sources can only be treated as tentative and should
be supplemented by studies of how teachers employ cultural tools in their practice.

What I am suggesting here is an approach to teachers' education and professional development which supports the view that in expert teaching uncertainty and
how one deals with it plays as important a role as the certainty that derives from
accumulated knowledge and experience. Some studies have been carried out
framed by this approach. They often use narratives, teachers' stories or video re-
corded episodes of teaching as the means for helping teachers to reflect on their
developing understanding of science and science pedagogy (e.g. Duckworth 1987;
Rosebery, 1998; van Zee, 2000).

Rosebery and Puttick (1998), for example, worked closely with fourteen newly
qualified primary teachers during the first four years of their teaching in order to
help them develop their understanding of science and the teaching of science. As
learners of science, teachers were asked to carry out investigations in areas such as
motion and acceleration, buoyancy and density. These investigations were often
initiated by the teachers' own questions about a phenomenon. They were conducted in small groups to enable them to get engaged in debate with colleagues
about their existing ideas as well as about current scientific explanations and theories. During this, they were encouraged to ask, and seek answers to, their own
questions; to explore problems and resources; to collect, analyse and interpret data;
to construct, juxtapose and interpret graphical representations; to compare their
methods and results with those of others; and to use the theories of others, including the standard explanations of science, as tools in their work. Teachers were encouraged to keep diaries about significant aspects of their learning, including any
confusions or dilemmas that occurred during their process of learning science and
how they went about resolving them. In turn, selected episodes of their learning
were discussed with other colleagues and with the researchers during unstructured
interviews.

As teachers of science, participants examined videotaped episodes of science
lessons from their own classrooms and explored dilemmas and confusion they had
about their students' learning, their practice and curricula. These included questions about the language the students used and what they did during a science activity as well as what could be learned from these about children's science thinking
and learning. To respond to such questions teachers were expected and encouraged
to draw upon multiple resources, including their own understanding of the phenomenon under study, their knowledge of individual children, their own understanding of learning and teaching as well as their pedagogical understanding.

One important finding from this kind of studies is that teachers' science subject knowledge develops over time in contingent ways, and facilitating this requires offering them opportunities not only to get deeply engaged with complex scientific ideas, theories, and practices but also to reflect on and think through ways of employing cultural tools to deal with well- and ill-defined problem situations. Moreover, it is argued that the development of teachers' understanding of science cannot be easily separated from their understanding of pedagogy. It is often found, for example, that during both the teachers' inquiries in science and their inquiries in teaching and learning, discussion of scientific ideas on the one hand and discussion about children's learning and pedagogical practice on the other occurred simultaneously. Rosebery & Puttick (1998), for example, argue that as teachers participated in their own scientific activity they found themselves questioning how they might teach a scientific phenomenon like acceleration to children. Similarly, in analysing aspects of their teaching, they questioned their own understanding of a particular scientific phenomenon. For instance, as one teacher considered her students' explanation that "air" was what allowed a big, heavy boat to float, she probed her own understanding of density and the role it played in buoyancy. This led her to further explore the complex ideas that explain flotation as well as to question and develop her own pedagogical practices. As teachers were gaining more experience in learning about and teaching science, they became more capable in using creatively cultural tools both in terms of developing their own learning of science and in developing their pedagogy and classroom practices.

Constructivist approaches to teacher expertise often associate teachers' confidence in their teaching with their possession of commodity-like subject and pedagogical content knowledge. A sociocultural approach to teachers' education aims to help teachers develop a deeper form of confidence: the confidence that comes with being able to deal with uncertainty and ambiguity.

At a time when teaching is dominantly configured in terms of universals, such as competencies and standards, it is perhaps important to emphasise the ways in which individual teachers necessarily create their own unique explanations and understandings of events. In the current climate of demands for transparent accountability, there is a tendency for teachers' professional development to be viewed as acquiring a set of concepts and skills that can ensure children's acquisition of scientific knowledge. Yet the practical nature of teaching, and the very character of scientific knowledge, means that this model cannot succeed. Instead, a much more flexible and resourceful approach is required.

REFERENCES

Abel, S. K., & Roth, M. (1992). Constraints to teaching elementary science: A case study of a science enthusiast student. *Science Education, 76*, 581-595.

Aikenhead, G. (2001). Student's ease in crossing cultural borders into school science. *Science Education, 85*, 180-188.

Alexander, R., Rose, J., & Woodhead, C. (1992). *Curriculum organisation and classroom practice: A discussion paper*. London: DES.

Appleton, K. (Ed.). (2006). *Elementary science teacher education*. New Jersey: Lawrence Erlbaum Associates.

ASE (1963). *Policy statement–Primary schools science committee*. Hatfield: The Association for Science Education.

Australian Foundation for Science (1991). *First steps in science and technology: Focus on science and technology education No. 1*. Canberra: Australia: Australian Academy of Science.

Ausebel, D. P. (1968). *The conditions of learning*. New York: Rinchart & Winston.

Axel, E. (1992). One developmental line in European activity theories. *The Quarterly Newsletter of the Laboratory of Comparative Human Cognition, 14* (1), 8-17.

Bakhurst, D. (1988). Activity, consciousness and communication. *The Quarterly Newsletter of the Laboratory of Comparative Human Cognition, 10* (2), 31-39.

Bantock, G. H. (1969). Discovery methods. In C. B. Cox, & A. E. Dyson (Eds) *Black Paper Two*. London: Critical Quarterly Society.

Barnes, B. (1974). *Scientific knowledge and sociological theory*. London: Routledge & Kegan Paul.

Barnes, B. (1982). *T. S. Kuhn and social science*. London: Macmillan.

Bauersfeld, H. (1988). Interaction, construction and knowledge: Alternative perspectives in mathematics education. In T. Cooney & D. Grouws (Eds), *Effective mathematics teaching*. Reston, VA: National Council of Teachers of Mathematics and Lawrence Erlbaum Associates.

Bell, B. F. (1981). When is an animal, not an animal? *Journal of Biological Education, 15* (3), 213-218.

Bennett, N. (1976). *Teaching styles and pupil progress*. London: Open Books.

Berliner, D. (1989). Implications of studies of teacher expertise in pedagogy for teacher education and evaluation. In *New Directions for teacher assessment*, Proceedings of the 1988 Educational Testing Service Invitational Conference, pp. 39-68. Princeton, NJ: Educational Testing Service.

Black, P. (1980). Why hasn't it worked? *Times Educational Supplement*, Oct. 3, 12-16.

Black, P. (1993). The purposes of science education. In R. Sherrington (Ed.) *The ASE primary science teachers' handbook*, Hemel Hempstead: Simon & Schuster.

Blenkin, G. M., & Kelly, A. V. (1981). *The primary curriculum*. London: Harper and Row.

Blyth, W.A.L. (1965). *English primary education: A sociological description - vol. II*. London: Routledge & Kegan Paul.

Blyth, W.A.L. (1978). The curriculum in the middle years. *Education 3-13*, 6 (2), 25-26.

Booth, N. (1980). An approach to primary science, *Education*, 8 (1), 3-13.

Bowden, P. & Tabor, D. (1973). *Friction: An introduction to tribology*. London: Heinemann.

Boyle, A. (1990). Science in the National Curriculum. *The Curriculum Journal, 1* (1), 26-37.

Bredo, E. (1997). The social construction of learning, In G.D. Phye (Ed.). *Handbook of academic learning. Construction of knowledge*. California: Academic Press.

Bredo, E. (1999). Reconstructing educational psychology. In P. Murphy (Ed.). *Learners, learning & assessment*. London: Paul Chapman Publishing.

Brown, A. & Campione, J. (1994). Guided discovery in a community of learners. In K. McGilly (Ed.) *Classroom lessons: Integrating cognitive theory and classroom practice*. Cambridge, MA: MIT Press.

REFERENCES

Brown, A. L., & Palinscar, A. S. (1989). Guided, cooperative learning and individual knowledge acquisition. In L.B. Resnick, L. B. (Ed.). *Knowing, learning and instruction*. Hillsdale: Lawrence Erlbaum Associates.

Brown, J. S., Collins, A., & Duguid, P. (1989). Situated cognition and the culture of learning. *Educational Researcher 18* (1), 32-42.

Bruner, J. (1966). *The process of education*. Cambridge, MA: Harvard University Press.

Bruner, J. (1986). *Actual minds, possible worlds*. Cambridge, MA: Harvard University Press.

Buckmann, M. (1984). The priority of knowledge and understanding in teaching. In L. G. Katz & L. J. Raths (Eds). *Advances in teacher education, Vol. I*. Norwood, NJ: Ablex.

Calderhead, J., & Miller, E. (1985). *The integration of subject matter in student teachers' classroom practice*. Lancaster: School of Education Monographs, University of Lancaster.

Claxton, G. (1990). *Teaching to learn: A direction for education*. London: Cassell.

Claxton, G. (1993). Interplay of values and research. In P. J. Black, & A. M. Lucas (Eds.). *Children's informal ideas about science*. London: Routledge.

Cobb, P. (1994). Where is the mind? Constructivist and sociocultural perspectives on mathematical development. *Educational Researcher, 23* (7), 13-20.

Cobb, P., Boufi, A., McClain, K., & Whitenack, J. (1997). Reflective discourse and collective reflection. *Journal for Research in Mathematics Education, 28* (3), 258-277.

Cole, M. (1985). The zone of proximal development: Where culture and cognition create each other. In J. W. Wertsch (Ed.) *Culture, communication, and cognition*. Cambridge: Cambridge University Press.

Collins, A., Brown, J. S., & Newman, S. E. (1989). Cognitive apprenticeship: Teaching the crafts of reading, writing, and mathematics. In L. B Resnick (Ed.). *Knowing, learning, and instruction*. Hillsdale: Lawrence Erlbaum Associates.

Collins, H. M., & Pinch, T. (1993). *The golem*, Cambridge: Cambridge University Press.

Conran, J. (1983). Primary science 1950-82: A personal view. In C. Richards, & D. Holford (Eds.). *The teaching of primary science: Policy and practice*. London: Falmer Press.

D'Andrade, R. G. (1981). The cultural part of cognition. *Cognitive Science, 5*, 179-195.

Darling, J. (1994). *Child-centred education and its critics*. London: Paul Chapmam Publishing Ltd.

Davydov, V. V. (1988). Problems of developmental teaching: The experience of theoretical and experimental psychological research. *Soviet Education*, xxx (2), 3-97.

Denzin, N. K., & Lincoln, Y. S. (1994). Introduction: Entering the field of qualitative research. In N. K. Denzin, & Y. S. Lincoln (Eds.). *Handbook of qualitative research*. Thousand Oaks: SAGE.

DES (1974). *Educational disadvantage and the educational needs of immigrants*. London: HMSO.

DES (1978). *Primary education in England and Wales: A survey by HMI Science Committee*. London: HMSO.

DES (1983). *Science in Primary Schools: A discussion paper by HMI Science Committee*. London: HMSO.

DES (1985). *Science 5-16: A statement of policy*. London: DES/WO.

DES (1988). *Science at Age 11: A review of APU Survey Findings 1980-84*. London: HMSO.

DES (1989). *Science in the National Curriculum*. London: HMSO.

DES (1991). *Science in the National Curriculum*. London: HMSO.

DfE (1995). *Science in the National Curriculum*. London: HMSO.

DfE (1998). *Science in the National Curriculum*. London: HMSO.

DfEE (1998). *Teaching: High status, high standards*. London: Department for Education and Employment.

di Sessa, A. (1988). Knowledge in pieces. In G. Forman, & P. Pufall (Eds.). *Constructivism in the computers age*. Hillsdale: Laurence & Erlbraum Associates.

Driver, R. (1975). The name of the game. *The School Science Review, 56*, 800-805.

Driver, R. (1984), A review of research into children's thinking and learning in science, In B. Bell, W. Watts, & K. Ellington (Eds.). *Learning, doing and understanding in science: The proceedings of a conference*, 8-21. SSCR. London: Woolley Hall.

146

Driver, R. (1989). Students' conceptions and the learning of science. *International Journal of Science Education, 11*, 481-490.

Driver, R. E., G. (1983). Theories-in-action: Some theoretical and empirical issues in the study of students' conceptual frameworks in science. *Studies in Science Education, 10*, 37-60.

Driver, R., & Easley, J. (1978). Pupils and paradigms: A review of literature related to concept development in adolescent. *Studies in Science Education, 5*, 61-84.

Driver, R., & Oldham, V. (1986). A constructivist approach to curriculum development in science. *Studies in Science Education, 13*, 105-122.

Driver, R., Asoko, H., Leach, J., Mortimer, E., & Scott, P. (1994). Constructing scientific knowledge in the classroom. *Educational Researcher, 23* (7), 5-12.

Driver, R., Erickson, G. (1983). Theories-in-action: Some theoretical and empirical issues in the study of students' conceptual frameworks in science. *Studies in Science Education, 10*, 37-60.

Duckworth, E. (1987). *The having of wonderful ideas.* New York: Teachers College Press.

Duit, R. (1981). *Student's notions about the energy concept-Before and after physics instruction,* International Workshop on Problems Concerning Students' Representation of Physics and Chemistry Knowledge. Ludwigsburg: Pedagogische Hochschule.

Engeström, Y. (1988). How to do research on activity? *The Quarterly Newsletter of the Laboratory of Comparative Human Cognition, 10* (2), 30-31.

Engeström, Y., Engeström, R., & Karkkainen, M. (1995). Polycontextuality and boundary crossing. *Expert Cognition Learning and Instruction, 5*, 319-337.

Ennever, L., & Harlen, W. (1972). *With objectives in mind.* London: MacDonald Educational.

Erickson, G. L. (1978). Children's conceptions of heat and temperature. *Science Education, 63* (2), 221-230.

Feasey, R. (1998). Effective questioning in science. In R. Sherrington (Ed.). *ASE guide to primary science education.* Hatfield: The Association for Science Education.

Feyerabend, P. (1975). *Against method.* London: New Left Books.

Forman, E. A. & Cazden, C. B. (1985). Exploring Vygotskian perspectives in education: The cognitive value of peer interaction. In J. W. Wertsch (Ed.) *Culture, communication, and cognition.* Cambridge: Cambridge University Press.

Foulds, K., Duggan, S., & Feasy, R. (1992). *Investigative work in science.* Durham: School of Education, University of Durham.

Gagné, R. M. (1970). *The conditions of learning.* New York: Rinehart & Winston.

Gagné, R. M. (1983). *The psychological bases of science: A process approach.* Washington: American Association for the Advancement of Science.

Gess-Newsome & Lederman, G. N. (1999). *Examining pedagogical content knowledge.* Dordrecht: Kluwer Academic.

Gilbert, J. K., & Osborne, R. J. (1980). Some problems of learning science. *School Science Review, 61*, 664-674.

Gilbert, J. K., Watts, M. (1983). Concepts, misconceptions and alternative conceptions: Changing perspectives in science education. *Studies in Science Education, 10*, 61-98.

Gomm, R., Hammersley, M., & Foster, P. (2000). Case study and generalisation. In R. Gomm, M. Hammersley, & P. Foster (Eds.). *Case study method.* Thousand Oaks: SAGE.

Goodwin, A., & Wastendge, R. (1995). The Nuffield junior science teaching project. *Didsbury Ideas, 5* (3), 65-89.

Gott, R., & Mashiter, J. (1995). Practical work in science – A task-based approach? In Murphy, P., & Selinger, R. (Eds.). *Subject learning in the primary curriculum.* Milton Keynes: Open University Press.

Gott, R., & Murphy, P. (1987). *Assessing investigations at ages 13 and 15.* London: DES.

Greenfield, P. (1984). A theory of the teacher in the learning activities of everyday life. In B. Rogoff, & J. Lave (Eds.). *Everyday cognition: Development in social context.* Cambridge MA: Harvard University Press.

REFERENCES

Greeno, J. G., Collins, A. M., & Resnick, L. B. (1996). Cognition and learning. In D. Berliner & Calfee, R. (Eds.) *Handbook of educational psychology.* New York: Macmillan.

Greeno, J. G., Pearson, P. D., & Schoenfeld, A. H. (1999). Achievement and theories of knowing and learning. In R. McCormick, & C. Paechter (Eds.). *Learning and knowledge.* London: Paul Chapman Publishing.

Guile, D. & Young, M. (1998). Apprenticeship as a conceptual basis for a social theory of learning. *Journal of Vocational Education and Training, 50* (2), 173-192.

Haliday, D. & Resnick, R. (2nd edn.). (1981). *Fundamentals of physics.* New York: John Wiley & Sons.

Haliday, D., Resnick, R., & and Walker, J. (4th edn.). (1993). *Fundamentals of physics: Extended with modern physics.* New York: John Wiley.

Hammersley, M. & Gomm, R. (2000). Introduction. In R. Gomm, M. Hammersley, & P. Foster (Eds.). *Case study method.* Thousand Oaks: SAGE.

Hammersley, M. (1977). *Teacher perspectives. Block II the process of schooling.* Milton Keynes: Open University Press.

Hammersley, M. (1997). Educational research and teaching: A response to David Hargreaves' TTA lecture. *British Educational Research Journal, 23* (2), 141-61.

Hammersley, M., Gomm, R., & Foster, P. (2000). Case study and theory. In R. Gomm, M. Hammersley, & P. Foster (Eds.). *Case study method.* Thousand Oaks: SAGE.

Hanson, N. R. (1965). *Patterns of discovery: An inquiry into the conceptual foundations of science,* Cambridge: Cambridge University Press.

Hargreaves, A. (1986). *Two cultures of schooling: The case of middle schools.* London: Falmer Press.

Harlen W. & Holroyd, C. (1996). Primary teachers' understanding of concepts in science: Impact on confidence and teaching. *International Journal of Science Education, 19* (1), 93-105.

Harlen, W. (1978). Does content matter in primary science? *School Science Review,* 59, 614-625.

Harlen, W. (1992). *Studies in primary education: The teaching of science.* London: David Fulton.

Harlen, W. (1995). Primary science from the 1960s to 1990s'. In P. Murphy, J. Bourne, M. Briggs, & M. Selinger (Eds.). *Primary education: The basic curriculum. E832 Study Guide.* Milton Keynes: The Open University.

Harlen, W. (1996). *Primary teachers' understanding of science and its impact in the classroom.* Paper presented at the British Educational Research Association, Lancaster: University of Lancaster.

Harlen, W. (1997). Teachers' subject knowledge and understanding and the teaching of science at the primary level. *Science Teacher Education,* 19, 6-7.

Harlen, W. (1999). *Effective teaching of science: A review of research.* Edinburgh: The Scottish Council for Research in Education.

Harlen, W. (2000). *The teaching of science in primary schools.* London: David Fulton Publishers.

Harlen, W., & Holroyd, C. (1995). *Primary teachers' understanding of concepts in science and technology.* Edinburgh: The Scottish Council for Research in Education.

Harlen, W., & Osborne, R. (1985). A model for learning and teaching applied to primary science. *Journal of Curriculum Studies, 17* (2), 133-146.

Harlen, W., & Qualter, A. (4rth edn.) (2004). *The teaching of science in primary schools.* London: David Fulton.

Harlen, W., Darwin, A., & Murphy, M. (1977). *Match and mismatch: Raising questions, fitting learning experiences in science to development for five to thirteen years old.* Edinburgh: Oliver and Boyd for the Schools Council.

Harlen, W., Holroyd. C., & Byrne, M. (1995). *Confidence and understanding in teaching science and technology in primary schools.* Edinburgh: The Scottish Council for Research in Education.

Hiebert, J., & Lefevre, P. (1986). Conceptual and procedural knowledge in mathematics: An introductory analysis. In J. Hiebert (Ed.). *Conceptual and procedural knowledge: The case of mathematics.* London: Lawrence Erlbaum Associates.

Hirst, P. H. (1983). Educational theory. In P.H. Hirst (Ed.). *Educational theory and its foundation disciplines.* London: Routledge & Kegan Paul.

Hodson, D. (1996). Laboratory work as scientific method: Three decades of confusion and distortion. *Journal of Curriculum Studies, 28* (2), 115-135.

Hodson, D. (1998). *Teaching and learning science: Towards a personalised approach.* Buckingham, England: Open University Press.

Hodson. D., P., & R. B. Prophet (1986). Why the science curriculum changes- Evolution or social control? In J. Brown, A. Cooper, T. Horton, & D. Zeldin. (Eds.). *Exploring the curriculum: Science in schools.* Milton Keynes: Open University Press.

Isaacs, N. (1955). *Piaget and progressive education.* National Froebel Foundation.

Jennings, A. (1992). *National curriculum science: So near and yet so far.* London: Tufnell Press.

Johnson, P. (1997). What should a science subject knowledge course for primary ITE look like? Proceedings of the 3rd Summer Conference for Teacher Education in Primary Science: *Developing the 'Right Kind of Teacher'* in Primary Science, pp. 133-138. Durham: School of Education, University of Durham.

Keller, C. & Keller, J.D. (1993). Thinking and acting with iron. In S. Chaiklin, & J. Lave (Eds.). *Understanding practice.* Cambridge: Cambridge University Press.

Kelly, G. A. (1955). *The psychology of personal constructs (Vol. 1 & 2).* New York: Wiley.

Kerr & Engel (1983). Can science be taught in primary schools? In C. Richards, & D. Holfords (Eds.). *The teaching of primary science: Policy and practice.* Lewes: Falmer.

Klausmeier, J. H., Ghatala, E. S., & Frayer, D. A. (1974). *Conceptual learning and development - A cognitive view.* New York: Academic Press.

Koch, J. (2006). Relating Learning Theories to Pedagogy. In K. Appleton (Ed.) *Elementary Science Teacher Education.* New Jersey: Lawrence Erlbaum Associates.

Kruger, C. & Summers, M. (1989). An investigation of some primary teachers' understanding of changes in materials. *School Science Review 71* (255), 17-27.

Kruger, C., Palacio, D., & Summers, M. (1990). A survey of primary school teachers' conceptions of force and motion. *Educational Researcher, 32* (2), 83-95.

Kruger, C., Palacio, D., & Summers, M. (1992). Surveys of English primary school teachers' conceptions of force, energy and materials. *Science Education,* 76, 339-351.

Kuhn, T. S. (2nd edn) (1970). *The Structure of Scientific Revolutions.* Chicago: The University of Chicago Press.

Kuhn, T. S. (1977). *The Essential Tension.* Chicago: The University of Chicago Press.

Lacey, C. (1977). *The Socialisation of teachers.* London: Methuen.

Larochelle, M., & Bednarz, N. (1998). Constructivism and Education: beyond epistemological correctness. In M. Larochelle, N. Bednarz, & J. Garrison, *Constructivism and Education.* Cambridge: Cambridge University Press.

Latour, B., & Woolgar, S. (1979). *Laboratory Life: The Social Construction of Scientific Facts.* Beverly Hills: SAGE.

Lave, J. (1988). *Cognition in Practice: Mind, mathematics, and culture in everyday life.* Cambridge: Cambridge University Press.

Lave, J. (1993). The practice of learning. In S. Chaiklin, & J. Lave (Eds.). *Understanding Practice.* Cambridge: Cambridge University Press.

Lave, J., & Wenger, E. (1991). *Situated Learning: Legitimate peripheral participation.* Cambridge: Cambridge University Press.

Layton, D. (1973). *Science for the people: The origins of the school science curriculum in England.* London: Allen and Unwin.

Lemke, J. L. (1995) *Textual politics: Discourse and Social Dynamics.* London: Taylor & Francis.

Lerman, S. (1994). *Metaphors for Mind and Metaphors for Teaching and Learning Mathematics.* Paper presented at the 17th Meeting of International Group for the Psychology of Mathematics Education, Portugal.

Lévi-Strauss, C. (1966). *The savage mind.* London: Weidenfeld & Nicolson.

Light, P., & Glahan, M. (1985). Facilitation of individual problem solving through peer interaction, *Educational Psychology,* 5, 217-225.

REFERENCES

Magoon, A.J. (1977). Consructivist Approaches in Educational Research. *Review in Educational Research, 47* (4), 651-693.

Mant, J., & Summers, M. (1995). Some primary-school teachers' understanding of the Earth's place in the Universe. *Research Papers in Education, 10* (1), 101-129.

Matthews, M. (1994). *Science Teaching: The role of history and philosophy of science.* New York: Routledge.

McGinnis, J.R., Parker, C., & Graeber, A. (2004). A cultural perspective on the induction of five reform-minded new specialist teachers of mathematics and science. *Journal of Research in Science Teaching. 41* (7), 720-747.

Millar, R. (1989). Constructive criticisms. *International Journal of Science Education, 11,* 587-596.

Millar, R., & Driver, R. (1987). Beyond processes, *Studies in Science Education, 14,* 33-62.

Millar, R., & Osborne, J. (Eds) (1998), *Beyond 2000: Science education for the future.* London: King's College London.

Ministry of Education (1961). *Science in primary schools.* Pamphlet No. 42: HMSO.

Murphy, P. (1999). Supporting collaborative learning: A gender dimension. In P. Murphy (Ed.). *Learners, learning, and assessment.* London: Paul Chapman.

Murphy, P., Bourne, J., Briggs, M., & Selinger, M. (1995). *Primary education: The basic curriculum, E832 Study Guide.* Milton Keynes: The Open University.

Murphy, P., Davidson, M., Qualter, A., Simon, S., & Watt, D.(2000) *Effective practice in primary science: A report of an exploratory study funded by the Nuffield Curriculum Projects Centre.* Milton Keynes: The Open University.

National Research Council (NRC) (1996). *National science education standards.* Washington, DC: National Academy Press.

Nelson, C., Treichler, P.A., Grossberg, L. (1992). Introduction. In L. Grossberg, C. Nelson, & P.A.Treichler (Eds.). *Cultural studies.* New York: Routledge.

Nichols, S., & Koballa, T. (2006). Framing issues of elementary science teacher education: Critical conversations. In K. Appleton (Ed.) *Elementary science teacher education.* New Jersey: Lawrence Erlbaum Associates.

Nuffield Chemistry (1967). *Handbook for teachers.* London: Longman / Penguin.

Nuffield Primary Science (1993). *Nuffield primary science (science processes and concept exploration) teachers' guides.* London: Collins Educational.

Nussbaum, J., & Novick, S. (1982). Alternative frameworks, conceptual conflict and accommodation: Towards a principled teaching strategy. *Instructional Science, 11,* 183-200.

OfSTED (Office for Standards in Education) (1995). *Science: A review of inspection findings 1993/94.* London: HMSO.

Ogborn, J. (1995). Recovering reality. *Studies in Science Education, 25,* 3-38.

Olson, J. (1992). *Understanding teaching.* Milton Keynes: Open University Press.

Osborne, J. (1996). Beyond constructivism. *Science Education, 80* (1), 53-82.

Osborne, J., & Simon, S. (1996a). Primary science: Past and future directions. *Studies in Science Education, 26,* 99-147.

Osborne, J., & Simon, S. (1996b). Teachers' subject knowledge: Implications for teaching and policy., Paper presented at the Annual Conference of the British Educational Research Association: Lancaster: University of Lancaster.

Osborne, D. M. (1996). Teacher as knower and learner: Reflections on situated knowledge in science teaching. *Journal of Research in Science Teaching. 35* (4), 427-439.

Osborne, D. M. (1999) *Examining science teaching in elementary school from the perspective of a teacher and learner.* New York: Falmer Press.

Osborne, R. J., & Gilbert, J. K. (1979). *An approach to student understanding of basic concepts in science.* Surrey: Institute for Educational Technology, University of Surrey.

Osborne, R., & Freyberg, P. (1985). *Learning in science.* London: Heinemann.

Osborne, R. J., & Gilbert, J. K. (1980). A technique for exploring students' views of the world. *Physics Education, 15,* 376-379.

Osborne, R. J., Schollum, B., & & Hill, G. (1981). *Force, friction and gravity: Notes for teachers, learning in science project. Working Paper No. 33.* University of Waikato. Hamilton, New Zealand.

Parker, J., & Heywood, D. (2000). Exploring the relationship between subject knowledge and peda-gogic content knowledge in primary teachers' learning about forces. *International Journal of Science Education, 22* (1), 89-111.

Parker, S. & Ward, A. (1978).*Sciencewise.* London: Nelson.

Parker-Jelly, S. (1983). Science 5-13: Reflections on its significance. In C. Richards, & D. Holford (Eds) *The teaching of primary science: Policy and practice.* Lewes: Falmer Press.

Pépin, Y. (1998). Practical knowledge and school knowledge: A constructivist representation of educa-tion. In M.Larochelle, N. Bedrarz, & J. Garrison (Eds.). *Constructivism and education.* Cambridge: Cambridge University Press.

Piaget, J. (1970) *Genetic epistemology.* New York: Columbia University Press.

Piaget, J. (1971). *Biology and knowledge.* Edinburgh: Edinburgh University Press.

Polanyi, M. (1959). *Personal knowledge.* Manchester: Manchester University Press.

Putman, R., & Borko, H. (2000). What do new views of knowledge and thinking have to say about research on teacher learning? *Educational Researcher, 29* (1), 4-15.

Redman, S., Brereton, A., & Boyers, P. (1968). Young children and science: The Oxford Primary Sci-ence Project. *Trends in Education, 12,* 17-25.

Redman, S., Brereton, A., & Boyers, P. (1969). *An approach to primary science.* London: MacMillan.

Richards, C. (1983). The primary curriculum and primary science. In C.Richards, & D. Holfords (Eds.). *The teaching of primary science: Policy and practice.* Lewes: Falmer.

Richards, R., Collis, M., & Kincaid, D. (1980). *Learning through science: Formulating a school policy.* London: MacDonald Educational.

Rogoff, B. (1990). *Apprenticeship in thinking: Cognitive development in social context.* Oxford: Oxford University Press.

Rogoff, B. (1994). Developing understanding of the idea of communities of learners. *Mind, Culture, and Activity,* 1, 209-229.

Rogoff, B., & Gardner, W. (1984). Adult guidance of cognitive development. In B. Rogoff, & J. Lave (Eds.). *Everyday cognition: Development in social context,* Cambridge Mass. Harvard: Harvard University Press.

Rosebery, A. (1998). Investigating a teacher's questions through video. In A. Rosebery, & B. Warren (Eds) *Boats, balloons, and classroom video: Science teaching as inquiry.* Portsmouth, NH: Heine-mann.

Rosebery, A., & Puttick, G. (1998). Teacher professional development as situated sense-making: A case study in science education. *Science Education, 82,* 649-677.

Roth, W.-M. (1993). Construction sites: Science labs and classrooms. In K. Tobin (Ed.) *The practice of constructivism in science* education. Hillsdale: Lawrence Erlbaum Associates.

Roth, W.-M. (1995). *Authentic school science.* Boston: Kluwer Academic Publishers.

Roth, W.-M. (1996). Art and artifact of children's designing: A situated cognition perspective. *Journal of the Learning Sciences, 5,* 129-166.

Roth, W.-M. (1997). The interaction of learning environment and student discourse about knowing, learning, and the nature of science: Two longitudinal case studies. *International Journal of Educa-tional Research, 27,* 311-320.

Roth, W.-M. (1999). Authentic school science: Intellectual traditions. In R. McCormick, & C. Paechter (Eds) *Learning and knowledge.* London: Paul Chapman Publishing.

Roth, W.-M., & Bowen, G. M. (1995). Knowing and interacting: A study of culture, practices and re-sources in a grade 8 open-inquiry science classroom guided by a cognitive apprenticeship metaphor. *Cognition and Instruction, 13,* 73-129.

Roth, W.-M., & et al. (1997). Why do students fail to learn from demonstrations? A social practice perspective on learning in physics, *Journal of Research in Science Teaching, 34,* 509-533.

Roth, W-M, Tobin, K., Ritchie, S. (2001). *Re/Constructing elementary science.* New York: Peter Lang.

Roth, W-M. (2006). *Learning science: A singular plural perspective. Rotterdam:* Sense publishers.

REFERENCES

Russell, T., D. Bell, L. McGuigan, A. Qualter, J. Quinn, & M. Schilling (1992). Teachers' Conceptual understanding in science: Needs and possibilities in the primary phase. In L. D. Newton (Ed.) *Primary science: The challenge of the 1990s.* Clevendon: Multilingual Matters Ltd.

Schön, D. A. (1987). *Educating the reflective practitioner.* San Fransisco: CA: Jossey-Bass.

Schön, D. A. (1983). *The reflective practitioner: How professionals think in action.* London: Temple Smith.

Schwab, J. J. (1962). *The teaching of science as enquiry.* Cambridge, Mass: Harvard University Press.

Schwab, J. J. (1969). The practical: a language for curriculum. *School Review, 78,* 1-24.

Scribner, S. (1985). Knowledge at work. *Anthropology and Education Quarterly, 16* (3), 199-206.

Sfard, A. (1998). On two metaphors of learning and the dangers of choosing just one. *Educational Researcher, 27* (2), 4-13.

Shulman, L. (1986). Those who understand: Knowledge growth in teaching. *Educational Researcher, 15* (2), 4-14.

Shulman, L. (1987). Knowledge and teaching: Foundations of the new reform. *Harvard Educational Review, 57* (1), 1-22.

Smith, R. (1994). Richer or poorer, better or worse? Has the development of primary science teaching been affected by National Curriculum policy?' *The Curriculum Journal, 5* (2), 163-177.

SPACE (1987-90). *Science processes and concept exploration (SPACE) project.* London: University of London, King's College and University of Liverpool.

Stake, E. R. (1995). *The art of case study research.* Thousand Oaks: SAGE.

Stead, K., & Osborne, R. (1980). *Friction. working paper No. 19.* Hamilton: University of Waikato, New Zealand.

Summers, M. (1994). Science in the primary school: The problem of teachers' curricular expertise. *The Curriculum Journal, 5* (5), 179-193.

Summers, M., & Kruger, C. (1990). Research into English primary school teachers' understanding of the concept of energy. In L. D. Newton (Ed.) *Primary science: The challenge of the 1990s.* Clevendon: Multilingual Matters.

Summers, M., & Kruger, C. (1992). Research into English primary school teachers' understanding of the concept of energy. *Evaluation and Research in Education, 6* (2 & 3), 95-111.

Summers, M., & Kruger, C. (1993). *A longitudinal Study of Primary School Teachers' Understanding of Force and Energy, Working Paper 18: PSTS project.* Oxford: Oxford University Department of Educational Studies and Westminster College.

Summers, M., & Mant, J. (1995). A misconceived view of subject-matter knowledge in primary science education: A response to Golby et al. 'Some researchers understanding of primary teaching'. *Research Papers in Education, 10* (3), 303-307.

Summers, M., & Mant, J. (1998). A view from the PSTS project. *Primary Science Review, 52,* 12-14.

Summers, M., Kruger, C., & Mant, J. (1997a). *Teaching electricity effectively: A research-based guide for primary science, Primary School Teachers and Science (PSTS) Project.* Hatfield: The Association for Science Education.

Summers, M., Kruger, C., & Mant, J. (1997b). A particle approach to the teaching of electricity and simple circuits. Proceedings of the 3rd Summer Conference for Teacher Education in Primary Science: *Developing the 'Right Kind of Teacher'* in Primary Science, pp. 325-338. Durham: School of Education, University of Durham.

Summers, M., Kruger, C., Mant, J., & Childs, A. (1998). Developing primary teachers' understanding of energy efficiency. *Educational Researcher, 40* (3), 311-327.

Teacher Training Agency (2001) *Qualifying to teach: Professional standards for qualified teacher status and requirements for initial teacher training.* London: TTA (available at http://www.tta.gov.uk).

Tobin, K. (1998). Sociocultural perspectives on the teaching and learning of science. In M. Larochelle, N. Bednarz, & J. Garrison, *Constructivism and education.* Cambridge: Cambridge University Press.

Tobin, K. & McRobbie, J.C. (1999). Pedagogical content knowledge and co-participation in science classrooms. In J. Gess-Newsome & N.G. Lederman (Eds) *Examining pedagogical content knowledge*. Dordrecht, The Netherlands: Kluwer Academic.

Torff, B. (1999). Tacit knowledge in teaching: Folk pedagogy and teacher education. In R. Sternberg, & J. Horvath (Eds) *Tacit knowledge in professional practice: Researcher and practitioner perspectives*. London: Lawrence Erlbaum Associates.

Turner, S. & Sullenger, K. (1999). Kuhn in the classroom, Lakatos in the lab: Science educators confront the nature-of-science debate. *Science, Technology and Human Values, 24* (1), 5-30.

Ussell, P. (1986). The changing aims of science teaching. In J. Brown, A. Cooper, T. Horton, F. Toates, & D.Zeldin (Eds.) *Exploring the curriculum: Science in schools*. Milton Keynes: Open University Press.

Van Zee, E.H. (2000). Analysis of a student-generated inquiry discussion. *International Journal of Science Education, 22*, 115-142.

von Glaserfeld, E. (1989). Cognition, construction of knowledge and teaching. *Synthese, 80*, 121-140.

Vygotsky, L. (1978). *Mind in society: The development of higher psychological processes*. London: Harvard University Press.

Warren, B., & Rosebery, A. (1996). 'This question is just too easy! Students' perspectives on accountability in science'. In L. Schauble & R. Glaser (Eds) *Innovations in learning: New environments for education*. Mahwah: NJ: Laurence & Erlbaum.

Wastendge, R. (1983). Nuffield Junior Science: The end of a beginning?' In C. Richards, & D. Holford (Eds.) *The teaching of primary science: Policy and practice*. Lewes: Falmer Press.

Wastnedge, R. (1968). Nuffield Junior Science in Primary Schools. *School Science Review, 61* (217), 342-348.

Welzel, M., & Roth, W.-M. (1998). Do interviews really assess students' knowledge? *International Journal of Science Education, 20* (1), 25-44.

Wertsch, J. V. & Stone, C. A. (1979). A social interaction analysis of learning disabilities remediation' Paper presented at the International Conference of Association for Children with Learning Disabilities, San Francisco.

Wertsch, L. S. (1985). *Vygotsky and the social formation of mind*. Cambridge, MA: Harvard University Press.

White, R. T. (1979). *Describing cognitive structure*. Paper presented at the Australian Association for Educational Research, Melbourne.

Whittaker, M.(1980). They're only playing – The problem with primary science. *School Science Review, 51* (216), 556-560.

Wilson, P. L, Shulman, L & Richer, A. (1987). '150 different ways' of knowing: Representations of knowledge in teaching. In J. Calderhead (Ed.) *Exploring teachers' thinking*. London: Cassell.

Wood, D. (1988). *How children think & learn*. Cambridge Mass: Basil Blackwell Ltd.

Wood, D. J., Bruner, J.S, & Ross, G. (1976). The role of tutoring in problem solving. *Journal of Child Psychology and Psychiatry, 17*, 89-100.

Young, M. F. D. (1976). The schooling of science. In G. Y. Whitty (Ed.) *Explorations in the politics of school knowledge*. London: Nafferton Books.

Zeichner, K. & Tabachnick, B.R. (1985). Social strategies and institutional control in the socialisation of beginning teachers. *Journal of Education for Teaching*, 11, 1-25.

SUBJECT INDEX

A

abstract concepts ...7, 22, 23, 38, 130
academic science...........................11
accountability........16, 131, 143, 153
act13, 35, 36, 38, 40, 55, 59, 99, 110, 138
active learners 53
adaptation..............................35, 131
adequate conceptual knowledge....28
adequate conceptual understanding
....25, 33
adequate level of subject knowledge
....17
ambiguity 30, 37, 143
ambiguous nature of knowledge ...54
analogies...... 43, 45, 48, 51, 125, 140
APU..9, 10
artificial situations.................40, 133
ASE 5
assessment.....................9, 10, 71, 78
asymmetry.....................................56
attainment targets 16, 17
authentic activities......39, 55, 57, 61, 139
autonomy......................86, 106, 108

B

behavioural objectives.....................7
bricolage.....................................139
  bricoleur 139, 142

C

case study ......xii, 65, 66, 67, 71, 134
certainty......................................142
child-centred tradition 22
class diary...69, 73, 93, 97, 109, 122, 137
classroom

interaction 54, 69
observation 68, 71
practice .. xi, 35, 54, 132, 141, 143
close questioning 96, 136
co-constructed..............................38
cognition...19, 26, 31, 34, 36, 38, 39, 40, 41, 130, 132
cognitivism 26
collaboration............. 23, 56, 84, 139
collaborative explanation........33, 34
commodity-like knowledge ... 34, 42, 60, 132
communication 20, 36, 38, 69, 72, 131, 133, 145, 146, 147
communities of practice.... xi, 25, 36, 37, 40, 41, 67, 71, 131, 133, 137, 140
community-of-learners 56
complex problems........................ 44
complex tasks 88, 91, 137
complexity 30, 40, 42, 54, 59, 67, 71, 132, 140
conceptual change 14, 15, 19, 32, 46, 49, 53, 130, 131
conceptual simplification............ 104
conceptual structures . 13, 27, 32, 46, 80, 83
conceptual understanding 15, 17, 18, 25, 32, 34, 53, 54, 86, 90, 104, 117, 122, 126
confusing situations 76
constructivism... xi, 3, 11, 12, 13, 15, 20, 25, 27, 30, 31, 33, 49, 54, 58, 60, 89, 90, 91, 124, 125, 130, 131, 132, 133, 134
constructivist learning 43, 48, 60, 90, 125, 131
constructivist teaching 16, 19, 22, 45, 125, 126, 137
content of primary science........ 9, 12
content of science 4, 7, 13, 14

contextual judgment 31, 139
contingent nature of teaching 140
continuing professional development
.... 19, 40, 41
continuity 16, 94, 103, 117, 124, 126
control .. 54, 57, 86, 87, 91, 106, 108,
   137, 149, 153
cooperative activity 32
cultural knowledge 57
curriculum
   developments 3, 4, 8, 11, 22
   materials 8, 9
   reforms 3

D

decisions 3, 12, 16, 29, 30, 31, 37,
   41, 47, 51, 55, 59, 60, 61, 123,
   133
decontextualised knowledge 58
dilemmas 55, 69, 138, 142
discourse 38, 39, 57, 58, 59
discovery learning 5, 10, 23, 74
dynamic process 36, 42, 55

E

eclectic 134, 139
effective primary science teaching . 3,
   66
elementary tradition 3, 4
elicitation .. 14, 20, 45, 47, 50, 58, 80,
   90, 124, 131, 137
email communication 139
enculturation 38, 55, 86
event 33, 34, 49, 51
everyday language 32, 39, 78, 95,
   111
everyday problem 95, 96
evolving spiral 36, 40
examples ... 13, 14, 19, 27, 29, 30, 38,
   43, 69, 70, 75, 111, 117, 126, 138,
   141
experimentation 5, 110

expert primary science practitioner
.... xi, 67, 129
expertise-in-action 141

F

fair testing 108
familiar problem 53
flexible 126, 143
forces 15, 66
function successfully 59, 136, 141

G

generalisations 30, 39, 67

I

ill-defined problems 31, 38, 133
inadequate scientific knowledge ... 30
inadequate teaching knowledge 44
individual knowledge 35, 146
initial teacher education courses .. 23,
   89
initial teacher training
   courses 17
instances ... 27, 28, 29, 30, 31, 39, 75,
   139
instances of knowing 139
interdependence 25, 123, 140
interpretation 7, 11, 12, 13, 34, 42,
   45, 47, 57, 58, 60, 76, 98, 102,
   111, 122, 130, 132, 133
interpreting evidence 33, 132
interviews . 29, 30, 31, 33, 40, 42, 66,
   70, 72, 73, 133, 134, 139, 142
investigative skills 17
iterative process 141

J

joint problem-solving event 55
judgments ... 31, 47, 48, 54, 135, 141
kind and amount of subject
   knowledge 18

K

knowledgeable20, 22, 33, 41, 57, 98, 127, 131, 132, 137
knowledge-base 140

L

language ... 13, 20, 30, 35, 38, 43, 57, 68, 78, 96, 127, 131, 133, 142
learning
   environment88, 91, 105, 124, 137, 151
   opportunity 87, 124, 125
   outcomes 44, 47, 50, 87, 139
   process.... 3, 4, 5, 6, 14, 15, 46, 48, 49, 53, 55, 60, 73, 83, 84, 90, 130, 134
local communities of practice 134
logical thinking 79

M

metacognitive awareness.. 75, 76, 80, 89, 90, 135
modest realist perspective 27
monitoring of standards 10
multiple resources 142

N

nature of science 17, 151
negotiation 39, 42, 133
network of links ... 33, 40, 49, 58, 73, 89, 132
non-examples 75
novel problem 53, 57, 108

O

operative knowledge 98

P

paradigms 39, 147

participation. 41, 61, 83, 90, 98, 112, 131, 134, 140
pedagogical content knowledge   xi, xii, 3, 19, 20, 21, 22, 23, 43, 47, 48, 50, 52, 53, 54, 55, 59, 60, 61, 67, 129, 130, 131, 133, 139, 140, 141, 143, 147, 153
pedagogical expertise 31, 131
pedagogical strategies 21, 31, 94, 124, 125, 136, 138, 139
Piagetian
   constructivism14, 15, 23, 130, 131
   staged theory 7
post-positivist philosophies of
   science 12
practical activities .. 8, 9, 12, 14, 15, 16, 20, 21, 22, 28, 45, 46, 48, 50, 52, 53, 54, 66, 68, 69, 74, 82, 83, 84, 86, 89, 90, 93, 124, 130, 131, 134, 136
practical character of teaching 135
practical investigations 4
practical science expertise 30
practical skills 26
primary school classrooms 74
primary science expertise xii, 19, 21, 22, 43, 47, 65, 66, 67, 71, 129, 130, 131, 132, 134
Primary Science National
   Curriculum 25, 68, 71, 73, 91
primary science practitioners 33, 130
problem-solving procedural
   knowledge 26, 31, 36, 41, 132
problem-solving situations 5, 34, 37, 76, 134, 136
procedural understanding 26, 32, 33, 34, 48, 50, 52, 53, 58, 60, 74, 80, 89, 90, 103, 106, 117, 134, 135, 136
process approach 5, 8, 11, 12, 14, 19, 22, 129, 130
professional knowledge 136, 138

R

ready-made scientific explanations45
reflective discourse.58, 59, 111, 126, 135
reflective practitioner . 138, 139, 142, 152
research knowledge 140

S

school science 11, 13, 58, 96, 137, 145, 149, 151
Science 5-13 .... 6, 151
science as a process of inquiry 6, 7
science as practice 37, 55
science classroom community21, 59, 137
science learning .. 5, 6, 21, 55, 56, 68, 78, 84
Science National Curriculum ... 3, 12, 16, 17, 22, 23, 25, 26, 29, 32, 34, 77, 125, 131, 137
science teaching4, 6, 7, 8, 10, 12, 15, 20, 22, 59, 65, 68, 69, 70, 75, 76, 80, 85, 89, 90, 129, 130, 137
scientific
    activities 8
    concepts .. 8, 11, 12, 18, 19, 22, 26, 27, 28, 31, 32, 33, 34, 35, 39, 45, 46, 49, 50, 58, 59, 66, 74, 75, 83, 86, 89, 90, 130, 132, 134, 139
    discourse.......... 39, 40, 42, 59, 102
    inquiry .. 23, 32, 91, 124, 131, 135, 136, 137
    language 45, 78, 96, 101
    orientation 18, 21, 25, 32
    procedures 34
    questions. 6, 52, 53, 74, 77, 81, 90, 136, 137, 141
    terms..... 43, 45, 51, 57, 78, 84, 90, 136
    understanding xi, 9, 18, 19, 20, 25, 28, 30, 31, 33, 41, 47, 48, 52,

53, 55, 59, 60, 69, 71, 73, 75, 76, 77, 78, 80, 82, 84, 85, 88, 89, 90, 91, 94, 102, 112, 123, 126, 127, 131, 132, 133, 135, 136, 137, 138, 141, 142
secondary science 5, 8, 11, 12, 15, 16, 73, 74
self-directed observations 5
sequential view of knowledge 26, 44
shared thinking 85
simplify scientific concepts .. 90, 136
situated 146, 149
situated cognition 40, 151
situated practice theory 38
small range of scientific concepts 18, 21, 60
social activity 35, 38, 40, 55, 133
social coordination 35, 131
social development of mind 35
sociocultural theory .... xi, 129, 132
standards-based education 21
subject knowledge .. xi, xii, 3, 17, 18, 19, 20, 21, 22, 25, 30, 31, 32, 34, 40, 41, 42, 43, 44, 45, 48, 49, 50, 55, 59, 60, 61, 65, 66, 67, 70, 71, 73, 89, 102, 129, 130, 131, 132, 133, 134, 136, 137, 138, 140, 141, 142, 143, 148, 149, 150, 151
    requirement 3, 18, 22

T

tacit understanding 38
teacher expertise ... xi, xii, 21, 22, 42, 43, 65, 67, 70, 71, 91, 124, 125, 131, 132, 134, 139, 140, 141, 143
teaching of science..... xii, 4, 5, 8, 13, 14, 16, 18, 19, 20, 21, 23, 44, 53, 54, 55, 58, 60, 66, 71, 73, 76, 77, 83, 129, 131, 133, 134, 137, 139, 140, 141, 142, 148, 152
tied to action 133
transmission teaching 47, 60
uncertainty 31, 40, 111, 138, 142, 143

Z

zone of proximal development 20, 34, 35, 49, 53, 56, 57, 91, 96, 124, 125, 126, 131, 135, 139

U

unique explanations.....................143
unstructured practical activities.....90
useful knowledge 7, 22, 129

AUTHOR INDEX

A

Abel, S.K.................................18
Aikenhead, G. 65
Alexander, R. 20
Appleton, K..............................21
APU.....................................9, 10
ASE.......................................5
Australian Foundation for Science 18
Ausubel, D. P. 12
Axel, E. 35

B

Bantock, G. H...........................10
Barnes, B................................30, 39
Bauersfeld, H. 86
Bennett, N. 10
Berliner, D..............................19
Black, P. 8, 10, 17
Blenkin, G. M.............................4
Blyth, W. A. L........................4, 16
Borko, H.................................36
Bowden, P. 96
Boyers, P. 7
Boyle, A. 8, 11
Bredo, E. 27, 30
Brereton, A................................7
Bruner, J...............12, 23, 31, 61, 75
Byrne, M. 18, 32

C

Calderhead, J............................18
Claxton, G. 4, 13
Conran, J. 4

D

Darling, J................................10, 16

Darwin, A. 7
Denzin, N.K...........................65, 139
DES 8, 9, 11, 12, 16, 17
DfEE......................................20
di Sessa, A. 85
Driver, R.........11, 13, 14, 15, 20, 83
Duckworth, E............................142
Duguid, P...............................36, 38

E

Engel, E. 8, 9, 13
Ennever, L. 7
Erickson, G.L............................13

F

Feasey, R. 110
Feyerabend, P. 47
Forman, E. A. 56
Foster, P................................67
Foulds, K. 111
Frayer, D.A..............................27
Freyberg, P. 13

G

Gagné, R. M. 12
Gardner, W. 57, 84, 96, 120
Ghatala, E.S.............................21
Gilbert, J. K. 12, 27, 29
Glahan, M. 56
Gomm, R. 67
Goodwin, A. 6
Gott, R. 10, 106
Graeber, A. 65
Greenfield, P............................56
Greeno, J. G............................26, 37
Grossberg, L. 139
Guile, D. 41

H

Haliday, D. 104, 111
Hammersley, M....ix, 67, 72, 96, 140
Hanson, N.R. 47
Hargreaves, A.................................4
Harlen, W... 5, 6, 7, 9, 10, 12, 15, 16,
   17, 18, 20, 25, 32, 33, 34, 42, 48,
   49, 50, 51, 52, 53, 66, 84, 105,
   110
Hiebert, J. 42
Hill, G. 96
Hodson, D. 4, 5, 21, 23
Holroyd. C.........................18, 32, 66

I

Isaacs, N. 5

J

Jennings, A.....................................16
Johnson, P. 18

K

Kerr 8, 9, 13
Klausmeier, J. H.............................27
Koballa, T.......................................21
Koch, J. 20, 129, 131
Kruger, C.............................18, 19, 29
Kuhn, T. S. 39

L

Lacey, C. 19
Latour, B. 37
Lave, J. 35, 38, 41, 65, 71, 98
Layton, D. 23
Lederman, N.G................................19
Lee, O...130
Lefevre, P.......................................42
Lemke, J..38
Lerman, S. 53
Light, P.....................................15, 56

M

Lincoln, Y.S...........................65, 139

Magoon, A.J. 12
Mant, J. 18, 19, 26, 27, 29, 42
Mashiter, J. 106
Matthews, M.................................20
McGinnis, J.R...............................65
McRobbie, J.C. 39, 58, 59, 105
Millar, R. 13, 14, 21
Miller, E....................................ix, 18
Ministry of Education.................. 4, 7

N

Nelson, C. 139
Nichols, S. 21
Novick, S. 14
Nuffield Chemistry 5
Nuffield Primary Science 15
Nussbaum, J..................................14

O

Ogborn, J. 20
Olson, J.......................................135

P

Palacio, D. 29
Parker-Jelly, S..........................7, 23
Pearson, P.D. 26, 37
Pépin, Y.......................................84
Piaget, J. 5, 6, 12, 13, 22, 27, 53,
   129, 131
Pinch, T. 37
Polanyi, M. 136
Prophet, R.B. 4
Putman, R. 36
Puttick, G...........................142, 143

Q

Qualter, A. 5, 20, 32, 50, 84, 105

R

Redman, S. 7
Richer, A. 19
Ritchie, S......21, 38, 55, 86, 105, 136
Rogoff, B........37, 56, 57, 84, 96, 120
Rose, J. 20
Rosebery, A.........................142, 143
Ross, G. 61
Roth, W.-M. ..ii, v, 18, 21, 27, 31, 37,
    38, 39, 40, 47, 55, 58, 86, 105,
    108, 136, 139
Russell, T. 18

S

Schoenfeld, A.H. 26, 37
Schollum, B..................................96
Schön, D. A. 138, 139
Schwab, J.J. 23, 135
Science 5-13 6
Science Processes and Concept
    Exploration (SPACE)................15
Scribner, S. 38
Sfard, A. 38
Shulman, L. 19, 130, 140
Simon, S...8, 18, 25, 66, 95, 99, 103,
    104, 105, 106, 107, 108, 111
SPACE 15
Stake, E.R. 67
Stead, K. 96
Stone, C.A. 57
Sullenger, K. 11
Summers, M...18, 19, 26, 27, 28, 29,
    30, 42, 44, 45, 46, 48

T

Tabachnick, B.R. 19
Tabor, D..96
Teacher Training Agency 23
Torff, B..47
Treichler, P.A. 139
Turner, S. 11

V

Vygotsky, L... 21, 23, 33, 35, 36, 38,
    42, 57, 131

W

Ward, A. 7
Wastendge, R.................................5
White, R. T. 27
Whittaker, M...................................8
Wood, D. 5, 61
Woodhead, C. 20
Woolgar, S.....................................37

Y

Young, M. F. D......................ll, 41

Z

Zeichner, K. 19

ALSO OF INTEREST

Education is Not Rocket Science
The Case for Deconstructing Computer Labs in Schools

David B. Zandvliet, *Simon Fraser University, Canada*

While computer labs are in some ways ideal for learning about technology or computer programming, they seem ill equipped to assist teachers with a lesson on language arts, geography or for helping students conduct a scientific experiment. As a result the huge investment in computers seems like so much wasted potential: labs are not influencing teaching in the ways we had hoped for and may even be harmful to students. These observations are based on 5 years of experience as the director of a centre for educational technology and on the results of three studies which the author conducted in Australia, Canada and Malaysia. The research indicates that school labs fail to meet even basic guidelines common to the workplace, and that they're often deficient in health related factors such as lighting, ventilation or workspace dimensions. The reality is that schools were not designed for so many computers, and therefore, are poorly outfitted to accommodate this sudden influx of technology. This research also shows that computers (in labs), can have an unexpected, de-socialising influence on students' lives. As educators, we need to discard the 'once size fits all' strategy which computer labs imply about teachers' instructional needs.

paperback ISBN: 90-77874-78-X
hardback ISBN: 90-77874-80-1
August 2006, 100 pp

Understanding and Developing Science Teachers Pedagogical Content Knowledge

John Loughran , Amanda Berry, and Pamela Mulhall, *Monash University, Clayton, Australia*

There has been a growing interest in the notion of a scholarship of teaching. Such scholarship is displayed through a teacher's grasp of, and response to, the relationships between knowledge of content, teaching and learning in ways that attest to practice as being complex and interwoven. Yet attempting to capture teachers' professional knowledge is difficult because the critical links between practice and knowledge, for many teachers, is tacit. Pedagogical Content Knowledge (PCK) offers one way of capturing, articulating and portraying an aspect of the scholarship of teaching and, in this case, the scholarship of science teaching. The research underpinning the approach offers access to the development of the professional knowledge of science teaching in a form that offers new ways of sharing and disseminating this knowledge. Through this Resource Folio approach (comprising CoRe and PaP-eRs) a recognition of the value of the specialist knowledge and skills of science teaching is not only highlighted, but also enhanced. This book is a concrete example of the nature of scholarship in science teaching that is meaningful, useful and immediately applicable in the work of all science teachers. It is an excellent resource for science teachers as well as a guiding text for teacher education.

Paperback ISBN 90-77874-23-2
SERIES: PROFESSIONAL LEARNING 1
April 2006, 240 pp

For more information on these and other titles visit
WWW.SENSEPUBLISHERS.COM

Printed in the United Kingdom
by Lightning Source UK Ltd.
116698UKS00001B/182